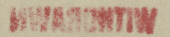

Apples on the Flood

Apples on the Flood

THE SOUTHERN

MOUNTAIN

EXPERIENCE

Rodger Cunningham

The University of Tennessee Press

Knoxville

Library of Congress Cataloging-in-Publication Data

Cunningham, Rodger, 1948–
  Apples on the flood.

  Bibliography: p.
  Includes index.
  1. Scots-Irish—Appalachian Region, Southern.
  2. Appalachian Region, Southern—Civilization.
  3. Appalachian Region, Southern—Social conditions.
  I. Title.
F217.A65C86   1987   975   86–19252
ISBN 0-87049-518-6 (alk. paper)

This book is dedicated to the people of Appalachia,
at home and in dispersion; and to all who work with
Appalachians toward preserving and advancing their
possibilities as mountain people and as human beings.

Go on, builders in hope: tho Jerusalem wanders far away,
Without the gate of Los; among the dark Satanic wheels.
—Blake, *Jerusalem*

ACKNOWLEDGMENTS

The course of my life has been quite varied during the conception and composition of this book. My study of my native region was self-directed and pursued largely in isolation for many years. I wrote the first draft of this work while surviving as a store clerk in Lemon Grove, California; my store manager, Joe Silvia, was as tolerant as he could be of conflicts between my job and my career. To George Brosi I owe the first reading of parts of my manuscript and my first advice and (very importantly) introductions. Others who then read early versions of my work include Bill Best, Archie Green, Loyal Jones, and Karen Simpkins; to each I owe much for continuing advice and encouragement. Discussions with Allen Batteau, Jerry Crouch, Richard Drake, and Mike Henson helped clarify points in my mind; a later version of the manuscript was the subject of fruitful communications with Ron Eller and Bob Snyder. Mike Maloney and Liz Lilly of the Appalachian People's Service Organization encouraged me greatly by showing me that my armchair reflections on the psychology of oppression and the like could be found relevant and illuminating by activists directly involved in helping "ordinary" people to understand and change their concrete situations. In this connection I also benefited from conversations with Evelyn Hurt and Billyie Smith of the Urban Appalachian Council. My work on the final version of the book was aided as well by the advice of Terry Birdwhistell and Anne Campbell. Also invaluable, of course, were the advice and assistance of my editors at the University of Tennessee Press.

I have naturally made use of the resources of many libraries. My original private studies in Appalachian scholarship were carried out at Indiana University in the interstices of "official" work in other fields. I wrote the first version of my manuscript using the resources of the San Diego State University Library; its excellent general collection contains many works that proved seminal in my thinking, while the understandable paucity of its holdings on Appalachia simply discouraged what might well at that point have become a self-defeating accumulation of readings and references. Later I was aided by the staff and resources of the Marshall University Library, both its general and its Appalachian collections, and especially by the latter's curator, Nancy Whear; by the Weatherford-Hammond Mountain Collection at Berea College; by the Indiana University Library once more; by the libraries of the Appalachian People's Service Organization and the Urban Appalachian Council; and by the general collections, the Appalachian collection, and the Frontier Nursing Service Oral History Project of the University of Kentucky Library. In consulting that library I was aided by a mini-sabbatical grant from the University of Kentucky Appalachian College Program. I also made much use of the Sue Bennett College Library, whose Appalachian collection, maintained by Julia Rose, is surely unsurpassed at any school of its size.

Prior to all my study of Appalachia, however, is my identity as a native of the region for many generations on both sides of my family in West Virginia, Virginia, Ohio, Kentucky, Tennessee, and North Carolina. This book is the product of long reflection not only on my own experience and on that of the people among whom I grew up in Kenova, West Virginia, but on that of my late parents, Don N. Cunningham and Mary Katherine Chapman Cunningham; of my late grandparents, Fred J. Cunningham, Emma May Crossen Cunningham, William McKinley Chapman, and Doris Clay Chapman; and of all their other descendants, as well as what I have been able to learn of their ancestors. I have above all striven to make this book true to their lives insofar as I have been able to share in those lives.

London, Kentucky
February 1986

CONTENTS

MAPS

Why did you have to do that?

—Last words of Hugh O'Connor,
film crew leader, shot for trespass
by Hobart Ison, Letcher County, Ky.,
September 1967

Our behaviour is a function of our experience. We act according to the way we see things.

If our experience is destroyed, our behaviour will be destructive.

If our experience is destroyed, we have lost our own selves.

—R.D. Laing, *The Politics of Experience* (emphasis original)

All things Begin & End in Albions Ancient Druid Rocky
    Shore,
But now the Starry Heavens are fled from the mighty
    limbs of Albion.

—Blake, *Jerusalem*

INTRODUCTION

What is now proved was once, only imagin'd.
—Blake, *The Marriage of Heaven and Hell*

It is a commonplace that the people of Appalachia are mainly "Celts" and largely of "Scotch-Irish" origin. Yet as well known as this fact is, it has attracted very little attention from serious scholars in recent times. The reasons for this neglect are plain. Not only does the subject carry a suggestion of racism, but the popular literature about "Celts" is one of the world's most fertile fields of nonsense. Any mention of the "Celtic" background of most Appalachians is liable to strike the serious student as irrelevant at best, and at worst dangerous.

And indeed, this kind of suspicion is certainly justified as regards the majority of popular writing both about Celts and about Appalachians. But that very fact should interest the alert observer. The "Celtic" nations of western Europe are, of course, oppressed and exploited in various ways, as is Appalachia; and much of the nonsense that has been written about each is a smokescreen for this fact. So then, if a parallel mystification has obscured the facts of oppression in both cases, then might not a penetrating look into the "Celtic" case illuminate facets of Appalachia's experience? And if there is in fact a historical connection between the "Celtic" peoples and Appalachian mountain people, then might not an examination of that history add a further dimension to the study of the Appalachian region? I intend, in fact, to show that the "Celtic" background of Appalachia is not only relevant in a politically and culturally serious context; it is perhaps relevant *only* in a serious context.

David Whisnant has noted how he had thought of the "Scotch-Irish" background of Appalachians as "essentially beside the point" until he learned of the Highland Clearances and "discovered levels of significance previously undreamed of in that romantic philosophy."[1]

But these levels are still analogical, not historical, for the Scotch-Irish were descended from Scottish Lowlanders, not Highlanders. Is there a significance here which is not only analogical but historical? I believe there is—a significance which adds a further dimension to Appalachian history, a dimension of repeated patterns of experience of at least eight hundred years' duration, and in some respects much longer. I am not referring to "racial memory" in some quasi-mystical telepathic or genetic sense. I mean, rather, patterns of individually learned social responses and ego-structures, existing on a high level of abstraction, shaped by very early experiences, and reinforced by sociocultural patterns so that they persist in spite of change in more easily graspable traits. Thus D. O. Mannoni, one of the greatest psychologists of modern domination, noted:

> There is a kind of psychological heredity whereby certain traits of character are handed down from generation to generation. . . . This form of heredity must be particularly persistent if it is true, as is claimed, that the characters of the various European peoples as described in antiquity are still recognizable today, even after all the intermingling they have undergone in the course of time, so much so that it is virtually impossible to link this constancy to any physiological heredity.[2]

My project, therefore, is an essay in exploring this "psychological heredity." It sets out to take the "Scotch-Irish" and "Celtic" aspect of the Appalachian people backward in its history and outward in its implications in ways which, to my knowledge, have not previously been attempted on this scale by serious students of the region. Instead of taking up the "Scotch-Irish" about 1600 on the eve of the Ulster Plantation, I shall show that the core of the Appalachian people was essentially formed by events which took place in the twelfth and thirteenth centuries, and which to some extent were prepared for by repeated patterns of events going back to the first agricultural settlement of Britain, five thousand years earlier. In the process I shall demonstrate that much of what has been written before about the "Scotch-Irish," let alone about Appalachia, is not only incomplete but seriously distorted by lack of such a perspective. My goals are: to separate the "Scotch-Irish" thesis from its embedding in false or irrelevant concepts of "Celtic traits" or "American stock"; to analyze these concepts in order to reveal their true import; to show how the latter is important for understanding the "Celtic," "Scotch-Irish," and Appalachian situations; and to demonstrate that the reality of the current situation of exploitation in Appalachia goes a great deal further back in time and outward in spheres of life than is usually thought, that it forms patterns of repeated motifs, and that its past helps explain a great many features of Appalachian life—indeed, that its application to the mountains illuminates the general theories of colonialism and allied forms of domination, of which the classic formulations are those of Mannoni, Albert Memmi, and Frantz Fanon.

In this process of tracing backward and outward, I have come across many parallels between ages and situations. Indeed, much of my intended contribution consists of adopting existing analyses of a given situation and trying it out on the others. My description of each historical locus thus contains elements which are somewhat conjectural. But the collective weight of these parallelisms seems to me considerable, especially as they have suggested details of correlation which I have later confirmed. And I hope that my generalist approach may have allowed me to notice elements and draw parallels which can suggest more detailed analyses by others. To many my approach will no doubt seem scandalously eclectic; but I hope that the reader may come to see my method not as circular but as spiral, progressing in a third dimension, advancing toward a goal and, I hope, defining a center.

The intellectual framework of this book is a synthesis of various strands of thought. By way of introduction, it seems best to say something about how this synthesis came into being. As a native of West Virginia, I first became interested in the concept of Appalachia as an exploited "third-world" region in the late sixties, when the subject was attracting widespread attention. Yet at the same time, I felt that the exclusively politico-economic approach to the subject was inadequate. Specifically, I also saw aspects of "Celtic" nationalism which seemed strongly relevant to the Appalachian "problem," but I remained puzzled as to how to integrate these two approaches. Each position seemed to contain valid criticisms of the other: thus I was repelled both by the nationalists' naïve or superficial approach to history and politics, and by the social activists' tendency to dismiss, ignore, or pigeonhole cultural questions. During the early seventies, while immersing myself for the first time in the growing scholarly literature on Appalachia, I devoted much thought to overcoming this dichotomy but without much immediate success. I had to be largely content with maintaining a tension between two independent trains of thought on the same subject. Meanwhile, the inadequacy of each side of that dichotomy, taken by itself, was being demonstrated more clearly every day in that era of drift and decline.

It was during 1973 that I first began to think seriously of writing a book about Appalachia. It would have been very different from this one, but I already knew that I wanted to discuss Scotland at least as far back as the late Middle Ages and that I saw a large element of psychological projection in attitudes of "outsiders" which were hampering modern Appalachians. As yet, though, these two facts remained as unconnected with each other as did the whole "Celticist" and "activist" currents of thought in which I had attained these insights. Nevertheless I persevered. In 1975 I read Geoffrey Ashe's *Camelot and the Vision of Albion*, a popularly written account of the ramifications of the Arthurian myth in both its historical effects and its analogues in other cultures. The book seemed suggestive of much more than it said—for example, in its treatment of Blake, an author I had been drawn to since the age of sixteen, and who had helped me to overcome another common dichotomy, namely that between myth and liberation. But I was dissatisfied with Ashe's wholesale romantic "Celticism" and with a certain lack of rigor in his historical scholarship. Then, in the later seventies, disillusionment and degree work in comparative literature at Indiana University drew me away from Appalachian studies and into scholarly (and personal) explorations that seemed to have nothing in particular to do with either Celts or Appalachians: Freud, Jung, R. D. Laing, Kierkegaard, Paul Ricoeur, Norman O. Brown, Ernest Becker, Joseph Campbell.

By now I was in San Diego, doing postdoctoral survival work two thousand miles from Appalachia and ten miles from the Third World proper, learning a great deal at first hand both about cultural systems and about the class system, national and international. At this time a rereading of Ashe's *Camelot* heightened my appreciation both of its inadequacies and of its suggestiveness. I felt that Ashe touched on and linked a great many themes which he treated rather superficially, and I began trying to use those links in a deeper exploration of those themes—to "misread" his work for political, psychological, and other ramifications far beyond his own point of aim. Meanwhile, my interests returned to my native region, but I was largely cut off from the new burgeoning of regional scholarship and writing which had begun just as I had left the East. I did what I could, however, to acquaint myself with what I could find of new works in the field, notably Whisnant's *Modernizing the Mountaineer* and Helen

Lewis, Linda Johnson, and Don Askins' *Colonialism in Modern America*
—a book which I later found had done much to spark that scholarly
revival, and one which led me, among other things, to a fresh reading
of Frantz Fanon and a first acquaintance with Memmi and Mannoni.
From Lewis' book I also became aware, via David Walls, of the economic peripheralization theory of Immanuel Wallerstein, which count-
ers liberal "development theory" with the thesis that a depressed and
exploited "peripheral zone" plays an essential role in the economic life
of a dominant metropolitan core—in short, that "underdeveloped" regions are victims of a process of "underdevelopment."

But it was while pursuing the "other" train of thought that I
made the vital connection. Browsing one day in the Celtic literature
collection of the San Diego State University Library, I came across a
misclassified work of social anthropology, Malcolm Chapman's *The
Gaelic Vision in Scottish Culture*. This proved to be a brilliant study of
what Chapman called the "symbolic appropriation" of a colonized culture by a dominant one. Chapman lucidly explores how English culture has enclosed Gaelic culture within its own categories, in such a
way as to create a stereotype of both that implicitly denies Gaelic and
all "Celtic" culture the attributes of adult competency to wield power.
It was, ironically, my literary and linguistic training which had prepared me for Chapman's use of semiotic concepts in a work of social
science. As soon as I had grasped Chapman's thesis, a great many of
my floating thoughts on many subjects began to crystallize. I had
found the tool with which to sort out the tangled strands of my conflicting ideas both about "Celts" and about Appalachians. Chapman
had made it clear just how to cut through the politically harmful aspects of "culturalist" stereotypes without denying the validity and autonomy—and the political significance—of culture and cultural distinctiveness as such.

It was now early 1981. For some months I had been making des-
ultory attempts at writing an article on the Scotch-Irish thesis and its
continued relevance to Appalachian studies. Now, my perceptions
sharpened and my approach more confident, I began writing in ear-
nest, and the "article" burgeoned to monograph length and beyond.
Then, while researching the settlement of Appalachia, I made a second set of vitally important connections when I read Michael Rogin's
*Fathers and Children: Andrew Jackson and the Subjugation of the American
Indian*. This Freudian psychohistorical study of Jackson's character
links it strongly to the frontier experience of which Jackson's life was
an exemplary part and to which it contributed. I found Rogin's thesis

greatly illuminating not only for the place and time he discussed, but for analogous situations—and, I began to realize, historically connected ones—reaching far back into the past and up into the present. Furthermore, I found myself going beyond Rogin not only historically but conceptually, while inspired by his basic method of drawing parallels between individual and collective experience. Thus it seemed to me that Rogin's drawing of connections between the geographical frontier and the ego-boundaries of individuals was not only powerful in itself but capable of extension along the lines of economic peripheralization theory. Again, Rogin's discussion of projective identification as a mechanism in the white man's view of the Indian suggested extensions along the lines of Chapman's "symbolic appropriation" and R. D. Laing's theory of attribution. Finally, the status of today's "Celtic" countries as peripheral regions of Britain, as explored by Michael Hechter in *Internal Colonialism*, suggested links between Wallerstein and Chapman, which in turn ramified through my whole burgeoning nexus of ideas concerning economics, culture, psychology, and history.

Thus the first draft of this book came into being in five months of intense thinking and writing—much of it on unsupervised Sundays in charge of the store where I worked. And there the matter sat for some time, due to my isolation and the pressure of other projects. But a year later, I returned to West Virginia and soon became aware of the many developments in the Appalachian studies field during my absence. I encountered the writings of Allen Batteau, Ronald D Eller, and Henry Shapiro, for example, as well as works in allied fields such as Bernard Sheehan's *Savagism and Civility,* Hugh MacDougall's *Racial Myth in English History,* and Joel Kovel's *White Racism.* I was gratified to find my own ideas confirmed, paralleled, and complemented rather than exploded or completely anticipated. When several participants in the 1983 Appalachian Studies Conference expressed interest in my work, I set out to produce a revised and expanded version of my manuscript. The ultimate result is the book you hold.

So then, how have I united all these concerns? To answer this question, and thus to set out for the reader the theoretical groundwork of this book, I shall first go into a bit more detail about the links and parallelisms I have used, and then I shall set forth my major theses. Finally, I shall briefly summarize the book as an expression of these theses.

In applying my literary training to a great variety of far-removed fields, I have tried to keep in mind the comparatist ideal of synthesis and of seeing connections among entities commonly thought of as separate. In this regard, as I have said, the most important aspect of my approach in the present study has been the drawing of analogies between group and individual experience, and in particular between social, cultural, and ethnic boundaries (frontiers, borders, peripheries) on the one hand and intrapsychic boundaries (personal identity as boundary of ego, ego itself as boundary of selfhood) on the other. Hence I connect unstable frontiers with insecure ego-boundaries, cultural invasion with intrusiveness, cultural stereotyping with false and labeling interpersonal perception, and so forth. On the latter point, I particularly emphasize the parallels between false concepts of "civilization" and false concepts of "maturity." Thus far I have been inspired by Michael Rogin, and in general I have freely used psychoanalytic and other psychological concepts without pledging allegiance to any particular "school." But on the collective side my view of the nature of attributions (both collective and individual) has been strongly affected by the symbolic anthropology of Malcolm Chapman and of his mentor Edwin Ardener,[3] while on the individual side my view of the effects of these processes (both individual and collective) has been informed by the attribution theory of the existential psychologist R. D. Laing.

But the development of my approach was not basically a matter of developing the parallels and then applying them to the situations. Rather, I derived the parallels from what seemed applicable to a given situation on different levels; indeed, they were generally inspired by what had been applied on that level to one or another analogous situation in the long and varied history of the exploitation of groups and individuals by one another. Thus there is little absolutely novel in the details of my approach as I have described it thus far, but I believe I have nevertheless made a contribution both to Appalachian studies and to the synthesis of approaches to domination and liberation.

In one way, though, I believe I have added a new dimension to my models. I have been moved to do this by consideration of Scotch-Irish and Appalachian history in terms of peripheralization theory. The frameworks I have invoked above are essentially dyadic; that is, they describe relations between pairs of subjects. But in the history of Appalachians and their ancestors, I distinguish *three* regions: a metropolitan core labeling itself as "civilized" (Rome, England, the East

Coast); an "outside" region labeled as "savage" or "barbarous" (the Celts, the "wild" Highlanders, the "wild" Irish, the "wild" Indians); and, all-important for my study, an intermediate region (the Scottish Lowlands, Ulster, Appalachia) that stands to the "civilized" core economically as a periphery, and politically and culturally as a frontier of expansion against the "wild" exterior. (Rogin's framework is tripartite in that he discusses England as the "mother country" but with a basically political and not economic emphasis.)

Recognizing the existence of this third zone, however, goes against the human mental tendency to perceive the world in terms of dichotomies—structural oppositions of "humanity" and "nature," "civilization" and "savagery," "order" and "chaos," and so on, all of these being versions of the primal distinction between "self" and "not-self." As a result, this intermediate peripheral zone and its inhabitants have constantly been misperceived by the "civilized" metropole—put into false positions, seen in false ways. And this misperception has been committed not only by the "civilized" insider but also by the "savage" outsider. To the metropolitan, the frontiersman was essentially barbarous; to the outsider, he was the foreign intruder. In short, each of these groups has tended to see the intermediate one—the peripheral dwellers—as a version of the other, and a particularly objectionable one at that.

My basic themes, then, are two: identity, both individual and collective; and peripheralization—what it means to be looked on constantly as someone on the fringe of things. And my fundamental thesis is that among Appalachians and their forebears, the second has had a pernicious effect on the first. Other writers have shown how the "civilized" person has created the image of the "savage" as a projection of that "civilization's" own rejected, repressed, and unsublimated infantile impulses. The result for the "savage," even when the latter has been spared physical extermination, has been psychic and sociocultural destruction. Again and again, a stable society of mature adults has been disrupted by "civilized" efforts (even, or especially, well-meaning efforts) to "raise" it from a state defined as "childish"—and these efforts have created a self-fulfilling prophecy of turmoil and dependency.

But what of the peripheral dweller? In this case—and especially if that periphery is also a frontier against "savagery"—people are subjected to a process somewhat more subtle but no less pernicious. For where a powerful "civilized" society is engaged in violence against a less powerful "savage" one, the frontier of the powerful society is identified with the unstable and violent ego-boundary of the individual, an insecure frontier which perpetuates the ego through violence.[4] But the peripheral dwellers, the frontiersmen, are also in a weak position with regard to the metropolitan core dweller. And thus they are also vulnerable to the effects of being identified with projected parts of the core dweller's psyche. Specifically, they are identified with the unstable, violent ego-boundary. Since their whole being is identified with another's boundary, they are not seen in all their dimensions; and since they are specifically seen as something violent and unstable, they are under pressure to let violence and instability permeate their whole psyches vis-à-vis the universe. The metropole then encourages them to take out this violence on the ones next in line, the "savages." Thus they are manipulated into carrying out the metropole's genocidal program while being culturally and socially destroyed themselves. They are encouraged to see themselves as the representatives of "civilization" against "savagery," while the metropolitan in fact looks on them as little, if at all, better than savages themselves. And they are seen in this way precisely because of that violence which the metropole itself has instilled in them by undermining their sense of autonomous identity and independent self-worth. They are never themselves but always versions of another, and always in a negative sense.

In exploring this theme of impaired identity, I have not only followed Freudian and existential psychology. I have also seen connections with the writings of Joseph Campbell and other mythologists who have studied the psychological meanings of rites, and particularly of the *rite of passage* as a formal transformation of identity. Thus I have formed the thesis that a peripheralized people is the victim of (among other things) distorted rites of passage which reinforce these insecure ego-boundaries and ego-foundations. It seems to me that this interpretation is in line with, and indeed integrates and brings out hidden aspects of, the classic theories of colonial domination. Here and elsewhere my approach attempts to transcend most social critics' blanket contempt for "myth" and also most mythologists' (including Campbell's) blindness or complacency regarding the effects of socioeconomic power on myth and ritual—effects that have given myth and ritual themselves what I consider an undeservedly bad name.

I have, then, attempted to trace the themes of identity and peripheralization among the forebears of the Appalachian people not only across spheres of life not previously linked together in this way, but also backward in time much further than has previously been attempted. Let me, then, proceed to a synopsis of my historical argument.

I begin by describing the Atlantic Zone of Europe, that distinctive though raggedly elongated "subcontinent" described so well in the works of the Irish geographer E. Estyn Evans. I briefly describe the various invasions of the area, analyzing later legendary accounts to show the psychological genesis of the dominating attitudes analyzed for modern cases by Memmi, Fanon, and their successors. While doing so, I narrow my focus first to Britain and then to the southwestern region of Scotland, the main home of what was to become the "Scotch-Irish." The Roman invasion frames a study of the Classical attitude toward Celtic and British "barbarians," and here I introduce the theme of "primitivism" as being a projection of one's own traits on the outsider. A key fact will become apparent here, and not by any means for the last time in this study: the basic identities and conflicts of the situation are not "ethnic"—at least not in any vulgar genetic sense—but *regional*, even in Europe and even at this remote date.[5]

Moving on into the early Middle Ages, I show how the Atlantic Zone in general and southwestern Scotland in particular were progressively transformed from a largely independent cultural and economic entity into a dominated periphery of mainland Europe. There follows what is in many ways the key section of the entire book, namely a discussion of the fundamental social and cultural trauma undergone by what was to become the Scotch-Irish and Appalachian peoples. This was the forcible feudalization and anglicization of the Scottish Lowlands in the late Middle Ages by a Scottish elite of Anglo-Norman culture. The region and its population were thus transformed from an integral part of one society into a subjugated fringe of another. In this period, economic peripheralization on the unstable frontier of western Europe—unstable because there were still unsubdued lands in Scotland and Ireland—led to the development, in individuals on the periphery, of a particular type of insecure ego-boundary. This insecurity, as I have said, was wedded to a false concept of both "civilization" and "maturity," and this peripheralized personality found its natural vent in projecting the self-to-be-subdued onto the outsider, who at this time was the Scottish Highlander. A few centuries later, these themes were repeated and reinforced in the Ulster Plantation, when the frontier of European power moved outward again and Appalachians' ancestors moved along with it, continuing to be "civilization's" manipulated advance agents against the "wild" Irish as they had been against the "wild" Highlanders.

I then outline the history of Appalachia itself from this viewpoint. First I show how, as the European periphery moved still further out, across the Atlantic, a large proportion of the Scotch-Irish moved along with it, transferring their aggression from "wild" Gaels to "wild" Indians—an old idea, but one which I explore in new ways. Then, as the Indian frontier retreated further west and the Scotch-Irish pioneers settled into the mountains, the ground was laid for the recovery of a stable, rooted identity. But this process ended up being seriously impaired.

First, in the Civil War and its aftermath, the rival lowland cultures and polities of North and South repeated the old pattern in a new way: each saw the mountaineer as a version of the other one, with disastrous effects both material and otherwise. Then, in the late nineteenth century, when the frontier closed altogether, the mountains began to be penetrated by industrial "civilization." At this point a fundamental shift occurred in the outside perception of the mountaineer. The frontier of white against Indian having faded from consciousness, the "frontier" concept was transferred to a newly important boundary—the one between industrial society and nonindustrial. Mountaineers were no longer on the fringe—instead they were altogether on the wrong side of this "frontier." Therefore, their stereotyped image now took on the essential features of their dark twins, the Indians. Like the latter, and like the Celts in ancient times, they were sometimes seen as detestable barbarians, sometimes as romantic noble savages; but these two constructs were simply versions of each other, and in neither case were they confronted as persons. Indeed the fact that they were seen as a version of the dominant culture—as "contemporary ancestors"—only accentuated the tendency to see them through projections rather than as they were, or are. I analyze some of the results in terms which unite the psychological insights of R. D. Laing, the social analyses of Memmi and Fanon, and the observations of some modern students and natives of Appalachia.

All this may seem to make Appalachians look like passive victims in an all too familiar way; but I hold that this impression is an artifact of the analytical method, since analysis itself is inherently a tool for exploring the bound and not the free, necessity and not possi-

xxvi   *Apples on the Flood*

bility, the fixed past (and the present as its result) and not the un-
decided future (and the present as its springboard). For the latter I
conclude by returning to the realm of myth, not deconstructing it
analytically as I had when exposing its distortions, but exploring it for
its suggestiveness. I contend that important insights may be derived
from certain "Celtic" (or Atlantic) mythic themes—insights regarding
the indestructibility of authenticity and wholeness beneath the distortions of power, and regarding the necessity of translating this insight into concrete action in the world.

Even though this book deals at length with some aspects of "Celtic" history, the reader will search in vain for explanations of history
and character in terms of so-called "Celtic traits," such as have been
attempted many times. Indeed, the reader will find little mention of
such "traits" at all. This fact may require an explanation.

To begin with, I disagree fundamentally with the basic assumption of much "ethnic studies," which treats culture as a more or less
arbitrary congeries of "traits" bagged together in a sharply defined
and defended "boundary."[6] As the reader will see in Chapter 6, I believe that when cultures do approach this state it is a sign of serious
trouble; and I think it is a sad commentary on our civilization that so
many students of ethnicity take such a condition for granted as the
normal human state of affairs. But I have been gratified lately to find
my criticisms of this view paralleled in a growing body of anthropological thought which sees sociocultural boundaries as secondary to
internal structures of meaning—and not only boundaries, but "traits"
themselves, so that "sociocultural *content* . . . does not persist . . .
and that flexibility makes the enduring collective identity system su-
premely adaptive."[7] This recent description of "enduring peoples"
and of what Mannoni would have called their "psychological heredity" certainly fits Scotch-Irish Appalachians, whose ancestors have,
for example, changed their language at least two or three times while
maintaining an unbroken identity since the Bronze Age or earlier.

And when cultures collide, it is incongruity between such structures of meaning, not simply the clash of more easily articulated "values," which makes misunderstandings so remarkably persistent and
so difficult to clear up. As Laing writes: "The history of heresies of all
kinds testifies to more than the tendency to break off communication
(excommunication) with those who hold different dogmas or opin-
ions; it bears witness to our intolerance of different *fundamental structures of experience*."[8] And when one group is materially stronger than

another, and conquest and/or domination take place, one result is that the dominated group's traits are fitted into the dominant's categories. Indeed, the imposition of such an alien set of meanings upon the dominated's own mind is one of the most profound effects of colonialism and other systems of domination and one of those systems' most effective agents of cultural and personality destruction, far beyond the overt imposition of "values."

Appalachia has been cited abundantly with regard to this fact, the fact "that dominated people often internalize the conceptual apparatus of the ruling elite."[9] Here, taking a structural approach to this Marxian insight, I shall analyze certain developments in Appalachia and elsewhere in terms of what Malcolm Chapman calls "symbolic appropriation." Chapman apologizes for the awkwardness of this phrase,[10] and I shall compound the awkwardness by preferring "sign-appropriation." (The more exact counterpart "semiotic appropriation" may perhaps obscure as much as it clarifies.) But I find myself forced to make this change by my belief that there is an important distinction between sign and symbol—a distinction vital to some of this book's modes of exploration, especially in the last chapter.

Thus what I wish to discuss is not a matter of cultural *content*, but of cultural (and political, economic, psychological, and so on) *process*. It is not a matter of "What came down through history?" but of "What sort of history came down?"—not of *what* was changed, but of *how* it was changed. The main contrast is not between some "Celtic" or "Atlantic" or "genuine Appalachian" culture (= good guys) and "English" or "Continental" or "American" culture (= bad guys). Much less is it between some static ideal and some inherently evil process of change. Change is of course an integral part of culture. The real contrast, rather, is between, on the one hand, processes of change which operate within a culture's inherent structures of meaning under conditions which respect human autonomy and integrity, and on the other hand processes of change which disrupt those structures and ignore those meanings under conditions of misperception, invalidation, and false justification of illegitimate power.

This primacy of *process* over *content* is, then, one reason I have not invoked traditional concepts of "Celtic" culture. A second reason is that, as I have said, the basis of the cultures in question is not "ethnic"—at least not in a simple sense—but *regional*: not "Celtic" but *Atlantic*. Indeed, I consistently use the word "Celt" in quotation marks because, especially as used with respect to the British Isles, it refers to something with an indirect and complex relation to the historic peoples called by that name among the Greeks and Romans during the Celtic heyday. Classical civilization never referred to the inhabitants of Britain as Celts; the word was almost unused in English until the eighteenth century; and the two areas of Britain where Celtic languages survive most vigorously today are Wales, where the population is mostly of pre-Celtic origin, and the Hebrides, where it is largely Norse in ancestry. (Indeed, language is really the only strictly correct context in which to use the word "Celtic" without qualification. Our modern notion of "Celtic nationality" is simply based on the populations which were still speaking Celtic languages, or had come to speak them, in the early modern period, when our social construct of "nationality" came into being. Hence the common misconception that the Scottish Lowlander and the Ulster Protestant are of fundamentally different ancestry from the Highlander and the Irish Catholic.)

The "Scotch-Irish" themselves experienced many admixtures of immigrants, especially English ones, both in Scotland and later in Ireland. And finally, of course, a goodly proportion of Appalachians themselves are not of "Scotch-Irish" origin at all but are derived from the original natives; from German, Welsh, English, Highland Scottish, and Black settlers; or from later arrivals. Nevertheless, just as all of these now share certain "American" characteristics, so by virtue of their choice of region and neighbors they have become part of that "Appalachian" culture which, by and large, is a transform of "Scotch-Irish" culture—and, in turn, they have contributed much to this "enduring people's" motifs without overwhelming the basic themes of its "psychological heredity," its "fundamental structures of experience." If, as Martin Buber said, it is unity of fate which makes a people, then the inhabitants of Appalachia certainly share such a unity.[11]

And the same is true at those historical junctures that are earlier than Appalachia. What made an Anglo-Scot or a western Englishman (themselves largely semi-"Celtic" to begin with) move in the first place to a burgh in southwest Scotland or a town in Ulster? The answer to such a question is not to be found in notions of "Celtic" versus "English" mentality, but in concepts such as Memmi's "small colonizer."[12] Hence the reader looking for descriptions of "Celtic consciousness" will instead find a great deal of discussion derived from studies of colonialism—discussion which might be thought irrelevant and/or anachronistic without this explanation. Hence, too, the reader will find a close discussion of the "Scotch-Irish" coexisting with a free admission that many other elements have gone into Appalachia. This might otherwise be thought contradictory, but I hope it is apparent now why I have chosen this treatment. To me, the "Scotch-Irish" element in Appalachian history—and before that, the "Celtic" or rather Atlantic element in the "Scotch-Irish"—are only a central thread, but an all-important one, in a cultural *process* whose bases are, first, a *regional* environment having a constant nature and, second, a *structure of meanings* with a great capacity to accommodate changes in "traits" and importations of "ethnic strains."

But where some may be momentarily puzzled, others may be relieved. When I have mentioned to my colleagues that I was working on the "Scotch-Irish," some have bristled as if I were trying to revive the racist and geneticist assumptions that marked such discussions in the first part of this century—the last time the question came up in Appalachian studies, until the decline of "race science," "eugenics," and nativism largely discredited the whole matter. But instead of resurrecting the discussion in these well-discarded terms, what I am trying to do is precisely to revive it on a modern basis, by reopening the question of mountaineers' European regional and cultural origins in terms of how European scholars today think of their own regions and cultures.

Appalachian studies has for some years been the scene of a debate between "cultural" and "political" approaches. Since this book has behind it a great deal of reflection on this matter, it seems appropriate to say a few more words here on the subject.

Richard Couto has called on Appalachian scholars to see culture as "a dependent variable" instead of "an accepted given, an independent variable,"[13] in order to avoid an apolitical approach which implicitly blames the victim. As a critique of "culture-of-poverty" theories, I think this is perfectly on target. But there is more than one approach to culture, and there is more than one definition of culture; and I think that as a general critique of all such approaches, Couto's injunction takes for granted a number of unnecessary dichotomies. The distinction between independent and dependent variables belongs to the realm of mathematics; elsewhere, and especially in the study of human interactions, it is a metaphor, and like all metaphors it is dangerous when not recognized as such. In a context such as this, I believe it is necessary to recognize that *all* "variables" are *inter*dependent—that there are *no* static "accepted givens." An *exclusive* concern with economic categories as the only "independent" reality can be as much of a mystification as any form of racism or "culturalism." Indeed, such an exclusiveness conceals the basic assumptions of the bourgeois rationality it sets out to combat.[14]

Allen Batteau has helped to clarify matters with an oft-quoted formula: "Culture is politically constituted, and politics are culturally structured."[15] But this formulation, though true in itself, may also seem to take for granted that structural dichotomy which sees "culture" and "politics" as a "given" polarity within which society, economics, psychology, and so on, must be subsumed. I suspect, however, that the whole intellectual problem of reconciling "culture" and "politics" is a fabrication arising from dividing a single process verbally into two aspects—for example, "culture" and "politics," "structure" and "function," "individual" and "collective," "inner" and "outer"—and then finding oneself under the necessity of elaborating verbal formulae to express the "relation" between these verbal constructs. In this particular case, the "political" side may become as trapped in verbal webs of its own making as the "cultural." *Any* vocabulary can be separated from its living context in thought and action and used for mystification.

I, at any rate, think that there is room for all these emphases as long as they are recognized as such—as emphases, not as exclusive keys to reality. To paraphrase Geoffrey Ashe: the real division in Appalachian studies, as in so many fields of scholarly and other endeavor, is not between, say, "action folk" and "creative people,"[16] or between Marxists and Christians (another dubious dichotomy), "but between Enclosers and Enlargers."[17] Appalachian studies can accommodate—indeed, it needs—any number of different types of Enlargers, but if it becomes the scene of a fray among different ilks and kidneys of Enclosers, then it is doomed, and deserves to be.

What I have to say in this book is not intended as an alternative to the researches of sociologists, economists, and the like. As a nonspecialist in many of the fields I deal with, I am not always precise in my own mind as to the relations among them. I remain confident, however, that my basic approach is sound. All the aspects I discuss tend to parallel and reinforce one another. Various forms of oppression (and of liberation) have a family resemblance, an abstract unity with very concrete manifestations. There is not one "reality" of which the other aspects are "metaphors"; rather, all aspects are "metaphors"—literally, carryings-over—of one another, and all as a whole make up the reality of which they are parallel aspects. This essay is simply a sighting shot at a new approach, and I hope a springboard for further discussion. I am attempting to encourage the reader to go forward from my speculations, rather than instructing him or her to take a seat in a certain spot. It is in this hope that I offer this work to all those who are interested in the Appalachian region and in the necessities and possibilities of the human spirit.

Apples on the Flood

1 *The Leap of Goemagog*

This backward movement is a forward movement, in so far as
going backward means going deeper into something.
            —Kierkegaard, *Concluding Unscientific Postscript*

Ceterum Britanniam qui mortales initio coluerint, indigenae
an advecti, ut inter barbaros, parum compertum. [Whether the
first mortals to inhabit Britain were natives or immigrants is an
open question, they being barbarians.]
            —Tacitus, *Agricola*, 11

Proprium humani ingenii est odisse quem laeseris. [A special
feature of human intelligence is to hate one's victim.]
            —Tacitus, *Agricola*, 42

   Histories of Appalachian settlement seldom go back earlier than
the arrival of settlers in America, and even histories of the "Scotch-
Irish" almost never penetrate beyond Scotland at the time of the Ulster Plantation under James VI. The most significant exception is
James Heron's "The Making of the Ulster Scot," but this essay dates
from 1910 and, though still useful, contains many obsolete assumptions and conclusions, especially concerning the relation of "Anglo-
Saxons" to other strains in the Ulster Scot's ancestry. The first part of
this historical survey therefore includes much detail which some may
doubt is relevant to Appalachian studies. But this material is presented in order to show that the history of the area in question—the
lowlands of Scotland, and in particular the western lowlands—*is* detailed and complex. The cliché view of British history, according to
which "Celtic" peoples inhabited the islands "at first" and were gradually and steadily driven back into remote regions by "Anglo-Saxons,"
is not only a wild oversimplification but a politically meaningful one,
a mystification. It is part of the wishful notion of "inevitable, irre-

sistible forces" which softens the guilt of conquest and destruction, and which even allows the conqueror to "appreciate" in a dissociated way the externals of the conquered's culture while watching its inner spirit disappear: the "Celt" as Vanishing European. It is closely connected with that strain of thought which associates the "Celt" with the dreamy, "mystical," and impractical, so that his disappearance seems as inevitable, and as ultimately desirable, as the individual passage from childhood to adulthood—of which, indeed, it is largely a projection.

This popular simplified view of "Celts" gradually rolling back before "Anglo-Saxons" is perhaps further from the truth in southwestern Scotland than in any other part of Britain. And as the popular view is a sentimental screen put up to soften the facts of exploitation, so the actual facts reveal a different pattern, a different unity of themes. Once more, the "Celtic" background of Appalachians is relevant in a serious context, not primarily (if at all) because of some "original" *content* of "Celtic" culture, but because of the *process* by which this identity has been modified over the centuries. The reader should look on what follows in terms of a process which first emerges in full clarity in the western Scottish lowlands in the twelfth and thirteenth centuries A.D. This is still long before the beginning of most histories of the subject, certainly of any of those which explore it from a perspective like the one taken here; but, with this culmination in mind, many elements of that process can be seen far earlier.

I shall be discussing lands and peoples which appear on most historical maps in pale italics stretching across wastes of dismissive off-white, cut off by the edges like bystanders in a group photograph; I intend to give them, in the reader's mind, the color, detail and centrality that belong to them as real participants in history. Scholars of Appalachia, even major ones, have referred to our subjects, if at all, in terms that seem derived from childhood memories of yellowing library books full of Victorian engravings. I intend to make those subjects stand out crisply in sharp relevance and in all their hues.

The Celts were far from being the first inhabitants of Britain, and the Roman and Anglo-Saxon invasions were far from the beginning of ethnic and regional oppression in those islands. The British Isles lie at the end of two different, and differently structured, paths of trade and conquest: a north-south sea route along the western European coastline to and from the Mediterranean and Africa, and an east-west land route across the northern European plain from the steppes of

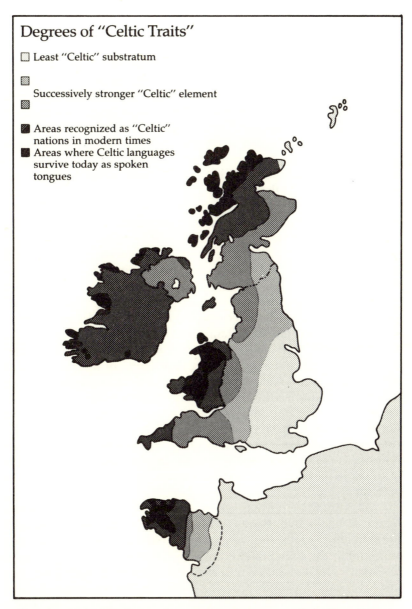

Degrees of "Celtic Traits"

☐ Least "Celtic" substratum

▨
Successively stronger "Celtic" element
▨

▨ Areas recognized as "Celtic" nations in modern times

■ Areas where Celtic languages survive today as spoken tongues

Note that "Celtic" background is a matter of degrees and shadings; there is generally a correlation with length of time since English or other conquest. The areas of modern-day "Celtic nationality" are simply, by and large, the areas which were still Celtic-speaking in the early modern period, when our social construct of "nationality" came into being. What we are dealing with is a *regional*, not an ethnic, phenomenon—or better, perhaps, the "ethnic" reality is at least as much regional as "hereditary."

Source: See Bickmore and Shaw, *Atlas of Britain*, 187; Edwards, *Atlas of Irish History*, 230; *Grand Atlas de la France*, 97; K. Jackson, *Language and History*, 220; Withers, *Gaelic in Scotland*, 93, 234.

central Asia. Before modern crops and methods of agriculture, this grassy steppe brought Asia into the heart of central Europe, often literally. Britain has frequently been influenced and invaded from both directions; but by and large, the flatter, wide-valleyed eastern parts of England have faced the continent, while the rougher, inlet-filled coasts of the west and north and of Ireland have formed part of a seaward-looking world that also includes Brittany and western Iberia in one direction, and Norway and the North Atlantic islands in the other. These areas, the "Atlantic Zone," formed a quite coherent entity in themselves, one which faded in unity and importance only in the past thousand or so years, as the growth of modern conditions led to the conclusive dominance of the land-based continental cultures. The parts of the Atlantic Zone are separated by stretches of water, but the greater ease of sea-based over land-based travel and communication made this fact all the more a basis for regional unity and distinctness. Some students of Spain are fond of saying that Europe ends with the Pyrenees; it could be said equally well that Europe ends with the watershed ranges of Britain, or even with the English Channel. Fanciful theories deriving the Megalithic cultures and so forth from the mythical Atlantis are inspired by the unity of this Atlantic Zone. Such a unity seems mysterious, in need of some extraordinary explanation, to moderns who think in continental European terms—who see the Atlantic Zone only as the series of broken fringes to which European powers have reduced it, and who thus have to project an Atlantis into the west to match Europe in the east, with the Atlantic Zone as the peripheral region of both. In fact, of course, it is nothing of the sort, but rather something central and valid in its own right, with its own principles of organization.[1]

The Atlantic Zone has a long human history, and from the beginning it is distinctive. Bands of hunter-gatherers, chasing the tails of the retreating ice sheets, were roaming Britain even before it became an island in the sixth millennium B.C. There is some evidence that on the west coast especially, the richness of the sea supported (as on the American Northwest Coast) a pre-agricultural society of unusual population density and cultural elaboration, and that this culture may have had strong influences on later arrivals. Some two thousand years after the opening of the English Channel, the earliest farmers arrived; they established what was to become a long-standing pattern by coming in two waves, one from Brittany into the west and southwest, and one from northern Europe into England, then Scotland and Ireland.[2] It was these Neolithic settlers who developed the British forms of the "Megalithic" cultures of Western Europe. Formerly thought to be inspired by Eastern Mediterranean models, their monumental religious and astronomical structures, such as Stonehenge, have been redated as earlier, native developments of the Atlantic Zone, which developed Mediterranean trade connections only in the culture's late stages. Then, shortly after 2000 B.C., bronze-using peoples started landing on the coasts of Britain and Ireland; rather than driving out the previous arrivals, they seem to have mingled gradually with them over the next thousand years.[3]

Recent research has suggested reasons for the social and political elaboration, unusual in its time, which was necessary for the creation of Stonehenge and other great communal works. As farming led to population increases, the inhabitants of this area on the edge of the West were not able to deal with overpopulation as other Europeans had, by emigration in that direction: "There was simply nowhere to emigrate to, and the demographic consequences had to be faced as best they might. . . . Devices favoring good social cohesion within small farming groups and ways of asserting one's right to farming land would be most useful."[4] If even at this remote date the Atlantic Zone was distinguished as an exception to a prevalent "frontier" mentality, this would be the beginning of a pattern which, as we shall see, was to be continued and repeated with profound effects up to the present day.

Of course we have no direct knowledge of the language or religious practices of any of these peoples. The earlier settlers presumably spoke languages of the "Atlantic" group or groups, whose sole survivor is Basque; some such tongue was still spoken many centuries later on the northern edge of Scotland and in the Orkneys, but it is known only from a few indecipherable names and inscriptions from the brief period between the introduction of writing and the Viking invasions.[5] Some of the Bronze Age settlers, if one can judge from durable words such as river names, may have spoken some dialect of the language of the warlike tribes from the grassy steppes who had invaded southeastern and central Europe in the fifth to third millennia B.C., apparently bringing the religion of the all-enfolding Sky-Father into what had been the realm of the Great Mother who brought forth crops from the earth.[6] These invaders may have called themselves Wiros, the Men or Heroes, but linguists call their language Indo-European—the old synonym Aryan having been spoiled by political misuse. Nevertheless the Bronze Age invaders of Britain seem to have adopted many of the customs of the older inhabitants, for pre-patriarchal forms of worship and social customs survived there until historical times. Too, it was the Bronze Age settlers of Wessex (who seem to have had an Indo-European social structure) that built the final and most impressive parts of Stonehenge, continuing the traditions of their Stone Age predecessors.

Then, starting about 700 B.C., Britain was invaded by a new wave of Indo-Europeans, a burgeoning tribe from the Rhineland, fortified by an aristocratic caste of kindred people from the Alps. Some of them at least called themselves the People of Strength, or Keltas.

The first Celtic invasions of Britain left a distinct legend that survived into modern times, and indeed was once regarded as history. According to Holinshed's sixteenth-century *Chronicles*, Britain was first settled after the Flood by "Samothean Celts," who were children of Japheth, Noah's third son and the ancestor of the European peoples. Then the island was invaded from the south by a race of giants descended from Ham, cursed ancestor of the Africans, and led by Albion the son of Neptune. (Albion is in fact the earliest recorded name for Britain.) These two mythical races are evidently stereotyped memories of the North European and Iberian strains in the pre-Celtic population. Then centuries later, when the giants had grown scarce, the British Celts came—or according to the legend, which Holinshed adapted from the twelfth-century Geoffrey of Monmouth's *History of the Kings of Britain*, a Trojan named Brutus, the great-grandson of Aeneas founder of Rome, left Italy, landed in southern England, killed most of the giants, drove the rest into caves in the mountains, named the island Britain after himself, and colonized it with fellow Trojans.[7]

Two points must be noted here. First, although the immediate pre-Celtic inhabitants of Britain (or Albion) were really a dense population of metal-users with towns and commerce, the legendary giants with "their beastlie kind of life"[8] sound like a distorted memory of more primitive peoples, even the Mesolithic hunter-gatherers. It looks as if the legends of each wave of invaders had been taken over by the next wave who intermarried with them, layering the stories together into one memory as the peoples themselves were layered and mingled together.

Second, although historically confused, this legend is symbolically highly structured and consistent, with a definite "message," as recast first by Christianity and then by the nascent imperialism of Renaissance Europe. The people whom the Celts conquered are looked on as giants—that is, frightening and monstrous. No cultural achievements are attributed to them, and in fact the Celts and even later peoples managed to grab the credit for Stonehenge until well into the nineteenth century. (Actually, contrary to what is still popular belief, there is no evidence that the Celtic Druids even used Stonehenge, whose final stages were already well over a thousand years old when the Celts arrived.) In its Christianized and imperialized form, these giants are called children of "the accursed race of Cham"[9] who had displaced children of Japheth: they are not simply monsters but niggers, hewers of wood and drawers of water, and usurpers as well—the "Trojans" who took their land were merely reclaiming it for the blessed white race. Again, these invaders are called Trojans in order to connect them with the legends of the founding of Rome, seat of the patriarchal authorities of Empire and Church, and the "origin" or filter of all high culture that was known to the West. (Concerning ambiguities in this father-identification, see the next chapter.) Giants are parent-figures, and hostile giants are projections of the feared aspects of the parents; surely it is significant that the warlike, patriarchal Indo-Europeans would attribute this nature to enemies with a much less patriarchal orientation, thus resolving an ambivalence toward their own parents by projecting the "bad" aspects onto a safe target: at once attacking the parents and learning to be like them. (We note that Geoffrey's Brutus was expelled from Italy for killing both his parents, his mother in childbirth and his father in a hunting accident.)

This legend of Brutus the Trojan contains another particularly illuminating detail. According to Geoffrey, the hugest and ugliest of the giants was one called Goemagog. The Trojan duke Corineus challenged Goemagog to a wrestling match, and threw him into the sea at a spot called Goemagog's Leap.[10] But in later versions, the name Goemagog was modified to Gogmagog,[11] after Gog and Magog, northern enemies of Israel mentioned in Ezekiel 38:2–16 and 39:1–11, who appear in the Apocalypse of John (20:8) as nations of "the four quarters of the earth" who will wage war on the saints in the last days. The "Trojans" and their Christian descendants resolved their parental conflicts, and thus defended their patriarchal personality structure, by projecting onto the enemy the threatening aspects both of the parental despotism and of their own rebellious response—that is, the negative aspects of both poles of the patriarchal dialectic. Albion's sons are children both of Ham and of Neptune: in historical (screen-) memory, dark people from over the sea; in mixed Hebrew and Greek mythology, embodiments of dark forbidden instinct (Ham had "uncovered his father's nakedness," i.e. raped or castrated Noah while the latter was drunk),[12] and of the dark chaos of the sea, so frightening to the land-oriented "Aryans" and Semites alike—for after the defeat of Gog and Magog at Armageddon, the Old Serpent shall be cast into the lake of fire, and there shall be no more sea. After the displaced nations of Albion were turned into monsters, and cast back into the dark sea from which they came, the very name of their defeated champion was corrupted into a reminder of the Chosen People's enemies. This is far from the last time we shall see such a process in action.

We can now narrow our focus from Britain as a whole to the main original home of the "Scotch-Irish" in the western Scottish Lowlands, for most modern scholars agree that the population of this area has, in the interior at least, remained substantially undisplaced since about the time we have reached. Interestingly, this quarter of Scotland appears to have been one of the last parts of Britain to be peopled at all. There is no sign of human habitation during the pre-Neolithic; Neolithic land clearings and Megalithic structures penetrate only gradually from the south coast and the east, and the region of the Clyde estuary itself, the natural focus of the region, was apparently not settled until the Bronze Age.[13]

Look at a map of Europe upside down. For those of us who are so used to the familiar outlines of maps that we see them as if they were faces, through a lens of ingrained assumptions, this simple trick can reveal much that is already before one's eyes. In Britain, one striking fact is that the Irish Sea is far from being a uniform channel: Ireland is nearly a peninsula of Scotland. Northern Ireland and southwestern Scotland are opposite ends of a raggedly broken bridge, and throughout history they have often had more to do with each other than with the rest of Ireland or Britain. In particular, the Scottish side and the area to the south of it are an odd corner of Albion's island, not on any major trade or invasion route but not isolated by great barriers.

Archeologically and historically, Scotland is divided into sections by two roughly perpendicular lines: an east-west line across the narrow neck between the Forth and Clyde estuaries, and a north-south line along the watersheds. Of the four quarters that this division forms, the southeast has the most connection with the continental European world, followed by the northeast. The northwest is emphatically part of the Atlantic Zone. But the southwest is ambivalent, "belonging" now to the west and the Atlantic, now to the east and the Continent. If the early history of Britain is more complex and ambiguous than most people realize, that of Scotland is the most complicated in Britain, and that of the southwest, what archeologists call the Clyde-

Solway area, is the most complicated, or at least hectic, in Scotland. This region is indeed, in a sense, the eye (or one such) of the whole storm of Western European history, reflecting its great shifts of current as if in a small convex mirror. Although the core of its population is apparently descended from people who were there twenty-six centuries ago, its language has changed at least three times.

There were several distinct Celtic invasions of Britain; this may be reflected in the way in which Corineus is made the head of a separate band of Trojan refugees that Brutus meets on his way westward. The first invasion, about 700 B.C., affected Scotland only along the east coast and evidently met stiff and often effective resistance; many of the invaders, not the natives, seem to have been reduced to living in caves and making crude pottery.[14] Eventually native and invader fused into a nation of highly mixed language and culture known later as the Picts.[15] In Roman and early medieval times they mostly spoke an archaic form of Celtic, but even at that late date they retained many pre-Celtic cultural features. For example, a woman could take several husbands (until, of course, the missionaries arrived); inheritance and royal succession were through the mother; and, as we have noted, many personal names—and the language of some inscriptions—were pre–Indo-European. Some of these inscriptions, which are mostly monuments, borrow the Celtic word for "son," suggesting that the older peoples of Albion had no way to speak of descent from a father.

The next wave of Celtic invaders came shortly after 500 B.C., being driven from their homes along the French and Dutch coast by other Celts from the south. These Celts were far more numerous than the first had been, and they had iron weapons. They overran and settled most of what is now England, and in the lower areas facing Europe their descendants apparently formed the bulk of the population whom the English in turn were to defeat.[16] Another invasion, though, occurred about two hundred years after this one, as part of the great expansion of Celtic peoples across Europe as far as western Russia, down across the mountains to sack Rome and invade Greece, and even to settle as far east as Galatia in Asia Minor. These Celts, the La Tène culture, had in turn been stimulated by the challenge of incursions from their Indo-European cousins, the Cimmerians and Scyths of the Eurasian steppes; the La Tène Celts had learned to beat the Scyths at their own game, adopting steppe horsemanship and chariot warfare as well as much of the Scyths' vigorous Asiatic art style, and developing these latter motifs into the brilliant flowering of what is now commonly known as "Celtic art."

After the first Celtic penetration, none of the later invasions seems to have had any profound effect on the population of the Forth-Clyde region, where (as in North Britain generally) archeological remains show a continuous tradition from the late Bronze Age onward,[17] though later invaders entered the area, imposed their own dialects, and formed a ruling class. Finally, in the last century before Christ, a fourth and final Celtic invasion brought the Belgae to southeastern England and may have pushed some earlier Celts northward into our area. In this period, the first real towns appeared in southern Scotland, and the first real forts. This movement came to an end in the eighties A.D., when the Roman invasion of Scotland "pacified" the area.[18] In A.D. 142, this area was consolidated as a frontier zone by Antoninus Pius.

The full-blown Celtic civilization is described for us in Latin and early Irish literature. There were three distinct classes: rulers, priests, and commoners—a pattern prevalent in Indo-European societies from Ireland to India, and especially in those two regions. Some features of Celtic society, as well as some words and grammatical features, are found only in cultures and languages isolated from one another along the fringes of the Indo-European world—Celtic, Latin, Hittite, Sanskrit, the Tocharian of ancient Sinkiang—pointing to a retention of archaic features among early offshoots. And archeology corroborates written sources in showing that as well as preserving archaic Indo-European features, Celtic institutions, especially religion, incorporated many features of pre–Indo-European cults and even pre-agricultural shamanism. This was especially true in Ireland and in western and northern Britain, where the climate and soil made agriculture less important than stockraising and hunting. Of the Celtic gods, the chief god of northern Britain was Maponos "the Great Son," son of Matrona "the Great Mother," who on the Continent was a minor deity of healing springs. He was a god of music and hunting, and appears in medieval Welsh legend as the hero Mabon fab Modron. While the southern British Druids, contrary to the imagination of Celtic romanticists, seem to have ignored Stonehenge, the northern Britons evidently dedicated to Maponos a major megalithic structure in southwest Scotland, the Clochmabenstane, and made it a tribal meeting-ground, later "officialized" by the Romans. Further, although the Celts had come to Britain from Gaul, Caesar states that the Druid religion came *to* Gaul *from* Britain, and that the Gaulish Druids still traveled to Britain to learn the deepest secrets of their religion. Lévi-Strauss notes: "If the Celts took certain of their legends from that sub-

Arctic civilization, of which we know almost nothing, we can understand why it is that the Grail cycle is closer to the Indian myths which flourished in the forests of North America than to any other mythological system." [19] It is worthy of note that, for all the modern-day interest in "British Celts," the Romans never referred to the inhabitants of Britain as Celtic; they reserved that word for the continental Celtic-speakers, though they recognized that the Britons spoke a similar language.

The Roman attitude toward these northern "barbarians" was a complicated one, and that attitude (or rather that range of attitudes) has important connections with modern attitudes toward "under-developed" peoples—connections both analogical and historical. Let us, then, step aside from our historical narrative so that we may examine these attitudes and begin to explore some of these connections. I call what follows an "incursus," not an excursus, since it takes us deeper into the theme of this book, which is the necessities and possibilities of the human spirit in its interaction with, and struggle against, history.

INCURSUS: *The Age of Saturn*

The Romans approached their "barbarian" neighbors and subjects with the same ambivalence that later colonizers would show toward their colonized peoples. And, as in later cases, this ambivalence simply oscillated between two sides of the same fundamental error.

On the one hand, the Romans had conquered most of the Celtic world, enslaving and exterminating entire tribes, and imposing their language and laws on the survivors. The common people kept their own gods (often represented in the guise of more or less equivalent Roman deities), and many of their own customs; but the Romans were intent on wiping out the native nobility and priesthood, and especially on abolishing human sacrifice—of which they had a particular horror because they had not totally abjured it themselves until the early lifetime of Julius Caesar, the conqueror of Gaul. As this fact suggests, we are dealing once more with a process of projecting one's own rejected qualities onto others, with exaggerated force and racist outcome.

But, unlike the early British invaders who originated the legends behind the story of Trojans and giants, the Romans had a literate,

highly complex culture with a sense of their own history, a consciousness of having adopted a great deal from the Greeks, and an ambivalent attitude toward their own simpler past—an awareness of having
lost as well as gained. Thus the Romans' mapping of attitudes toward
their own earlier existence onto their view of the Celts and other "barbarians" had a positive as well as a negative side—though this did not
make the "positive" side any truer to the reality of the subjects, or any
closer to confronting them dialogically as persons. As often as the
Celts were looked on as a wild and bloodthirsty race, they were seen
on the other hand as a breed of noble savages, as free of corruption as
they were of riches, where the wise were elected to positions of authority, since social relations were still on that human scale which was
already being lost in the urbanized Mediterranean world.

(The texts documenting this process are discussed by Stuart Piggott in *The Druids*, chapter 3, "The Druids in the Classical and Vernacular Texts." Piggott's work is a painstaking study of the image of
the Druids, and of the Celt in general, in European thought, with special attention to this question of "soft" versus "hard primitivism."
Piggott's framework, however, is skewed by a tendency to identify soft
primitivism with a "subjective" or romanticized view and "hard"
primitivism with an "objective" or empirical view. In actuality, both
soft and hard primitivism are equally subjective, depending as they
do on the construct of "primitivism" in the first place, a construct
which Piggott does not adequately criticize. His work should be read
in conjunction with Bernard Sheehan's *Savagism and Civility*, which
treats a different case of the same process, the early years of the
Jamestown colony, through the equivalent concepts of "noble" versus
"ignoble savagism." Sheehan clearly recognizes these categories as
polar aspects of the same projection, and as equal failures to engage
"the particularities of a real social order,"[20] "a traditional society
made up of real people"[21]—in short, as notions which "merely fed the
white man's internal needs."[22] At this point the student of Appalachia
will no doubt be seeing that the roots of misperception and domination
of mountain people go much deeper than one might have supposed.)

In the Roman attitude toward the Celts and other "barbarians,"
we see reflections of the Romans' own previous existence as simple
Italian villagers, beyond the western edge of what had been the civilized world, as the Celts later stood with relation to them. But as we
also see, conditioning the Romans' views of their own history as well,
reflections of the backward depths of individual existence in child-

hood. The Romans' harsh child-rearing practices were notable even in their own time, and the Romans were aware themselves of the connection between these and their urge to conquer their neighbors. They liked to say that the name *Roma* was derived from the Greek *rhome*, force. Normally, the Empire was identified subconsciously with the Good Parent and the barbarian with the Bad; thus the Roman pattern of conquest provided a resolution of conflicting attitudes toward the parents—a false resolution, of course, and an unstable one which constantly demanded new worlds to conquer—one which broke down when the Empire's frontiers reached their natural limit at the edge of intensive agriculture.[23] (This is, incidentally, the reverse of the notion that a Roman "failure of nerve" *caused* the Empire to stop expanding— a notion which also has its parallels today.)

At the same time, though, the urbanized elaboration of Roman culture led, in more sophisticated minds, to a more complex approach to the parent conflict. The repressed joy of childhood had for ages been reflected in legends of the Golden Age before the dawn of history, when the heavenly rule of Saturn and the Titans had not been replaced by that of the sky-father Jupiter and his rapacious and despotic children. In a society becoming anonymous and bureaucratized on a scale comparable with our own, authority came to seem not only despotic but totally inaccessible and irrational, and the nostalgia for the age of Saturn became a yearning for a simpler, human-scaled world, seen (not entirely without truth) in the tribal societies which Rome was busily wiping out. The imperial byword was Virgil's *Tu regere imperio populos, Romane, memento:*[24] "You, Roman, be mindful to rule the peoples by command." (Aeneas, ancestor of the Romans, is told this by his father's spirit as part of a speech in which the latter contrasts Roman talents defensively with the cultural achievements of the Greeks.) But when the Roman mind became capable of self-criticism to a degree literally unthinkable in most traditional oral societies, it was into the mouth of a Caledonian chieftain that it put this dry characterization of the Roman legions: *Ubi solitudinem faciunt, pacem appellant:*[25] "They make a wasteland and call it peace." This is the complaint of any subjugated barbarian, and also of any Roman child smarting under the harshness of his *paterfamilias*, made doubly arbitrary and unjust by the parents' anomic loss of their own bearings in a society elaborated beyond human scale. And on a higher level of integration, it is the voice of the parents' conscience, and of the Roman citizen's.

Nevertheless, this voice speaks not for the barbarian's benefit but for the Roman's, and this in two senses of the word "benefit." It is part of an internal dialogue from which the other is excluded, and also it does not engage the other so as to do him any good. This, too, has its parallels in later history up to the present.

Let us continue, then, to explore that history. The limit of effective Romanization in Britain was, as I have noted, the limit of intensive agriculture in the southern and eastern part of the island. The north and west were occupied militarily rather than settled. After A.D. 142, the Scottish lowlands were a military frontier zone between the two Roman walls—the stone one of Hadrian and the earthen one of his successor Antoninus—and the highlands and the east, though invaded, were never conquered at all. Their inhabitants, the semi-Celtic Picts, responded to Roman and Romano-British attacks by uniting into a confederation, and as the Empire began to crumble, the Romanized British tribes came under increasing attack from them, and from Ireland and Germany.

In A.D. 407, amid the chaos of the collapsing Western Empire, a Roman general in Britain declared himself emperor and left for the Continent, taking the legions with him. The Romanized and largely Christianized Britons were now on their own. They elected a native overlord or Vortigern (probably a title rather than a name), who took the fatal step of seeking help against the Picts and Irish from some of the German pirates, the Angles and Saxons. The latter's homeland was further away, and the Britons had no idea how many of them there were; by the time they found out, it was too late.

Sentimental Celtophiles are fond of saying that the Celts, in their battles against the Germanic tribes, were hampered by "Celtic traits" such as "individualism" and "lack of organizing spirit." This is usually said as if to lament their passing in a sentimental sense, while at the same time distancing oneself from it by making it seem inevitable, a law of nature. The student of Appalachia will see the dismal parallel. In actuality, the earlier Celts were a good deal more highly organized than the Germans. The latter were the ones known to the Romans for their feuding spirit;[26] and linguistics shows that much of the organization the Germans did have was borrowed from the Celts themselves, as shown by their adoption of Celtic words like *Reich* ('kingdom'),

Recht ('law'), *Amt* ('office'). What gave the Germans the edge over the Celts was simply that the Germans were located in much more heavily wooded territory, and further from the Romans, who overwhelmed most of the Celts before they had a chance to organize themselves effectively. This gave the Germans the chance, first, to overrun the remainder of the continental Celts beyond the Roman frontier, and then to imitate Roman organizational models to their own advantage.

The Anglo-Saxons quickly made great inroads in Britain. Raiding bands of them even crossed the whole country from sea to sea from their settlements on the east coast. Unlike most of the Britons, but like the Picts and Irish, they were pagans, and so primitive that they thought the great Roman temples and baths had been built by the giants who, they gathered, had once lived in Britain. After the Vortigern was deposed, the Britons never again had a central government; but, faced with the military threat of the Saxons, and of the Picts to whose side the Saxons had switched, they agreed about the year 500 to form a unified military command under a Romanized British warrior. This battle chief, Artorius, was a genius who brought the Anglo-Saxons to a halt for a generation or more. The Christian Britons enjoyed fifty years of peace, to the point where the priestly writer Gildas attacked their complacency. But the peace was unstable; there was a plague, the Saxons went on the march again, and this time there was no stopping them—for fourteen hundred years. Bur Artorius became a popular hero whose fame long outlasted his success; for of course he became "King" Arthur, the greatest hero of medieval literature.[27]

Britain was now divided into tribes again, each a separate small Christian kingdom with a royal line descended from Roman-recognized frontier chieftains. The English entered what is now southeastern Scotland about A.D. 600, invading the territory of the Votadini (Guotodin, Gododdin). The king of the Gododdin, Mynyddog Mwynfawr ("Mountaineer Mercy-Great"), whose court was evidently at Edinburgh, had mounted an expedition southward in the 590s to battle the English at Catraeth (now Catterick in Yorkshire). The Gododdin, vastly outnumbered, had been soundly defeated, but their court poet, Aneirin, one of the few survivors, sang their exploits in a 103-stanza poem, which most scholars believe to have been preserved in southwestern Scotland before it reached Wales. Kenneth Jackson, dean of Celtic linguists, has called the *Gododdin* "the oldest Scottish poem";[28] with only a bit more stretching, it might be called the first work of Appalachian literature.

North Britain, Political Units and Languages, AD 142

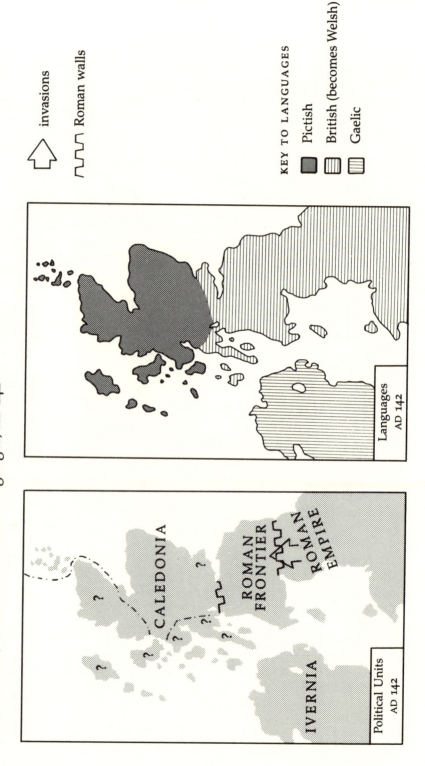

invasions

Roman walls

KEY TO LANGUAGES

Pictish

British (becomes Welsh)

Gaelic

IVERNIA

CALEDONIA

ROMAN
FRONTIER

ROMAN
EMPIRE

Political Units
AD 142

Languages
AD 142

North Britain, Political Units and Languages, AD 407

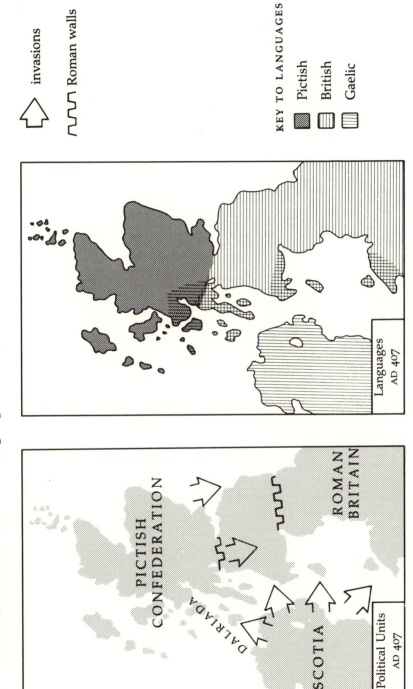

invasions

Roman walls

KEY TO LANGUAGES

Pictish

British

Gaelic

PICTISH CONFEDERATION

DALRIADA

SCOTIA

ROMAN BRITAIN

Political Units
AD 407

Languages
AD 407

Meanwhile, the opposite side of the country was being attacked by the Féni of Ireland, a Celtic group which had only recently taken possession of that whole island from earlier arrivals, both British and non-Celtic.[29] These Féni, whom the Romans called Scoti or Pirates and the British called Gwyddyl or Wild Men—whence the word Gaels— invaded the Atlantic shore north of the Clyde and established the Kingdom of Dalriada, which straddled both shores in Scotland and Ulster. It is one of the many ironies of history that these Gaels or Scots, commonly thought of as the "original" inhabitants of Scotland, were in fact the last Celtic group to enter the country. In Roman times three languages were spoken in today's Scotland: pre-Celtic Pictish, Celtic Pictish, and British. A thousand years later there were also three, but they were three entirely different ones—Gaelic, English, and Norse—which had completely replaced the first three! Further- more, since *Scotia* originally meant Ireland, the name Scotland means "land of the Irish"; but the Gaelic name of the country is Alba, which originally meant "Britain," being the same word as Albion.

In the fifth century, these Irish pirates carried off to their island a young nobleman, probably from southwestern Scotland, named Patricius. He later bought his freedom, joined the Christian priest- hood, and returned to Ireland as a missionary. He succeeded so well that a hundred years later, Ireland and not Britain was the chief center of Christianity in the "British" Isles. Irish monks not only evangelized the Picts and "Scottish" Scots, but traveled widely in England and on the Continent. (The Britons themselves never sent missionaries to the English, preferring them to go straight to Hell.)

But during the period when western Britain and Ireland had been severed from the Continent by the heathen English, Christianity there had diverged from that of Rome. In part this was a matter of con- servative features, such as the use of an old dating for Easter and, less conspicuously but more importantly, a more restricted idea of the powers of the Pope; but there were also innovations, such as a pro- found organizational adaptation to a society based on tribes rather than provinces, and on dispersed farms rather than villages. There was also a much less hostile attitude toward native languages and tradi- tions. Too, the British theologian Pelagius gave a higher place to human effort in obtaining salvation than the view that finally was accepted at Rome, though Pelagianism had once been influential throughout the West.

The result of all this was that, for what was to be the last time in history, the Atlantic Zone (or the central, British part of it) formed a

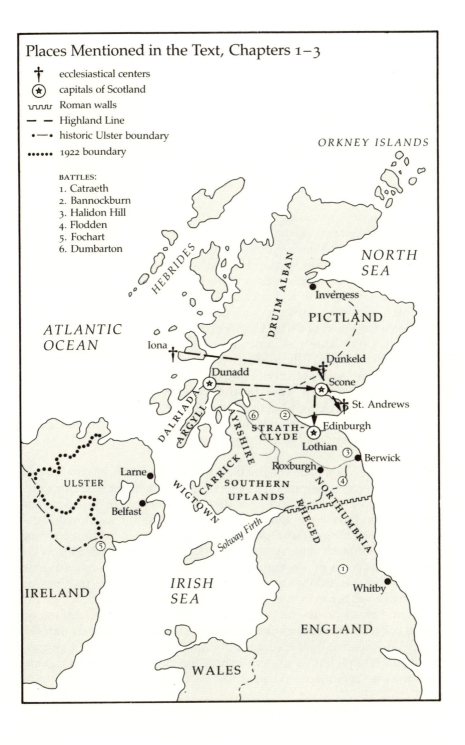

Places Mentioned in the Text, Chapters 1–3

✝ ecclesiastical centers
✪ capitals of Scotland
〜〜〜 Roman walls
— — Highland Line
•—•—• historic Ulster boundary
•••••• 1922 boundary

BATTLES:
1. Catraeth
2. Bannockburn
3. Halidon Hill
4. Flodden
5. Fochart
6. Dumbarton

ORKNEY ISLANDS

NORTH SEA

ATLANTIC OCEAN

HEBRIDES

DRUIM ALBAN

PICTLAND

Inverness

Iona

Dunadd

Dunkeld

Scone

St. Andrews

DALRIADA

ARGYLL

AYRSHIRE

STRATH-CLYDE

Edinburgh

Lothian

Berwick

Roxburgh

CARRICK

WIGTOWN

SOUTHERN UPLANDS

Solway Firth

RHEGED

NORTHUMBRIA

Larne

ULSTER

Belfast

IRELAND

IRISH SEA

Whitby

ENGLAND

WALES

distinct cultural unit over against the Continent. The form of Christianity that was the conceptual vehicle of that culture is now called the Celtic Church, but this name did not exist then. Its members simply called it the Church, and its opponents simply called it heresy. The quarrel between the two came to a head when Roman missionaries from southern England met Irish missionaries in northern England, and the king and queen of Northumbria ended up celebrating Easter a week apart. Collisions were also occurring in Germany and even further east.[30]

Loyal Jones has said, "No group in the country . . . has aroused more suspicion and alarm among mainstream Christians than have Appalachian Christians, and never have so many Christian missionaries been sent to save so many Christians than is the case in this region."[31] This statement needs only to be extended to Appalachians' ancestors—and not for this occasion only but, as we shall see in later chapters, for many. The bitterness of the controversy was reflected in the fierce invective of Bede, born eight years after the official end of the controversy. That end came in A.D. 664, when a council was held at Whitby on the Northumbrian coast and King Oswiu decided in favor of Rome. Almost the only immediate result was a plague spread throughout the British Isles by clergy returning from Whitby; but within the next couple of centuries one part of the islands after another submitted to Rome, and the balance between the Atlantic Zone and the Continent was permanently tipped.

Thus the homeland of the bulk of Appalachians' ancestors was part of a region which had many analogies to their present one—including a general confusion as to its very existence. Its principles of organization have been generally ignored, belonging as they do to a framework of thought and perception fundamentally different from the now dominant one. And as Mediterranean civilization grew to overshadow most of the world of Appalachians' ancestors and their cousins, the conditions of empire led, as we have seen, to types of systematic misperception which have reappeared later in history with the same types of destructive results. The successive repetitions of these patterns are not sheer coincidences, nor are they merely parallel cases. The historic linkages among them will become clear, as we proceed in the next chapter to explore how the parts of the Atlantic Zone became the "mountainous backyards" of various empires.

2 *Counting in Indian*

Much may be made of a Scotchman if he be caught young.
—Samuel Johnson

What we call "Western civilization" was now taking shape; and with it, the distinctive elements in the repeated pattern that forms the history of the core of the Appalachian people. In this chapter we shall see how the homeland of mountaineers' ancestors was progressively transformed from an integral and central part of Atlantic culture into a subjugated fringe of "the West." We shall then explore some of the lasting evils to which this process gave rise.

Michael Rogin, in *Fathers and Children*, has explored the connection between the boundary of a nation or culture and the ego-boundaries of its members. He discusses this phenomenon with regard to the early American frontier; but the frontier is a feature not only of American culture and society, or even of "Anglo-Saxon," but of Western civilization in general in both ancient and modern times. Therefore the frontier psychology, with its unstable ego-boundary and its tendency to respond to the existence of others as a threat to its own being, is a fundamental part of American consciousness and of that of the West as a whole.

All the world's civilizations have pictured themselves at the center of things, but Western civilization has given this notion a particular edgy militancy, in direct proportion to its lack of foundation. We have always known ourselves to be "the West." Even at the height of the Roman Empire, Rome herself and Carthage right across the Mediterranean were the westernmost real cities in the world, and the only ones in the Western Empire. The Romans' high culture was from Greece and their eventual religion was brought by Greeks from Palestine. We have remarked already on the Romans' own consciousness of being a rough frontier people, and their ambivalent defensiveness about this fact vis-à-vis the peoples next in line for "enlightenment."

(And the Greeks themselves, centuries earlier, had suffered a major intellectual crisis when they had encountered the stretches of Egyptian history, reaching back beyond their own dating for the origin of the world.) Rome was not even the natural center of her own empire; when the West was overrun by the "barbarians," the more populous and settled Eastern half got along perfectly well without it. Indeed, the East had deliberately sold the West out to ensure its own survival, and then managed to reconquer a great deal of the western Mediterranean world before the Arabs rushed in from the other direction. During the Middle Ages, when Westerners twitted the Byzantines for calling themselves "Romans" when they spoke not Latin but Greek, the Byzantines replied disdainfully that they had no need to learn a "Scythian dialect" in order to represent the world's legitimate order. The West returned the compliment with the Fourth Crusade, in which it destroyed the majority of what ancient Greek literature had survived the Muslims.

The Romans, being so little removed from barbarism themselves, had treated the more openly "barbaric" peoples within their sphere with an overcompensating intolerance unknown in the East. Greek culture had spread into civilizations as elaborate as the Greeks' own, and complex amalgams were common. This was nowhere more conspicuous than in religion, where the Christian Church was affected by the older religions of Asia Minor, and where newly evangelized nations had the liturgy translated into their own languages. In the West, by contrast, the Roman Empire and the Roman Church had simply bulldozed the less elaborate societies, cultures, and religions in their path—*ubi solitudinem faciunt, pacem appellant*. Only the Atlantic Zone formed an exception—unconquerable, unsettleable, and already full of archaic survivals due to previous invasions' having come up against the same barriers and having filtered through in complex patterns of assimilation and adaptation rather than rolling over. Again, in terms of the new Christian world, we can see this most clearly in the distinguishing marks of the "Celtic" Church, such as its extensive calendar of local saints, who (just as in the East) included slightly edited versions of ancient deities. Ireland's greatest woman saint, Brigit, is the goddess Briganti, "The Exalted One," the same word as the Hindu divine epithet Brihati.[1] Too, besides features that may have been derived from Druidism, the monastery-centered "Celtic" Church included features, clearly reflected in art motifs, which were derived from Greece and Egypt via the old sea-routes without Western European intermediaries.[2] And although the Celtic Church used Latin, it had its own highly distinctive pronunciation.[3]

Even in the so-called "Dark Ages," the "West" was still on the move. The fall of Rome had not stopped the grassroots spread of small-scale technology; more advanced agricultural methods, and hence more complex economic systems, filtered north and east into Germany and beyond, aided by techniques introduced from the other direction. While high culture tumbled down, everyday life continued to become *less* primitive for most people outside the Roman area. The economic center of western Europe therefore shifted northward dramatically; indeed, Western Europe as we know it came into being for the first time. Thus, although Charlemagne derived his symbolic authority from Rome when, in A.D. 800, the pope crowned him emperor of the West, he established his practical power by siting his capital at Aachen, seven hundred miles to the northwest in what had been Rome's wild frontier. Modern economic studies by the Common Market show that the most centrally located city in Western Europe is still Aachen.

But this development had little effect in the Atlantic Zone, where the soil was still wetter and thinner, and where forests had been given way to overgrazed pastureland since the Stone Age. The Atlantic lands, into which Romanization and Christianity had gradually percolated and adapted to the landscape, retained their old rhythms of life, now even more different from those of "the West," which was bursting with change and dynamism even in these "Dark Ages." And what were the mental effects of this dynamic? Frederick Jackson Turner remarked in 1893 that "up to our own day American history has been in a large degree the history of the colonization of the Great West";[4] but we have seen that this process, and the mentality that goes with it, were already two thousand years old in 1893, if not three times that. The discovery of America was only to be the last great fluke in a succession of repeated stimuli which formed and continually reinforced the distinctive "Western" mentality.

Turner himself, in his classic essay, wrote that "what the Mediterranean Sea was to the Greeks, . . . the ever retreating frontier has been to the United States directly, and to the nations of Europe more remotely."[5] But except for almost offhand allusions, Turner treated the frontier of Western colonization as if it were the edge of inhabited territory—as if the "empty" lands beyond had not been inhabited by human beings and often, in fact, settled agricultural nations, which had to be driven out or exterminated to make room for "settlement." Certainly, in discussing the effects of the frontier on the American character, he ascribed little if any effect to this destructive kind of social contact; he took for granted the frontiersman's own view, as he saw it, that the frontier was a place to escape social contact altogether. He does say, in a celebrated passage, that "the wilderness masters the colonist. . . . He shouts the war cry and takes the scalp in orthodox Indian fashion."[6] But he writes as if this were simply a parallel result of similar conditions, somehow imposed by The Land itself; he might as well be comparing American frontiersmen with Siberian tribesmen, or Australian aborigines, or Martians. "All European thought," said Fanon, "has unfolded in places which were increasingly more deserted and more encircled by precipices; and thus it was that the custom grew up in those places of very seldom meeting man"[7]—*meeting*, that is, *encountering* as a person.

Turner was able, I think, to repress this genocide, as did most of his countrymen, because the genocidal habit of mind was so all-encompassing in Western civilization that he failed to notice it as a figure against a ground.[8] The ground of his perceptions *was* Western civilization, and the figure was the difference between America and Europe. But America is no escape from Europe and from history. Precisely on this point and in this aspect it approaches what Sartre called it, a "super-European monstrosity."[9] And it was on Western frontiers far older than America's that the arts of genocide, both bodily and cultural, were first perfected, along with the art of repressing that genocide—and *ipso facto* of turning it against the self. Jules Henry spoke of "the immemorial insatiability of Man-in-the-West";[10] one of my purposes is to bring the immemorial into memory, to help make the unconscious conscious and, perhaps, more accessible to change.

With the events which made possible modern Western civilization, then, the stage was set for a confrontation which could have only one outcome. Europe's center of gravity was now in northern France and the lower Rhineland—the very region which had always been a major staging area for continental invasions of Britain. Measured from the new center, the Atlantic culture area centered around the Western sea routes made an intolerable dent in the territory of "the West." The new Western culture had to fight off invasions from the pagans of the east and north, and from the Muslims of the south; the constant necessity of such defense had a deep effect on the nascent Western mind. Fighting these pagans and Muslims was one thing, for their homes were far away, their beliefs plainly distinct, and their habits aggressive. But what the West's new focus of experience really could not tolerate was the close presence of a sister culture, "white" and Christian yet different, whispering right in its ear that alternatives were possible. Defense was necessary, not so much against physical aggression as against the ontological threat which the Atlantic culture posed. And in the Anglo-Saxons, the new Western culture found an ideal expression of its defensiveness; for the best defense is a good offense, and the Anglo-Saxons were in the perfect position to embody this.

For in Britain, after the English adopted Roman Christianity, the bearers of Westernization *were* the invading hordes from outside. Instead of struggling in mutual opposition as they did for centuries on the Continent, the two great forces—Western culture and alien invasion—were united in Britain into a single force with double strength. The English alone perceived no conflict between the two great impulses that warred in the breast of every continental ex-barbarian. The English became, literally, Westerners with a vengeance. All the oedipal aggression which the continental Christian projected onto the attacking barbarians, the Anglo-Saxons directed against the defending culture—a culture whose very existence he denied, whose uniqueness and centered wholeness were invisible to him, which he could see only as a broken jumble of peripheral fringes. In short, he blamed the victims of his own aggression, treating the defending Britons as if *they* were the aggressors, like the pagans and Muslims of the Continent. To English writers like Bede, even their pre-Christian ancestors could be baptized retroactively with the honor of having spread civilization. Thus Bede writes of the Northumbrian king Aethelfrith's overrunning of much of southwestern Scotland: "He ravaged the Britons more cruelly than all other English leaders, so that he might well be compared to Saul the king of Israel, except of course that he was ignorant of true religion. . . . One might fairly apply to him the words of the patriarch Jacob's blessing of his son: *Benjamin shall ravin as a wolf: in the morning he shall devour the prey, and at night he shall divide the spoil.*" [11] This Chosen People imagery is applied to a *pagan* king's invasion of *Christian* territory.

In the seventh century, then, the English reached the western sea in two places, cutting Welsh-speaking Britain into three pieces. The northernmost, Cumbria (the same word as *Cambria*, "Wales"; the British word means "Allies" or "Citizens"), was by now organized into the kingdoms of Rheged, in what is now northwestern England and the adjacent Scottish coast, and Alclud (Strathclyde) in inland southwest Scotland. Rheged was soon overrun by Aethelfrith, but its local lords were semi-independent for centuries, and—the important point—though the Cumbrian-Welsh (British) language was gradually replaced by English, the Cumbrian-speaking population does not seem to have been substantially replaced by Anglo-Saxons. Into modern times, shepherds in that area used a distorted but recognizable form of Welsh numerals to count their sheep, believing that normal English numerals would be unlucky. To understand the origin of this, one need only try to count something important in a foreign language; the feeling tends to persist that the count is somehow unreal, unreliable, or at least not "solid." (These Cumbrian numerals have also been found being used in children's games in the United States; the children call this "counting in Indian.")

Meanwhile, on the other side, the Irish invaders of Dalriada pushed eastward over the watershed which they called Druim Alban, the Spine of Albion. In A.D. 841, Kenneth MacAlpin, king of the Gaels, also became king of the Picts, who had already been under strong Gaelic influence for centuries, and he changed the name of his kingdom from Dalriada to Alba, usually translated from then on as Scotland. But at the same time the Vikings had invaded the north end of the island, and soon they were raiding and settling down the northwest coast, so like their native land. Before long they had conquered the whole area of the old kingdom of Dalriada. Thus, ironically, within a couple of generations, the area ruled by the Gaelic kings had shifted entirely from one side to the other of Druim Alban. Scotland more and more became an eastward-looking, continental-model kingdom, while the Viking rulers of the northwest adapted to the local clan system and became chiefs of a realm—at first the independent earldom of Orkney, then a province of Norway, then a part of Scotland as the autonomous Lordship of the Isles—whose language and culture were more Gaelic than the kingdom of Scotland itself. (So much, again, for racist notions of "Celt" versus "Teuton," whether biased toward the one or the other. What we are dealing with here is already, once more, a clear matter of regional culture and "psychological heredity," not of "race.")

Strathclyde, meanwhile, tucked away in its valley and able to play off its diverse neighbors against one another, managed for centuries to remain independent of the Norse, the Scots, and the English. Its rulers are known in Welsh legend as *Gwŷr y Gogledd*, the Men of the North. Outside a few genealogies, historical records are sketchy, for reasons which will become clear; but in addition to the *Gododdin*, a sizable proportion of the oldest Welsh tradition is of Northern British origin.[12] This includes the earliest versions of the story of Merlin, originally a man-of-the-woods figure unconnected with Arthur and seeming to reflect a much older Subarctic shamanism. There is also a medieval list of magical talismans called "the Thirteen Treasures of the Island of Britain, which were in the North";[13] their ownership is mostly attributed to kings of Strathclyde and Rheged, and Rachel Bromwich notes of the term *Y Gogledd* that "the Treasures were designated by it as belonging to a most ancient sunbstratum in the bardic tradition."[14] Kenneth Jackson conjectures that "the Celtic literary institutions flourished more, in the conditions of Roman Britain, in the North than they did in Wales precisely because Wales was part of Roman Britain and for most of the time the North was not."[15]

But Strathclyde, pressured from all sides, could not last forever. After overrunning Dalriada, the Vikings rolled on south; and, though their stay was not as permanent as it was further north, they caused much destruction. They invaded Strathclyde in 870 and made a puppet of its king, Arthgal, who was assassinated in 872 by order of the king of Scotland. In 875, to avoid being caught between Viking and Scot, a large proportion of the Strathclyde nobility fled to Wales, presumably taking with themselves the *Gododdin* and other works.[16] To ward off collapse, the remaining Strathclyde Welsh ruling class resorted to close and unequal alliances with the kingdom of Scots; the upper classes became heavily Gaelicized by intermarriage and outright immigration. Strathclyde became politically revitalized, but at a high cultural cost; it gained power but more and more as an arm of Scotland.

Meanwhile, the English-held south coast was invaded by Irish and Hebridean Gaels mixed with Vikings—the Gall-Ghàidhil, or Foreign-Gaels, who gave their name to the district, now called Galloway. Strathclyde was able to profit from the confusion by conquering Galloway and even a slice of what is now England; but in 945, in return for Scottish help, her kings swore loyalty to those of Scotland, and the process of Gaelicization gathered momentum and filtered down socially.

The two kingdoms together now outflanked the English settlements on the east coast. In 973, England gave Scotland a slice of the Anglo-Saxon land north of the Tweed in return for Scottish fealty; when the Danish king Canute invaded England in 1016, the Scots repudiated the fealty, kept the territory, and went after more, overrunning England as far as the Tweed. And in 1018, the same year as this

North Britain, Political Units and Languages, AD 664

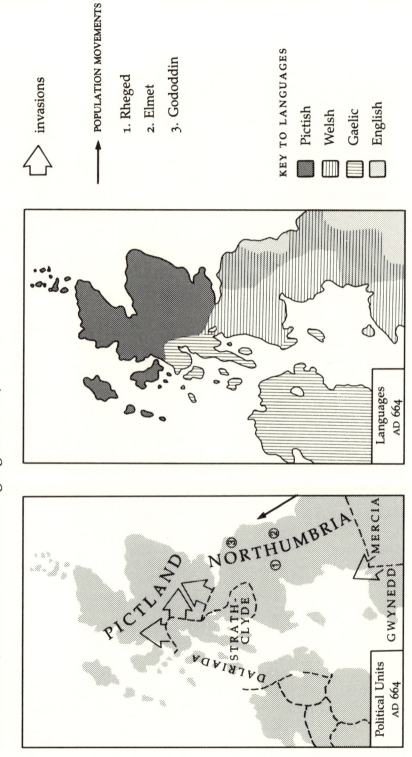

invasions

POPULATION MOVEMENTS

1. Rheged
2. Elmet
3. Gododdin

KEY TO LANGUAGES

Pictish
Welsh
Gaelic
English

Languages
AD 664

PICTLAND

NORTHUMBRIA

DALRIADA

STRATH-
CLYDE

MERCIA

GWYNEDD

Political Units
AD 664

North Britain, Political Units and Languages, AD 900

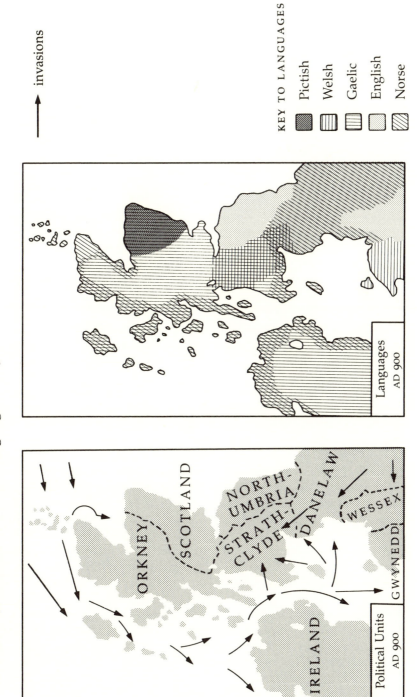

invasions

KEY TO LANGUAGES

Pictish
Welsh
Gaelic
English
Norse

Languages
AD 900

ORKNEY

SCOTLAND

NORTH-
UMBRIA
STRATH-
CLYDE

DANELAW

WESSEX

GWYNEDD

IRELAND

Political Units
AD 900

process was finalized by the battle of Carham, the last native king of Strathclyde (Owain) died, and the kingdom came under a Scottish prince, Duncan, who sixteen years later became king of Scotland. Strathclyde had ceased to exist as a separate entity. Eventually Welsh died out in the North, being last spoken by the common people in the remote, impoverished Southern Uplands, where Galwegian legends refer to them as "Kreenies" (Britons) and "Gwassogs" or "Gossocks" (serfs).[17] So far had the *Gwŷr y Gogledd* fallen—and largely at the hands of other "Celts."

But worse was in store. The Scots may have conquered English territory; but, to put it another way, Scotland now included a sizable component of unassimilable Anglo-Saxons, occupying the best land in the kingdom—and, as we have seen, with a powerful logic of events behind them, pushing their culture toward the heart of Scotland. In biting off the northern tip of England, Scotland had taken culturally deadly bait.

In 1058, the Scottish king Macbeth, who had murdered Duncan in 1041, was deposed in turn by Duncan's son, Malcolm III Canmore. In actual history, Macbeth seems to have been an able and popular king, and his own succession had been no more irregular than that of many another Scottish king; but history was henceforth to be written by the other party.

Malcolm, placed on the throne by an English invasion, laid the country wide open to English influence. After the Norman conquest of England, his court became a refuge for Anglo-Saxon nobles, including his second wife, Margaret. This redoubtable lady had been steeled to "European" attitudes during a childhood in Hungary, her mother's homeland, where Christianity was recent, the vernacular still unwritten, and Central Asian shamanism still a rival to the Church. Margaret never learned Gaelic, spoke to her nobles and bishops through her husband, and made it her project to begin purging the Scottish Church of its remaining "Celtic" features. (For these efforts, she was later canonized as St. Margaret of Scotland.) Her confessor, Turgot, became the first English archbishop of St. Andrews; her children were all given non-Gaelic names; and the functions of the government began one by one to be moved from Scone, in Gaelic Perthshire, south across the Forth to Edinburgh in English-speaking territory.[18] Now the seat of the Scottish kings had moved twice, from northwest to northeast and from northeast to southeast, into successively more continental-oriented areas. The Scottish court was now located in an English-speaking area that had not even been part of Scotland a few generations earlier. Parallel with this process, the seat of the Scottish Church had moved from Iona in the Western Isles to Dunkeld on the east edge of the Highlands, and then southwards to St. Andrews—and with the last movement, the patron of the kingdom was changed from the Gaelic St. Columba to the apostle Andrew, brother of the first bishop of Rome. The veneration of Andrew had reached Pictland from England.[19] There were anti-English revolts after Malcolm's time, notably under his own brother and successor Donald III (Donalbain), but the anglicized party had the balance of power on its side.

The areas of Strathclyde and Galloway became particular victims of this process. Even in Malcolm's time nearly the only Gaelic place names to be found in Anglo-Saxon Lothian were those of forts and the like; Margaret's youngest son David I (1124–1153), tiring of the gradualism of his two brother-predecessors, took the opposite tack entirely. David, "polished from his boyhood," as an English chronicler put it, "by his intercourse and friendship with us,"[20] inaugurated a policy of wholesale feudalization of Scottish law and society, and punished anti-feudal, anti-anglicization revolts in the backlands. This was especially true in the southwest. Galloway in particular was in continual revolt and was nailed down only barely by the thickest concentration of forts in the country.

Behind Anglo-Saxon influence came Norman influence, as lands were taken from rebel chieftains and given to Anglo-Norman freebooters. For the Norman elite of England, Scotland became a frontier zone, a sort of medieval Texas—"a land of opportunity for sons whose fathers had not yet died, for younger sons with no patrimony to inherit."[21] Some of these freebooters were truly desperate characters such as Hugh de Morville, the chief murderer of Thomas à Becket, who fled to southwest Scotland and became the lord of Kunegan.[22] Prominent local families established their loyalty by intermarrying with the Normans, and some went a step further by anglicizing their names: MacFergus—Fergusson; Kunegan—Cunningham.

(Let us pause for a moment to consider the Normans and their character. Bursting out of their French province in the eleventh century, they had revolutionized the political makeup of Europe. Scotland was not the first country which they had changed profoundly by adapting the techniques of feudal lords to the service of centralized elite power of a hitherto unknown kind and degree. Their original experiments in England and Sicily "were, outside Islam and Byzantium,

the first states to be effectively organized since the fall of Rome." [23]
Yet the Normans were no French Latins; they were, as their name indicates, Northmen. They had invaded France in the late ninth century—at first, it seems, in a movement almost entirely made up of
upper-class males [24]—and there they had established their own state,
owing only the remotest feudal loyalty to the king of France and often
battling him with Viking help. Nevertheless, these Northmen had
changed their religion and even their language within a few generations, and thereafter they were enthusiastic proselytizers for their
own form of Western civilization—so enthusiastic, in fact, that their
French nickname gives us the word "bigot." It was the old story we
have seen before and will see again: having adapted to others, they
had no patience thereafter for others who would not adapt to them.
Like the Anglo-Saxons before them, they presented themselves to Europe as both the invading horde and the bringers of "civilization"; and
when their fresh bigotry was added to English attitudes, the resultant
Anglo-Norman amalgam pressed into new territory with redoubled
force.)

It was David, then, with his Anglo-Norman friends, who set out
to make Scotland over into an "effectively organized" state on the Norman model. He imposed feudal sheriffdoms on the old Celtic tribal
districts, and in a parallel development, he changed the principle of
church organization from the monastery-based Celtic system to the
Roman diocesan system. [25] And it was he who introduced into Scotland, through his Norman followers, the chief technological vehicle of
feudal rule: the motte-and-bailey castle. This type of structure, developed in northern France two centuries before, had been introduced to
Britain on the first day of William the Conqueror's invasion and had
not been seen in Scotland until David's time a lifetime later. A deep
ditch was dug, and the earth thrown inward to form an eminence (the
motte) on which a wooden castle was built; alongside this a lower
ditched and palisaded enclosure, the bailey, was filled with outbuild-
ings. These artificial hills, rising over the rolling countryside, marked
a new relation between the people and their authorities. Whereas in
pre-feudal times defensive works had expressed the self-defense of
the people, now an important purpose was the defense of the lords
from the people, and the aggression of the lords upon the people.
"From having been more or less self-sufficient [the peasants] found
themselves tied to the *châteaux* and their seigneurs and forced to pay
taxes to these new overlords." [26] Pre-feudal fortifications had needed
to be built on large natural features in order to sprawl over an area big

enough to hold the local peasantry during a siege, but the motte-and-bailey castle could be constructed almost anywhere because it was a small, tight refuge for the elite. In Scotland, mottes are rare both in the unsubdued Highlands and in the longtime English-speaking areas of the southeast; they are thinly scattered even along the English border. But they are thickly concentrated in a broad band covering the southwest and stretching up the east coast.[27] Even from this simple fact, their function is plain: not to defend Scotland but to defend feudalism; not to defend the people but to defend *from* the people.

Towns, called burghs, were founded in the vicinity of some of these castles. Here an important difference existed between the core of Europe and its periphery. In France, the motte had come into being in early feudal times and had proliferated by stages as the creation of independent lords; the French bourg grew up around it as a "fortuitous union,"[28] and "villages without *châteaux* remained more numerous than villages with them."[29] In peripheral Scotland, by contrast, the mottes were built by royal command out of Edinburgh; the Scottish burgh was a deliberately founded and chartered entity from the beginning—a planned "growth center," to coin a term—and was sometimes built simultaneously with the castle. "The burgh, in effect, did not arise or grow. The burgh was made."[30] Furthermore, while on the Continent the bourgs were basically concentrations of local people, in Scotland and Wales the burghs and their mottes were deliberately settled with Anglo-Norman colonists.[31] And while the growth of this feudal society in France was a historical process covering centuries, in Scotland it was essentially imposed from above during the reigns of two kings, David I and his son Malcolm IV. (It was under the latter that the Anglo-Saxon and Cumbrian-Welsh territories were first officially included in the phrase "Kingdom of Scotland," as distinct from subject territories.)[32]

We thus see that this type of regional "development"—belated, compressed, and accompanied by great cultural shock—is not confined to modern "peripheral" regions but has its roots in centuries of oppression. David's "development" of Scotland is an analogue of that "accelerated development" which W. G. Frost benevolently wished on Appalachia, "so that they may pass through in a single generation the changes which more favored communities have passed through in several generations"[33]—a "development" which entrepreneurs of Frost's time were able to impose in their own terms.

With this change in way of life came a change in ways of social control, a change also imposed and equally catastrophic. Throughout lowland Scotland the old systems of "Celtic" law, dating back to the unwritten judgments of pre-Christian times and the frontier regulations of the Romans, were replaced by European feudal law, administered in the burghs by sheriffs who were largely of Norman extraction and who conducted their proceedings in English. The "natives" were thus forced to learn English in order, literally, to defend themselves,[34] and in order literally to learn to think in terms of a new value system which had declared their own laws worthless. Furthermore, feudalization and agricultural development brought a growth in trade, and the burghs became commercial towns with legally defined marketing territories—what later "developers" of another region would call "local development districts" composed of a "center" and an "associated hinterland." "Both castle and burgh were new; and the new burghs were settlements of new men, or of men who had broken away from the feudal ties of lord and land."[35] The budding money economy of the burghs—the first Scottish coinage is that of David I,[36] and the king's incomes from the burghs were not in feudal services but in hard cash[37]—meant that the newly enserfed peasant could escape serfdom in the burghs (where he was officially "free" after a year and a day's residence),[38] but only by moving "forward," not "backward," and thus by paying a double cultural and psychic price.

A merchant class developed—the bourg-eoisie or burgh-ers—and power and wealth could be gained by commoners who possessed a sense of economic rationality and calculation. This sense was already well-developed among the Anglo-Norman colonists, whom the "Celtic" natives had therefore to copy assiduously, putting their old way of life behind them at whatever pain and cost, if they wished to share in the spoils. English already had a vocabulary and phraseology (itself largely French in origin) that facilitated thinking of this sort; Gaelic or Welsh did not, and thus a change in culture brought with it a change in language if one was even to be able to think in terms of the new instrumental "rationality." The study of medieval charters reflects what happened as a result. The earliest are signed by people with names derived mostly from Gaelic, and to some extent from Norse, with English and French in the minority. As time goes on, the non–Anglo-Norman names disappear, first the Norse and then gradually the Gaelic, giving way to names of English and French derivation. But this is not simply a matter of immigration: we can also trace families from generation to generation, and see fathers with Gaelic names imitating Malcolm III by giving all their sons Anglo-Norman ones.[39] This and other facts contradict the widespread notion that

"Anglo-Saxons" simply replaced "Celts" in the Scottish lowlands. The genocide was of a different sort.

We must not suppose that the anglicized party in Scotland was pro-English in politics; far from it. Malcolm III himself invaded England three times, David I briefly annexed a large chunk of that country, and the rest of the Middle Ages was marked by repeated wars between the two countries as England attempted (at times successfully) to reoccupy the Anglo-Saxon territory north of the Tweed and even the Gaelicized Welsh lands of the southwest, and to reduce the Scottish kings to English vassalage; while Scotland fought just as fiercely to regain her independence and even to annex more English territory. The final boundary between the two countries was the product of so many compromises that the town of Berwick ended up in England, while the county of Berwickshire, which it had ruled, remained in Scotland. The neighboring county of Roxburghshire was retained by Scotland, but the town of Roxburgh had been permanently wiped off the map.

These wars, though, were fought on the Scottish side by men whose cultural "traits" often had more to do with the English than with the surviving Gaelic princedom of the Northwest, the Lordship of the Isles, against which incessant wars were also fought. It is just at the same time as Scotland's most serious conflicts with England that we see this distinction developing clearly. "Lawrence Minot, an English poet of the mid-fourteenth century, in his account of the battle of Halidon Hill [at Berwick] (1333), wrote of Scots both 'wild' and 'tame'";[40] while "in John of Fordoun's chronicle (c. 1387) the Lowlanders figure as 'domesticated folk', dependable and urbane, while the Highlanders and Islesmen are 'wild folk', uncouth, undaunted, comely in person but unsightly in dress."[41] The two great medieval Scottish heroes, William Wallace and Robert Bruce, were both from Anglo-Norman families; and several chronicles imply that the Scots frequently lost battles due to quarrels between the English- and Gaelic-speakers in their ranks.[42] Thus at the same time that feudalism was unifying the Scottish state politically, its effects were dividing the country into two culturally.

All these entanglements and paradoxes are outgrowths of a basically simple underlying pattern—a *process*, again, with a *regional* basis—energized by events on the technological and economic levels. Let us take a brief look both backward and forward at this process and its implications.

We have alluded to the processes which moved Europe's center northward from the Mediterranean to the Rhineland; let us examine these processes in more detail. At the time that Christianity was spreading northward and eastward through the Germanic and Slavic territories, three of the world's most momentous inventions were introduced into those lands from the other direction. The first was the heavy plow; the second was the horsecollar, which greatly increased the amount of force a draft animal could apply to a pulled load; and the third was the iron horseshoe.[43] These three inventions revolutionized agriculture in the heavy, rain-soaked soils of northern Europe. The two-field rotation system was replaced by an accelerated, three-field system. Forests started to melt away; the little clearings in which the Germanic and Slavic tribes had lived gradually knitted together into continuous areas in which the forests were the patches; population could rise without triggering disruptive migrations. This agricultural revolution formed the economic basis of the feudal system, and gave that system and Western culture a penetrating power which extended beyond mere physical conquest. On one edge of the West occurred the German penetration of western Poland and Bohemia—a situation restored to its previous state in 1945—and the beginning of the reduction of the hinterland (note, a German word) to a supplier of grain and raw materials to the West, while the Hungarian grassland became a fully settled agricultural region and the West began pushing the steppe cultures back toward Asia. Meanwhile, on the other edge of the West, in Britain, the West's frontier advanced westwards and northwards beyond the actual frontier of English settlement or even English conquest, up to the edge of the Scottish highlands and the Irish Sea. Beyond this line the thin acid soil, torrentially wet climate, and physical barriers stymied even the new agricultural technology and precluded the feudal complexity which these inventions supported and made possible. Thus the Gaelic society of Ireland and Highland Scotland remained essentially in Iron Age stockraising tribalism. (The Irish, in fact, were notorious for still hitching their plows to their horses' tails in the sixteenth century.[44])

In the northwest, then, the zone between the old Anglo-Saxon frontier and the new feudal frontier corresponds almost exactly with the area of the kingdom of Scotland, and in particular with the band in which mottes are concentrated. And this coincidence is no coincidence. Due to the early medieval "green revolution," the edge of Western Europe in this area had simply run so far ahead of England so fast that another power, coming from the opposite direction, had

had time to organize itself before the English could overwhelm it altogether as they had the older cultivated area of southern and eastern Britain. Scotland remained politically non-English for centuries, until the Union of Crowns in 1603 or even the Union of Parliaments in 1707; but culturally, matters were not the same.

The Scottish state was fiercely opposed to English domination, but nevertheless it owed its very existence to a technology and economy that were spreading northward from England. Thus there was tremendous pressure for a whole culture and way of life to spread northward as well. The English in Scotland might be a minority, but they were the most "advanced" people in the country. The Scottish upper classes, as the keepers of a state "ripening" into feudalism, were attracted to European culture, and the most conspicuous bearers of that culture were the English and the latter's Norman conquerors. Furthermore, what did Gaelic stand for? When the new agricultural revolution reached its limit at the edge of the highlands, the remaining patch of Atlantic civilization in Britain was reduced to an impoverished rump of its former self: one, furthermore, which was as politically hostile to the Scottish state as the English had ever been—and often, ironically, in actual league with the English. The anglicization of the lowlands of southern and eastern Scotland was due to factors as much cultural and psychological as economic. By the twelfth century the new technology had been available for centuries but not fully exploited in this corner of the world; chroniclers agree that it was only with David I, "the Maker of Scotland," that large areas of the lowlands began to be cleared and drained for agriculture. The reasons why this development took place at just this time are social and cultural as well as economic, and the dynamic of this change has its psychohistorical roots among others. Let us, then, depart for a space from our historical narrative again in order to examine these roots of history in the human psyche.

INCURSUS: *Outside the City Wall*

The twelfth century was a time of great ferment in Scotland and Britain, and in Western Europe as a whole; many historians speak of a "twelfth-century Renaissance." Trade, capital accumulation, and state power grew at a fast clip, aided by the Crusades. In intellectual life, establishment Western thought began to assume its definitive form with the translation of Aristotle's works from Arabic and the gradual rise of Aristotelianism in the next two centuries from heresy to the official philosophy of the Church, replacing the Platonic philosophy which had come down from Augustine. Aristotle was the tutor of Alexander the Great and was the last great Greek philosopher before Alexander's imperial spirit of bigness strangled Greek originality of thought; it was basically he who originated the desacralized view of the universe, the notion of detached observation, and the spirit of "rational" manipulation, with the vocabulary which has structured what most Westerners have taken for granted as common sense for the past seven centuries.

In primitive thought, the foundation of cities had been seen as a repetition of the universe's creation in the beginning of time: the foundation stone of the city was the center of the world, corresponding to the navel of the human microcosm; the attackers outside the city were the forces of primeval chaos and disease. The first town-fortifications, says Eliade, were set up not against physical foes but against the ghosts and demons of the forest and wasteland.[45] We see a memory of all this in the story of Corineus and Goemagog.[46] But Europe, as we have seen, had never been its own center; from early times it had seen itself as "the West." And by the high Middle Ages, in the decentered, peripheral and peripheralizing civilization of Western Europe, the sacral world-view had become more and more strained, less and less compatible with what educated people knew of the origin and nature of their culture. Medieval scholars, observing the passage of civilization from Mesopotamia through the Near East, Greece, and Rome to Northwestern Europe, conjectured that they were seeing a universal process of degeneration, and that when the brushfire of high culture finally left Western Europe and swept out to sea, the whole world would lapse into chaos and the end would come. As early as this, Westerners no longer saw themselves at the sacred center, one with the beginning, but rather at the edge of both space and time. This consciousness must have played a large part in the abandonment, or rather repression, of the sacral world-view among the medieval Western intelligentsia, and in the Western Church's adoption of Aristotelianism, in which the human mind does not participate in the universe by identification but observes it with pure detachment.

One particular manifestation of the new mentality is especially striking, but before discussing it we must first remove a misconception. It is commonly said that Copernicanism, in the sixteenth and seventeenth centuries, deflated the medieval's exalted view of himself as a being "at the center of the universe." This notion persists among the vast majority of people who think about the matter at all, in spite of its having been shown by Lovejoy in *The Great Chain of Being* (1936) to be precisely the reverse of the case. The fact of the matter, as Lovejoy amply documents, is that Copernicus was reproached for unduly *exalting* humanity from its position which was seen not as the *center* but as the *bottom* of the universe.[47] This humbling is part and parcel of the Christian view of things, and of many other views; but in the late Middle Ages it took a new symbolic form.

The earth was already known to be round; this fact had never been entirely forgotten (especially not in the Atlantic lands), and it became common knowledge among the literate minority after the revival of Aristotle. At this point some thinkers apparently began to feel that the geocentric model of the universe did indeed suggest "centrality" and "exaltation" too strongly; they started to say that to understand the world properly, one should visualize it turned inside out, with God at the center, Heaven gathered around Him, the heavenly bodies revolving around Heaven, and the earth as a hollow sphere on the edge of the universe, beyond which lay the Outer Darkness. "Outside the city wall" is the significant phrase used for our world by the Anglo-Norman writer Alanus ab Insulis.[48] This was of course not an alternative physical model but a metaphorical suggestion for seeing through the "spiritual eye." But two things should be noted about it. First, it strikingly expresses exaltation and humiliation in terms not of up and down, but of center and periphery. And second, it is one of the first appearances in Western thought of the use of conceptual space-models, an important scientific tool and one which is an outgrowth of Aristotelianism and its distancing of mind from the immediate. Can it be a coincidence that an image with these features appears at just this moment in history—simultaneously drawing on a strong underlying fear of being left out and on the edge of things, and demanding the cultivation of an intellectual detachment which negates the basis of that fear?

And it is precisely this detachment, this desacralization, this repression of the archetypal symbolic mode of thought, which cleared the way for the wholesale alliance of thought with power-structures. In this case, the city's own subjects were identified with the external forces of chaos, and acts committed against them were justified in the name of "order." Meanwhile, the human psyche was restricted to the functions of cognition; the other functions of the organism—not only sensuous but emotional and imaginative—were relegated to demonic

status; and, within cognition itself, the functions of reason and calculation were restricted to the uses of instrumental rationality. This
was to be far from the last time this process occurred in Western civilization. The Aristotelian world-view, and the change in consciousness
that it accompanied and gave direction to in the twelfth and thirteenth
centuries, paved the way for the achievements of the West in the suc-
ceeding eight hundred years; but the price of this, the other side of
this dialectic, was that it sowed the seeds of that positivism through
whose sights, as R. D. Laing said, violence cannot be seen.[49]

We have mentioned Geoffrey of Monmouth's story of Corineus
and Goemagog. Let us now examine some aspects of Geoffrey's work
that are relevant to our discussion, with regard to this period and to
the continuous and repeated pattern of our subject in general. Our
theme is the interaction of the human spirit with history; history survives in that spirit as memory. Geoffrey's massive fictional manipulation of that memory has its element of genius, but it is a sinister
genius which played its part, over centuries yet to come, in a vast
crime against the human spirit.

Geoffrey was a Welsh aristocrat of Norman affiliation and possible Breton ancestry, who stood between his two cultures, consciously and drastically reworking the old legends to present the
"Celtic" viewpoint in a form palatable to the overlords of the expanding civilization in general and the Angevin Empire in particular. He
based his work partly on that of Nennius, who had written his *Historia Brittonum* three hundred years earlier, in the age of Charlemagne.
The different manuscripts of Nennius contain two distinct versions of
the story of Brutus, the founder of Britain. In one, he is an early Roman consul who conquers Britain in the name of Rome; the purpose
of this story, as Hanning says, "is clearly to attach the Britons to the
ancient world and make them the heirs of Roman greatness."[50] In another manuscript tradition, however, Brutus is cast out of Rome because his mother died in childbirth and he shot his father in a hunting
accident, thereby fulfilling a prophecy that he would kill his parents.
In this way Britain becomes "a nation freed by its founder from the
burden of hatred imposed by the old world."[51]

It is this second version which Geoffrey takes up, adding a further significant motif. Brutus goes to Greece; there, rather than being
expelled for being a Trojan, as in Nennius, he liberates a colony of Trojan prisoners from the Greek tyrant Pandrasus, and in classic hero
style wins Pandrasus' daughter as his bride.[52] "The new Britons are

Trojans reborn: a nation rises from the wreckage of a preexisting nation. The conditions for rebirth as Geoffrey presents them are the desire for freedom and a leader to implement that desire."[53] Here we have a fascinating prism for reflections and refractions on the tensions between the "old world" centered on Rome and the "new world" centered on Aachen. Nennius' two versions of the Brutus story, dating from the heyday of the court at Aachen, exhibit the polarity of ambivalence toward the parent-culture. In that sense both legends are "true" because they embody the two sides of the paradox by which one emulates and incorporates the parent in the very act of rebelling. There is also a theme of progress toward maturity, as the Oedipus-like motif of parent-slaying shows forth the contrast between the mentality of primitive defilement which accuses Brutus and that of moral responsibility which declares him innocent. This thematology, appearing here amid the twelfth-century expansion of the "frontier," has obvious parallels with the archetypal themes which would later emerge in the discovery and conquest of America.

And in that connection, there is yet a further motif of Geoffrey's story, one evidently originating with him, which provides even more striking parallels with the repeated motifs of later history. When Brutus and the Trojans revolt against Pandrasus, they flee to the forests, living as hunters and gatherers, and send Pandrasus an ultimatum asking him *first* to let them remain there, and only if he cannot, to let them emigrate.[54] In the event, Pandrasus does neither, and the Trojans must fight a war to escape; but the original choice itself is remarkable. Hanning observes:

> Its exaltation of freedom takes new, antisocial forms. The traditional defiance of tyranny by a freedom-loving nation was a social act. . . . But the Trojans are clearly ready to live outside society indefinitely, if necessary. . . . Geoffrey, in short, raises a disturbing question about the relationship, so basic to the Christian tradition of early medieval historiography, between the quest for personal *salus* and the maintenance of national *salus:* can man always find his happiness within society? His inspiration for this idea may have been Gildas, who described the Britons' flight to the woods [during the Saxon invasions] as a result of oppression. For Gildas, though, this movement from society was unnatural—a punishment from God—and not a state to be enjoyed.[55]

Here for the first time appear parallels with later experience which are striking and do not need to be belabored. And what is the ultimate destiny, not yet manifest, of Brutus' people who have "lit out for the territory" for their liberty? The Great Goddess tells Brutus that "a race of kings will be born there from your stock and the round circle of the whole earth will be subject to them."[56] The Righteous Empire is older than one had thought—and indeed, we will later see the ideological ramifications of this very passage. Born simultaneously with people's urge to flee the city and its subject countryside as a place of oppression was the necessity of taking the city's internalized ideals with them. (The boy on whom Huckleberry Finn was based ended up as a justice of the peace in Montana. He had "lit out for the territory" indeed—with the "sivilization" on his back.)

In another mode, we can say that Geoffrey's hero accomplishes his archetypal withdrawal from society to undergo his trials and transformations, but that his return to that society is anomalous and incomplete; it is not accomplished in space but by recreating the society in another place, out of the hero's own internal images. The hero-myth thus takes on a narcissistic aspect—a reflection of that "increasingly obscene narcissism" which Fanon ascribed to European thought from its having "unfolded in places which were increasingly more deserted and more encircled by precipices."[57] And the relation to the parents exhibits a failure of necessary identification with them, with society, and with the transcendent which only strengthens the negative aspects of the parental relationship.[58] "Living myths," says Campbell, "are not mistaken notions, and they do not spring from books. They are not to be judged as true or false but as effective or ineffective, maturative or pathogenic."[59] These aspects of the myth as constituted by Geoffrey are pathogenic and anti-maturative; but not, alas, ineffective or defunct.

Geoffrey was one of the first in the long line of co-opted native intellectuals of the West's possessions. His writings, seemingly so archaic and primitive in their *motifs,* are actually a strong reflection in their *themes* of a mentality "advanced" for its time, a mentality destined to thrive and to expand vastly and catastrophically in following ages. Indeed, we shall see that Geoffrey's writings were not only a reflection of that mentality, but would one day be an agent in that expansion.

Let us return, however, to our thread of time and place, but let us do so with continued attention to the psychohistorical themes I have outlined above.

We have seen that the same forces which had made possible the unity of the Scottish state had deeply modified and divided Scottish culture. The twelfth- and thirteenth-century Highlands were still essentially outside the European orbit; their divisions, Argyll, Moray, Ross, and Caithness—to say nothing of Galloway in the southwest— were self-proclaimed "kingdoms" which took centuries for Edinburgh to subdue. Even then the same situation obtained in the Isles, won on paper from Norway in 1266. But the Lowlands, in contrast, were now distinctly part of Europe in a particular function: that of economic periphery. The forced feudalization of northern and western England, Wales, and the Scottish Lowlands had produced an area in which "civilization" had a different face than it did in the metropole of southeastern England and the Continent. The periphery became largely a supplier of raw materials—wool, hides, furs, and so on— and when skilled industry was developed, it was largely in the hands of immigrants. In the twelfth and thirteenth centuries, so many linen-weavers were brought in from Brabant in the Low Countries that the Gaelic word for weaver became *breabadair*, "Brabander." [60] The history of the area, and of its natives who left for Ireland and America in turn, strongly supports the thesis that an economic periphery is not simply a "developing" area suffering "growth pains," but rather that the periphery *as periphery* performs an important function in the economic life of the core—that "underdeveloped" regions are victims of a process of "underdevelopment." Thus whatever the ambiguities, the gains and losses, of the "modernization" process, it was the losses that hit with particular force in peripheral regions, in the twelfth century as in the twentieth.

We are now, however, primarily concerned with exploring some of the cultural and psychological aspects of this process. We have noted the connection between collective social frontier and individual ego-boundary, as an element fueling the dynamic of Western expansionism and racism from ancient times. It is plain how this essentially paranoid mentality dehumanizes and destroys those beyond the frontier, but the dwellers inside the frontier are themselves victimized in a more subtle but also deadly way. Peripheral dwellers—as inhabitants of the zone which the more "central," metropolitan core dwellers identify with the boundary between themselves and the environment [61]—are subjected to forces which tend to shatter their own sense of identity. They are seen by core dwellers not as beings in their own right, but as aspects of the latter's own selves—and of the most confused aspect of those selves, the insecure boundaries. Thus *the periph-*

eral dweller suffers not only insecure boundaries but an insecure sense of fundamental individuation—at least (an important qualification) insofar as he or she accepts the identity, or lack of it, imposed by the metropole. And he or she tends to be trapped into doing so, for the weaker the sense of autonomous selfhood becomes, the stronger is the tendency to lean upon the very other who is robbing that selfhood.[62]

Thus the Scots, their society sandwiched between a wild, windswept Iron-Age Gaeldom and a glittering feudal England, must have inclined toward feeling like adolescents with unformed identities, trapped between childhood and adulthood. It must have come to seem like an inevitable fact of life that they must outgrow the primitive "Celtic" state of being, which existed side by side with them like their childhood memories and menaced them with disruptive Highland raids and backland rebellions like outbursts of childish impulse. They must abandon a state of being that the new economic system, with its towns and commerce, linked with childish ineptitude in dealing in "abstract" terms and being competitive for survival in the "real world." They must grow out of this and grow into the more highly organized "mature" edifice of feudalism, by imitating as well as they could the parent-figures—the Anglo-Normans and Scotto-Normans for whom "the centre of civilisation was the centre of England"[63]—and thus attaining the only mature identity their society allowed them to see as possible.[64] In this interpretation, the warfare between England and Scotland may have served only to complete, in the back of the aristocratic and bourgeois Scottish mind (for what we are saying applies, at this stage, mainly to these classes), the picture of the English and Normans as parent-figures, conflict with whom served only to reinforce identification. For, as was later to be said about Appalachia, the process was all "an investment of emotional energy upward, toward the superior, rather than horizontally toward one's peers."[65]

(We have up to now emphasized the patriarchal aspects of domination, but here one thinks of the words of Fanon: "On the unconscious plane, colonialism . . . did not seek to be considered by the native as a gentle, loving mother who protects her child from a hostile environment [the demons of the wasteland, externalized], but rather as a mother who unceasingly restrains her fundamentally perverse offspring from managing to commit suicide and from giving free rein to its evil instincts [the demons of the wasteland, internalized]. The colonial mother protects her child from itself, from its ego, and from its physiology, its biology, and its own unhappiness which is its very

essence."[66] This familial change parallels the social change from peasant versus enemy to lord versus peasant. Too, one cannot help thinking of St. Margaret and her fanatical youngest son, so "polished" by
the English, and one may even speculate about some personal psychohistorical connection in this regard. A colonial city is, after all, a *metropolis*; and, as we have seen, the Scottish colonial city, the royal
burgh, was to an unusual degree wedded directly and deliberately to
the mottes, the man-made eminences which consolidated and imaged
forth the intrusive power of Anglo-Norman authority. To win his
"freedom" from the new feudal serfdom, the peasant had to enter the
confining enclosure of the burgh, in the shadow of the castle, and remain within its walls for a year and a day before being reborn as a
"citizen" [city-dweller] of the new society. The dialectic of oppression
and liberation is a matter of motherland versus intrusion, but also
of patrimony versus metropole. Oppression and liberation are not
gender-marked, but like other human phenomena they naturally express themselves in these two modes.)

All this may seem remote from mottes, coinage, and the horsecollar; but it seems to me that psychological factors are not only historically important in themselves, but particularly so in conditions
such as the ones we are examining. As Rogin says: "Infantile sexuality
and prolonged infant dependence shape the human personality.
These forces do not finish their work in childhood. Crises in the life
cycle return the ego to its early roots. Adult traumas—war, depres-
sion, death of a parent—do so as well. Crises open fissures in the ego,
making it particularly vulnerable to disorienting contemporary experience, and bringing childhood longings into play. Primitive forces
also take decisive shape from the culture into which the individual
matures."[67] Thus, though many of the processes we are discussing
were given special force by shocks in the economic and political
spheres, it by no means follows that the psychological processes are
merely surface phenomena of the politico-economic ones. They have a
life of their own that redounds back upon the historical process, is
equally a part of the historical process in which economics and politics are embedded.

So much, then, for the Scottish nobility and (perhaps especially)
the nascent bourgeoisie; but why did anglicization and "domestica-
tion" spread down to the peasantry? We have already discussed some
of the material advantages of learning the English language and adopting the feudal culture. But these pressures, I think, were made effective by a deep underlying mental process belonging to the basic nature

of feudalism. What changes, then, did feudalism make in the peasants' world of experience, and how were these changes reflected in their fundamental structures of experience?

Under the old "Celtic" system, land had been owned individually or collectively by those who worked it, the heirs to nine generations of the original owner; the lord had simply been the leader of the peasants, and all the free ones had been thought of as related to him. Under feudalism, by contrast, the lord himself held sole title to the land, and all others were reduced to being tenants, holding their fields only in return for services. This radical change in the relation of the people to their land was surely among the biggest factors in the breakup of "Celtic" culture in the Lowlands—not only for narrowly construed economic reasons, but for profound psychological ones as well.

The old relationship of the peasant to the land, unbroken for nearly two thousand years, had often been disturbed by famine and invasion, but it had formed a constant background to the peasant's expectations and hopes. The relation with the earth which gave life had been perceived as one of unconditional motherly support, mediated through the collectivity; the leader derived what authority he had, great though it might be, solely from being the embodiment of that collectivity and the indirect and symbolic channel of that nurturing support. As Robert Coles was to say of the Scottish peasant's descendant, "he sees himself and his family and his kin and his friends as . . . part of something well nigh everlasting, something that continues, goes on, stays, is *there*, however hard and difficult and miserably unfair 'life' can get to be."[68]

Now, though, the land became an inanimate substance; all its psychic energy of nurture became concentrated upon the feudal lord, a foreigner in fact or in mind, elevated upon his man-made hill, and possessing in his own person both the land and the services of his tenants. Existence itself now became an object given in return for particular reified conscious actions. The complicated feudal structure of layer upon layer of "holdings-from," leading from the local lord to the king, must have made real authority seem all the more remote. Furthermore, the feudal lord himself did not come into possession of the land through the old system by which a chieftain inherited leadership of a distinct people with its compact district of land; the Norman freebooters were given their lands from higher authority, for personal loyalty to the king and his men and in units corresponding to strategic considerations—units further distorted from their original shape by marriages of convenience which transferred lands according to the laws of feudal inheritance as a pre-capitalistic "medium of exchange."[69] Thus, for example, by the time of James VI a map of the Cunningham lands looks as if the original district of that name had been blown or torn to bits and scattered over a wide area of the southwest.[70].

The natural result of all this was an acute collective outbreak of separation anxiety, resulting in a mass breakdown of the old society and its re-formation as the lower stratum of the new order. In this new order, the peasants were cast in the role of children being socialized all over again, and those peasants clutched at the figures of their "betters" as the only stable things in a collapsing world—even though those "betters" were part of the problem. The peasants were deprived of their land as a source of Eriksonian "basic trust," as what for their descendants in Appalachia would be described as "a matrix for their lives,"[71] as "the crucible for continuously unfolding life."[72] They were encouraged to transfer this conviction of motherly support to the proto-capitalistic metropole, but the latter restored their freedom and security in a way that was primarily negative and at any rate too different in form for them to assimilate at the pace demanded by the crash program of belated feudalization to which they were being subjected. The result was an outburst of unsublimated and ego-threatening rage at the suddenly untrustworthy mother—a rage which could only be mastered, in the absence of possibilities for a vital reconnection to land and community, by a rigid assertion of autonomy and an acceptance of the concept of land as a commodity, as mere matter drained of identification as a source of trust and subject to manipulation as a product of the self.[73] Insofar as the image of the land resisted this affective neutralization, it tended to do so only at the cost of remaining the object of that primitive rage which encouraged the subject to treat it not neutrally, let alone positively, but negatively—as a breast to be aggressively scooped out.[74] The expression of this attitude was not fully realized until centuries later, in America, when vast stretches of untitled, "free" land became available to be perceived—regardless of its being other people's homes—as a wilderness to be subdued.

Rogin notes how, in nineteenth-century America, "the stage before private property was, in the liberal view, the stage prior to the development of active, individuated egos."[75] The pioneering feudal lords of twelfth-century Scotland, and still more the burghers, seem to have held attitudes parallel to this formulation, equating property with identity, having with being, *meum* and *tuum* with *I* and *thou*. For they themselves were victims of the same attitude, and their unawareness of their own true selfhood apart from possession—apart from the "properties" of their egos—is of the same nature as the degradation they help impose on their "propertyless" victims. The regressive distress which must have threatened to overwhelm the peasants' psyches at this time can thus be seen as an example of the self-fulfilling prophecy—of a pathological process of attribution parallel to the economic process of "underdevelopment." That is, in classic style, the peasants fled for security to the very figures who had robbed them (or through whom they had been robbed) of whatever security they had once enjoyed.[76] Furthermore, since degradation is the first stage in the rite of passage, that very fact cemented the union with an iron band and confirmed the personal identification which, in this case, led to a tremendous inner need to be resocialized, to "grow up," as the colonizer himself desired to "grow up"—that is, to be Anglo-Norman. In this patriarchal discourse, at least, rage at the metropole generated a desire to subdue the land, while rage at the father-lord worked in the same direction, generating a desire to match him by emulation.

What the lowland Scottish peasant experienced fitted the pattern of a rite of passage from the mother-world to the father-world. But instead of being also, as in normal passages, a move out of the world of subjection to the uncomprehended will of the father and into the fellowship of the brothers, it was just the opposite. The call to "grow up," addressed to adults, is implicitly infantilizing and hence double-binding—it imposes, that is, a contradictory situation in which the subject cannot succeed and from which he cannot escape as long as he accepts the given terms.[77] The feudalization/anglicization process was thus a distorted rite of passage, and one which was to have disastrous consequences in a repeated context of similar conditions. As a distorted initiation into "adulthood," it fostered an impaired sense of personal autonomy and hence of ontological security; it filled the peasant with the need to validate himself by invalidating others. As Simone Weil said, "Whoever is uprooted himself uproots others. Whoever is rooted in himself doesn't uproot others."[78]

Three centuries or so of this process had a drastic effect on the Scottish lowlander. Let us next examine this effect, with particular emphasis on one of its most striking aspects: language. During those three centuries, the Scottish lowlanders fitted the description given of the Irish four centuries later still: "They had been brought up in the belief that English was the topnotch of respectability, the key that opened Sesame, and they were determined that their children should not be left without a boon so precious."[79] By the late Middle Ages, consequently, the English language was general among the Scottish upper classes, and understood by nearly everyone else in the lowlands and along the "development corridor" up the east coast. Late medieval Scottish literature and history contain several instances of noblemen gravely insulting their rivals by deliberately addressing them in Gaelic.[80] The use of Gaelic had never been actively penalized as it was in the Highlands in later times, but it had committed suicide voluntarily, out of shame.[81] "The story told is not so much one of outright deception and swindles (although there were plenty of them) as it is a subtle and deadly process by which a people were convinced of their own worthlessness, and thus, in many cases, gave up efforts to defend themselves and their ways of life."[82] The subject of this quotation is not Scotland but Appalachia.

Nevertheless, in the western Lowlands, Gaelic long survived in the southwestern corner, Carrick ("Cliffs") and Wigtown.[83] In 1505, Scotland's greatest English-language poet, William Dunbar of Anglo-Saxon Lothian, trading joking insults with his rival Walter Kennedy of Carrick, calls him a "gluntoch" (*glùndubh* or "black-knee," i.e. a plaid-robed Highlander)[84] and states (using a form of insult typical of the dawning capitalist era) that he, Dunbar, can fart English better than Kennedy can speak it:

> Sic eloquence as they in Erschry use,
> In sic is sett thy thraward appetite.
> Thow hes full littill feill of fair indyte:
> I tak on me, ane pair of Lowthiane hippis
> Sall fairer Inglis mak, and mair parfyte,
> Than thow can blabbar with thy Carrik lippis.[85]

But Kennedy retorts:

> Thou lufis nane Irische, elf, I understand,
> Bot it suld be all trew Scottis mennis lede;
> It was the gud langage of this land,
> And Scota it causit to multiply and sprede,
> Quhill Corspatrick, that we of tresoun rede,
> Thy fore fader, maid Irisch and Irisch men thin,
> Throu his tresoun brought Inglis rumplis in;
> Sa wald thy self, myght thou to him succede.[86]

North Britain, Political Units and Languages, AD 1090

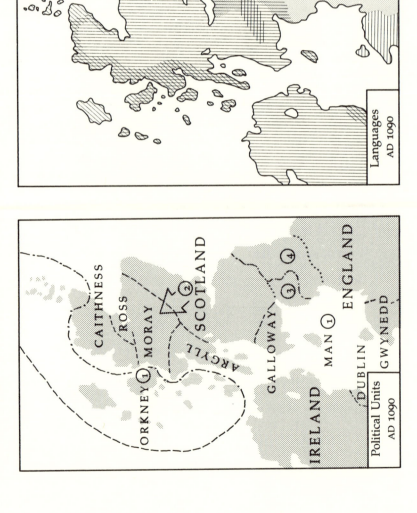

1. to Norway 1098
2. invasion 1078
3. to England 1092
4. to Scotland 1134–1153

KEY TO LANGUAGES

▥	Welsh
▦	Gaelic
▨	English
▧	Norse

Languages
AD 1090

ORKNEY ①
CAITHNESS
ROSS
MORAY
② SCOTLAND
ARGYLL
IRELAND
GALLOWAY
③
④
MAN ①
DUBLIN
GWYNEDD
ENGLAND

Political Units
AD 1090

North Britain, Political Units and Languages, AD 1411

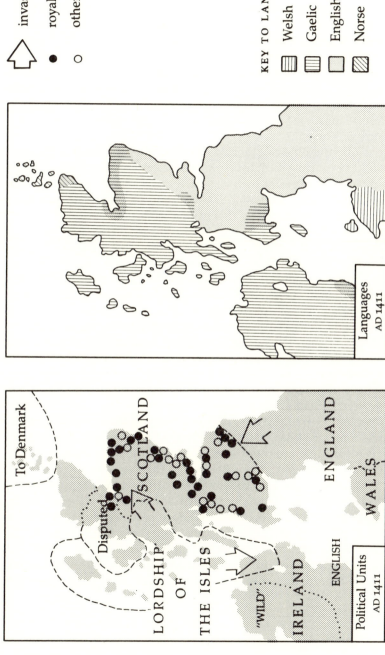

invasions

● royal burghs

○ other burghs

KEY TO LANGUAGES

Welsh

Gaelic

English

Norse

To Denmark

Disputed

SCOTLAND

LORDSHIP OF

THE ISLES

"WILD"

IRELAND

ENGLISH

ENGLAND

WALES

Political Units
AD 1411

Languages
AD 1411

This has been called "perhaps the first instance of linguistic nationalism to be found in Scottish literature,"[87] and it has also been stated that this mode of satire "probably came into the Scottish court from Gaelic tradition before the time of Dunbar."[88] But what kind of nationalism is it? Kennedy states that Gaelic "suld be all trew Scottis mennis lede," but he also correctly calls it "Irisch," as it was called until the eighteenth century, and its speakers "Irisch men." When he wrote, the languages spoken in Scotland—Gaelic, English, and the dying Norse—had, as we have noted, all been introduced within the past thousand or so years. Gaelic had itself replaced several other "gud langages," before it had started succumbing in turn to the pressure of English.

By the time of Dunbar and Kennedy, the latter could at least no longer be accused of disloyalty for defending Gaelic, since the Gaelic-speaking northwest had just been stripped of the last of its autonomous political power with the abolition of the Lordship of the Isles in 1493, after a particularly destructive war, and the flight of the Lord of the Isles, the Macdonald, to his holdings in Ireland. The king at this time, James IV, was probably the last Scottish king who could speak Gaelic.[89]

(Incidentally, it is notable that *gluntoch,* as an insult applied to Gaelic-speakers, is itself a Gaelic word—and therefore originally, one may presume, an epithet applied to some Gaelic-speakers by others. Evidently it was once thrown at the plaid-wearing Northwest Highlander by people from the more "domesticated" parts of Gaelic Scotland—people whose descendants, ironically, found themselves subjected to the same insult for speaking Gaelic at all. The word thus reflects in its tiny mirror the ironic turnabouts of the whole medieval Scottish situation. Compare the way in which modern American city-dwellers in the Midwest disparage Appalachian migrants as "ridge-runners" or "briar-hoppers." These words refer to characteristics not visible in Cincinnati or Chicago; plainly they originate in the attitudes of more "civilized" Appalachians to their up-country cousins.)

Meanwhile, the sixteenth-century southwest was still a buffer zone where raids from the Highlands and Isles had wrought nearly as much havoc as the continual warfare between the area's two leading families, the Cunninghams and Montgomeries. It was the Ayrshire laird Alexander Montgomerie, who had spent several years in Gaelic Argyll, that, a century or so after Dunbar's flyting with Kennedy, wrote a satire giving his own version of the origin of Gaelic culture:

God and Sanct Petir was gangand be the way,
Heiche up in Ardgyle, quhair thair gait lay.
Sanct Petir said to God in a sport word,
"Can ye nocht mak a Heilandman of this horss tord?"
God turned owre the horss turd with his pykit staff,
And up start a Helandman blak as ony draff.
Quod God to the Helandman "Quhair wilt thow now?"
"I will down in the Lawland, Lord, and thair steill a kow."
"And thow steill a cow, cairle, thair they will hang the."
"Quattrack, Lord, of that? For anis mon I die." [90]

Here the despised Other is neatly identified with the animal and the excremental in a single image; he is even called "blak" and compared with "draff" (dregs). [91] To complete his identification as an antitype of the merchant-capitalist ideal, he has no regard for property—including his own life. In further demonstration of this disregard, the Gael next steals God's knife—repeating, by the by, Ham's crime against his father's potency—but the weapon falls out of his plaid. Then:

"Fy," quod Sanct Petir, "thow will nevir do weill!
And thow bot new maid sa sone gais to steill."
"Umff!" quo the Helandman, and swere be yon Kirk,
"Sa lang as I may geir get will I nevir wirk." [92]

To be sure, no love had ever been lost between highland northwesterner and lowland southwesterner. Nine hundred years before Montgomerie, the Strathclyde singers of the *Gododdin* had rejoiced at the Lowland ravens which gnawed the head of Domnall Brecc, slain king of Dalriada and ancestor of the Macdonalds. Thus the inhabitants of the southwest had been defending themselves against Highland warriors and raiders since time immemorial—but always in their own name. Now, though, their land was someone else's line of defense, a buffer zone. One of the two greatest fortified royal burghs in medieval Scotland was at Dumbarton, the old capital of Strathclyde just outside the south edge of the Highlands. (The other was at Inverness, holding down the other end of the Highland Line.) Alexander II (1214–1249) had given Dumbarton its burgh status for its services against the "men dwelling in the neighboring mountainous parts"; this is the first surviving mention of Dumbarton since the Viking invasions. [93] The people of Strathclyde were only too glad to render that service, since it was incidental to their age-old pattern of defending themselves. But what was incidental to Strathclyde was central to

Scotland, and vice versa. The Scottish court was interested in Strath-clyde's self-preservation only for its own purposes. A "modernized" Dumbarton, no longer a capital, was a foreign-speaking instrument of a larger power indifferent or hostile to local interests. The Britons had called it Alclud, the Rock of the Clyde; the name Dumbarton, Fort of the Britons, is of Gaelic origin, given it by the Highland raiders who had so often besieged it, and becoming the normal name after the Scottish annexation. This was the name that stuck, but to an English-speaking city whose language came to dominate the countryside as the common people needed to deal with their masters. This process is emblematic of what happened to the whole area and its culture. Physical self-preservation had become the vehicle of cultural self-destruction. As Memmi notes on the individual level: "If the small colonizer de-fends the colonial system so vigorously, it is because he benefits from it to some extent. . . . To protect his very limited interests, he protects other infinitely more important ones, of which he is, incidentally, the victim." [94]

By the end of the Middle Ages, the linguistic shift from Gaelic to English had produced a change in the very name of the languages. Medieval Latin documents referred to Gaelic as *Scotica*, "Irish," and the new Lowland language simply as *Anglica*, "English." The fifteenth-century Lowlanders still referred to their own new language as "In-glis," and to Gaelic as "Irisch" or "Erse"—but, as if to clarify matters and put the Gaels in their place, the latter was now rendered not as *Scotica*, recalling the name of the kingdom, but as *Hibernica*, a more restrictive word for "Irish." [95] Then, by 1500, Lowland writers began to clarify matters further, setting themselves off from their hostile neighbors in both directions, by referring to their form of English as "Scottis" or "Scots," [96] while the English of England was called "South-ron." Thus the very word "Scot," and with it the national sense of identity, was removed from a Gaelic dialect and awarded to an English one. As for the Gaels themselves, meanwhile, their word *gall*, for-eigner, came to be an exact synonym for "Lowlander." (It was in this period that our modern concept of "nationality" was coming into being; hence the widespread misconception that the Highlands and the Lowlands are inhabited by two distinct "nations," one "Celtic" in origin and the other "Anglo-Saxon.") We have seen how Dunbar could inaccurately call his neighbor Kennedy a "black-knee" simply for being bilingual: this illustrates the fact that, though it still survived in "backward" areas outside the Highlands, Gaelic was by this time definitely associated with the stigma of being a wild, "blak," dirty, strangely clad, present-oriented ("For anis mon I die," I've got to die sometime), thieving Highlander.

But, as we have seen, three areas can actually be distinguished: England, the Highlands, and the anglicized but non-English area in between which had essentially become the kingdom of Scotland. This latter, central area was part of a region of northern and western Britain, including Wales and parts of England, which had recently been reduced from an integral part of one civilization to a peripheral region of another.[97] Around the end of the Middle Ages, when the Western world in general was suffering great turmoils, peripheralized and deculturated Scotland suffered a collective identity crisis, and became determined to forge a new identity out of the shattering events of the past few centuries. The linguistic effect, as we have seen, was an assertion of the English of Scotland as the "Scots" language. Scottish authors boasted of their writing without "Southron" words and constructions.

But no sooner did this consciousness arise than it in turn received heavy blows. For one thing, after the Scottish defeat at Flodden in 1513, literary and artistic activity declined in sixteenth-century Scotland as rapidly as it blossomed in contemporary England. The Reformation too (of which more below) interacted in a complex manner with economics, culture, and individual psychology to lay waste Scottish art. And in 1603 came the final irony as James VI of Scotland became James I of England and set out to impose on all his English-speaking subjects a single translation of the Bible—into "Southron" English. This was no new departure: the Scottish Reformers had all used London English translations because they were already available. But the King James Version of 1611 was the death-blow of Scots as a literary language. Scots broke up into a conglomeration of seldom-written dialects; while at the same time, in the seventeenth century, the remnants of Gaelic speech in the southwest were making their last stand against those dialects.

By such a process were the Lowlanders shamed out of the linguistic expression of their culture. Here, with King James, we see the same process beginning again in new terms—and not for the last time, of course, in the lives of Scotsmen and of Appalachians. Let us conclude our examination of this process by looking briefly at its effect on another vital expression of a people's consciousness: its religion.

For it is within this context of oppression and invalidation that we might begin to understand the extreme nature of the Scottish Reformation, when the Lowland Scottish mind caught fire with the

most extreme notions of divine sovereignty and human responsibility. Analogous reactions occur time and time again among peoples
whose center of experience is threatened, who are resisting the role of
being a stained mirror of others. The wholeness and authenticity
which transcend circumstances come to be seen as accessible *only* in a
relation between absolute individuality and absolute transcendence.
This point is not weakened but strengthened by the fact that many of
what we commonly consider the dour features of Scottish Presbyter-
ianism date from the Kirk's early Lutheran and Episcopal phases and
even, in some cases, from before the Reformation—even from Queen
Margaret's time.[98] In the sixteenth century, the extreme Calvinism of
John Knox and Andrew Melville did not penetrate the Highlands, but
it swept the Lowlands in general and the southwest in particular,
catching up all social causes in its net. Besides making the country's
politics still bloodier and more complicated, its attitude toward "Popish
and pagan mummeries"—toward socially mediated contact with the
transcendent—largely helped to cut the people off from what was left
of their traditional history and collective ritual. Further, Calvinism's
emphasis on the absolute sovereignty of God produced, in many, a
largely negative "individualism"—with what were often disastrous
effects on human autonomy. Individuals saw themselves as nothings
and felt that guilt had made them so; they could experience their own
freedom and goodness only by assigning these qualities entirely to
their heavenly Father, who could then give them back. To anticipate
our history a bit, accounts of early Scottish missionaries' "revivals"
in Ulster could have been written among their descendants in Appalachia three hundred years later. Thus a seventeenth-century observer
writes of a Mr. Glendinning:

> God made use of him to awaken the consciences of a lewd and secure
> people thereabout, his preachings being threatenings; and being of a
> forward zealous temper according to his light, . . . this man, seeing the
> great lewdness and ungodly sinfulness of the people, preached to them
> nothing but law, wrath, and the terrors of God for sin; and in very deed
> for this only was he fitted, for hardly could he preach any other thing;
> but behold the success! . . . I have seen them myself stricken, and
> swoon with the Word—yea, a dozen in one day carried out of doors as
> dead, so marvellous was the power of God smiting their hearts for sin,
> condemning and killing.[99]

Thus, between the twelfth and sixteenth centuries, the Scottish
lowlands were transformed—indeed, "the Scottish Lowlands" were
created, and so was the Scottish Lowlander. From a central and nor-

mal part of one civilization, the western Lowlands in particular were changed into a peripheral and devalued part of another, and its inhabitants felt this change painfully and adapted as they could or must. I have of necessity emphasized the negative aspects of these changes, and some of the negative features of the people's adaptations to them; and I shall have to continue to do so in later chapters. Nevertheless, it must be remembered that this is only part of the story—the part, perhaps, which *can* be discussed in terms of "forces" and "adaptations." Creativity, like violence, "cannot be seen through the sights of positivism"; and mountain people and their forebears, despite attacks on their "traits," have endured both in their innermost core of being and in their innermost sense of meaning. In later chapters we will continue to explore both their adaptations to their necessities and their furtherance of their possibilities.

This chapter has covered a thousand years of complex history, and has approached that history from so many different perspectives as to sweep up a congeries of details whose interrelation may be hard to grasp in one look. Nevertheless, what we have dealt with, for all its changing circumstances and varied aspects, is a single process moving in one basic direction. Its central feature is the feudalization of southwestern Scotland in the twelfth and thirteenth centuries. As for what came before, sentimental primitivism is out of the question— indeed, part of the problem; the growth in the complexity of our civilization is a matter of both gains and losses whose nature and relative importance is properly a matter of endless debate. But I think it certain that in the area we have discussed (among others), where "our" civilization was an outside imposition upon a region that was peripheral in several senses, the central facts are that this imposition was external, that it was belated, and that it was accelerated to such an extent that it placed inhuman strains on great numbers of people. Once more, the problem lies not in the *content* of what was imposed but in the *process* by which it was imposed.

Hence my references to "anglicization" and language change should not be thought of as implying a Celtic nationalist position. It is by a sort of optical illusion that the lines of oppression and domination seem to converge on England or the English, or in a simple sense to *any* particular group as a final villain. It was the Scots who "anglicized" themselves as part of an internalized system which the English neither originated nor, by and large, deliberately imposed—in a process aided and abetted by the fiercest fighters for Scottish inde-

pendence and resisted by England's allies in the far northwest.[100]
Analogous criticisms can be brought against various forms of regional
and "ethnic" chauvinism today, and in a later chapter I shall do so.

Much of what I have said about the psychological and other
aspects of this process in the British Isles is conjectural, but I am
convinced that its basis is not a fantasy. The student of Appalachian
history, or simply the observer of contemporary Appalachian experience, can draw analogies to all I have discussed. We shall see that
these analogies, striking in detail, are also historical connections.
And in both cases, it is vital to remember that the forces discussed
here are only part of the story, and that human integrity, both individual and social, has never entirely succumbed to them.

In both the twelfth-thirteenth centuries and the nineteenth-
twentieth, the causes as well as and the results of this process have
aspects which are economic, psychological, and so forth. I find no
reason to suppose that this whole flock of chickens hatches from a
single egg laid either at the point of production or at the point of inner
experience. "In any case," with Memmi, "before attacking this *final
analysis* I intend to show all the real complexities in the lives of the
colonizer and the colonized."[101]

Thus we have arrived at the period in which most histories of the
"Scotch-Irish" begin—that of the Union of Crowns and the eve of the
Ulster Plantation. For example, James G. Leyburn's *The Scotch-Irish: A
Social History,* the only general work in print on the subject, starts
with a section titled "The Scot in 1600." Leyburn notes correctly that
"Scotland lay, geopolitically, on the northwestern periphery of 'civilization'";[102] but he does not use the word "periphery" in our sense.
He discusses the poverty and squalor of Lowland Scottish life with
the unspoken assumption that its deficiencies were simply due to a
failure of "civilization" to penetrate more effectively; in short, he
takes for granted the "development" model. He attributes Scotland's
grim condition to an excess of traditionalism, in a society whose cultural tradition had in fact been disrupted repeatedly over many centuries—the parallel with Appalachia today is hardly farfetched. For
example, he attributes the warfare among local elite families to a con-
gruence between feudalism and the clan system—in an area where,
in fact, the Highland clan system had never existed. He asserts, indeed, that due to the supposed clan system, "David [I] had little
trouble in introducing feudalism to Scotland"[103]—a statement whose
accuracy the reader may now judge. Too, alluding to later history, he
notes: "The story of the Scotch-Irish (as of Scotland itself) is one of

progress from something near barbarism in 1600 to civilization . . . in the space of two centuries. . . . So did the Scots . . . transform themselves into a nation whose philosophers, literary men, and manufacturers were the admiration of the world." [104] He does not ask whether there might be some connection between this development and the movement of the frontier of "civilization" another layer outward, to the Highlands, Ireland, and the hinterlands of the colonies—including largely Scotch-Irish Appalachia. Let us, then, begin to examine the results of this movement.

3 *Apples on the Flood*

No more let *Ireland* brag, her harmlesse Nation
Fosters no Venome, since the Scots Plantation. . . .
Had *Cain* been *Scot*, God would have chang'd his doome,
Not forc'd him wander, but confin'd him home.
Like Jewes they spread, and as Infection flie,
As if the Divell had Ubiquitie.
  —John Cleveland, "The Rebell Scot"

Let us turn our attention, as King James did, to Ireland. At this time, a thousand years after the birth of "the West," Ireland, like the Scottish Highlands, was still not part of it. Indeed, her cultural and other differences from England and the Continent were probably greater in 1600 than at any time since the pre-Celtic Megalithic period. Although a Christian country, Ireland could no more be called "European" or "Western" in culture and society than Ethiopia.

Although not predominantly rough in terrain like the Scottish Highlands, Ireland is bowl-shaped, with low coastal mountains surrounding a central plain. After the Celtic invasions which gave her her language and many of her customs, the first successful invasions were those by the Vikings in the ninth century. The effect of these on the coastal monasteries was terrible, but the inland regions continued much as they had, and many of the major works of Irish art were produced during this time. The Vikings founded the first towns, but they were all on the coast and were eventually conquered by the native Irish kings. In 1169, the Normans invaded under authorization from the pope (an Englishman), but even their attempt at subduing the country went awry; Ireland was too different and too remote to be feudalized. What happened instead was that wave after wave of Anglo-Norman lords, after struggling to stamp out the quicksand of Irish culture, was gradually absorbed into the elite of the native system. The newcomers learned the Irish Gaelic language and battled England as vigorously as the older families—though for some time their position was ambiguous. Thus a fourteenth-century Anglo-Norman writer lamented, in a poem in the Irish language:

The English call us Irish,
The Irish drive us from our homes. . . .
We run along like apples on the flood.[1]

Nevertheless, when the acid test came as Henry VIII took over the Church in 1536, the Anglo-Normans, now called *Sean-Ghaill* "Old Foreigners," proclaimed their Irishness by remaining loyal to the pope. Ireland now presented itself to the Continent as a "wild" country whose social, political, and cultural structure had remained largely unchanged since the pre-Christian Iron Age, and on which successive invasions had had the main effect of furnishing it with improved weapons of defense. It was after the Reformation, then, when an intrinsically weak Ireland lay on the other side of a new kind of line across Europe, that she came to constitute a serious political threat to England—as a potential staging ground for military invasions by Catholic powers.[2] It was then that England set out seriously to destroy Irish culture and society.

To the English there was in fact no "culture" in Ireland, nothing they could recognize as anything but a savage chaos, to whose distinctive features they were blind. Seven hundred years of invasions had, after all, obscured many of Ireland's highest achievements. And the English were particularly blind to Irish cultural values because they were so similar to those out of which English culture had developed. Recognizing their worth would thus have gone against the process of repressive "growth" into "maturity."

Indeed the most "civilized" of the English were precisely those who advocated the most savagery toward Ireland. English authorities in and on Ireland defended the most violent acts of force and grisly terror against Ireland in the very name of "civility."[3] And we must note that it is just here, in the sixteenth century, that the very concept of "civility" or "civilization" first takes shape. Let us examine that development as an aspect of this colonial situation—a development which, once more, will continue and will grow in significance in later similar situations.

In previous chapters I have occasionally used the word "civilization" in a loose sense—and, increasingly, in an anticipatory way. In fact, though, before the Renaissance, there was no "civilization" and no "barbarism"—that is, these concepts did not exist, and it was "civilization" that brought "barbarism" into being. The Romans had spoken of *Romanitas* versus barbarians, medieval Europe of Christendom versus "Heathenesse," but these are simply classifications of Us versus Them. There had been no clear, common way of distinguishing the set of all countries with a certain degree and kind of technical and economic elaboration from the set of all others. The Romans had known that the inhabitants of Iran, India, and (very vaguely) China were what we would call as "civilized" as the Romans themselves were, but they still called them "barbarians," a neutral or vaguely opprobrious word which simply meant "foreigners." Medieval Western Europeans (like ancient Greeks) knew that many other countries were richer and less disorderly than their own, but Western Christians were not interested in making that kind of distinction between one "heathen" country and another: such distinctions were not philosophically useful to anything they wished to say about human societies.

The use of the words "civil" and "civility" where we would now say "civilized" and "civilization" is no more than four centuries old. It dates from the period when Western Europe, having reached around Africa and almost simultaneously stumbled upon America, found itself suddenly shifted from the edge to the center of the known world and forced to reconsider its notions of its own superiority—or rather, to recast these within a much wider and less manageable framework. The same events which had brought Western Europe into intellectual confrontation with other equally elaborate societies had also given it overwhelming political and economic power over many of the simpler ones. Now, the difference between these two types of society—the kind Europe could impose itself upon, and the kind it as yet could not—came into being as a primary distinction with a name.

The word "civilization," like the idea, has a complex and instructive history. The Latin word *civis* meant "citizen," one who participated in the political life of a city-state, as opposed to a slave or a countryman. One such city-state, Rome, grew to an empire, but the word *civitas* always kept behind it this concept of membership in an urban elite. In the Middle Ages, when Western town-life started over again, *civitas* followed its Romance cognates in changing its meaning from abstract "citizenship" to concrete "city" (the same word as *civitas*), replacing *urbs*; for with the absence of urban slavery under feudalism, a city-man was the same as a citizen: *Stadtluft macht frei*, city air makes free. "Civil" law came into being to regulate the relations among these "citizens," who were neither nobles nor serfs. All our other meanings of "civil" derive from this distinction between town and country, which (especially on the periphery, as we have seen) became the distinction between a dominant minority and a subject population. Words for city-dwellers give us *polite, civil,* and *urbane;* words for country-dwellers give us *boor* (a farmer), *clown* (Latin *colonus,* a settler), and *villain* (*villanus,* a worker on a villa or estate). In the sixteenth century, then, Westerners began seeing the world in an inflated version of this paradigm: the first English instances of the new senses of "civil" and "civility" date from that century, and from works dealing with America and Ireland.[4]

The opposition of civilization and barbarism had thus developed out of an opposition of town and country; the underlying image was that of an opposition between order and turmoil. We have already seen how the developing Western culture of the "twelfth-century Renaissance" had led to the development of the town/country opposition in economic and cultural terms, in tandem with the growth of the technical-instrumental world view. The intellectual horizon of the time precluded the insight that the "order" of the towns might *create* the turmoil of the countryside, that the "order" of the core might contribute to the turmoil of the periphery, that the "order" of the "civilized" world might help produce in the "barbarous" world that disorder which then became the excuse for the imposition of more "order." The Western concept of "civilization" thus laid the groundwork for the self-defeating and ever-expanding compulsion of New Worlds To Conquer which has plagued us ever since.

In Ireland, these attitudes manifested themselves in various ways, some vicious and some patronizing but none helpful to the natives. The Irish were undoubtedly not civilized by Western European standards; and since the ideology of the time held that a civilized nation could be non-Christian but a Christian nation could not be barbarous, it followed that Ireland could not be really Christian either. The surviving "Celtic" variances in Church practices, the abundant survivals of pre-Christian customs, and the positive indifference to the Church caused by the latter's identification with feudalism were used to show that the Irish were pagans with no real religion at all[5]—a form of perception which we have seen before in this history and which we shall see again. They were frequently compared to Scyths and Tatars; their practice of transhumance, leading their flocks and herds to different areas with the seasons, was confused with rootless nomadism.[6] Concepts were borrowed from Spanish accounts of the New World to characterize the Irish—at times they were even accused of cannibalism[7]—and the natural conclusion was drawn that the English should deal with the Irish as the Spanish were dealing with the natives of America.[8] Wrote one of Good Queen Bess's most powerful favorites, Robert Dudley: "Temporising warres are to be used with civill and expirt men, but savages and those rurall raskells are only by force and fear to be vanquished."[9] After all, if Christianization was the most important thing of all, and if it was impossible without civilization, then the Irish must be "civilized" by any means necessary.

In practice, of course, "Christianization" was indefinitely postponed as the ferocious measures taken to "civilize" the Irish failed somehow to attain their goal; and the Irish were eventually "Christianized," not by the English but by the underground Jesuit missionaries of the Counter-Reformation. These men worked directly to instruct the Irish in contemporary Catholicism without attacking the basis of their culture, and they succeeded in producing the world's most staunchly Catholic country—with, of course, the unwitting help of the Protestant English themselves. The grimly guilt-centered Catholicism of Ireland has been called "Protestant," and this paradox expresses an important fact: like Scottish Calvinism, as pointed out in the last chapter, Irish Catholicism became the chief psychic mainstay of a people whose collapsing social system was cutting them adrift.

Besides the Spanish model, however, many apologists for the English conquest of Ireland invoked the example of the Romans. This was especially the tack of the most "progressive," "humanitarian," and "developmentarian" spokesmen (to use our modern terms), whose most elaborate ideologue, Sir Thomas Smith, remarked "how this contrey of England, ones as uncivill as Ireland now is, was by colonies of the Romaynes brought to understand the lawes and orders of thanncient orders whereof there hath no nacion more streightly and truly kept the mouldes even to this day than we, yea more than thitalians and Romaynes themselves."[10] Note that, contrary to the assumptions of many "Celtic" nationalists, English imperialism in Ireland at this stage did not appeal to any sense of "Teutonic" or "Saxon" racial superiority to "Celts"—in fact it derived its strength precisely from denying or ignoring any such distinction and putting the matter strictly in sociopolitical and cultural terms. Distinctions between Germanic and Celtic peoples were not very clearly made in Elizabethan times; interest and pride in the Germanic and "Anglo-Saxon" background of the English were in their infancy and did not begin their wide spread until the seventeenth century.[11] Rather, the thrust of the colonizers' argument was precisely that Ireland was as Britain had been, and that as Rome conquered Britain for her own good, Britain (conceived of as essentially the same nation as in ancient times) must do the same to, or for, Ireland—to her "contemporary ancestors," to coin a phrase. All racial prejudice is based largely on projection of the subject's own denied qualities onto the victim; here this dynamic becomes conscious as part of a thought-out, indeed a "progressive" and "developmentarian," ideology.

Indeed, it was only after the growth of the concept of "civility" that all the "civil" inhabitants of England, Wales, and Scotland began widely, under James I, to call themselves "Britons." Only then did they form a conceptual unit over against the remaining fragments of the Atlantic Zone, newly stigmatized as "barbarous." This concept of "Britishness" had been worked out during the previous century as an adjunct of Welsh Tudor supremacy in England. It was first popularized in 1521 by the Lowland Scot John Major in his punningly titled *Historia Majoris Britanniae*, and was elaborated by Elizabethans such as Sir Robert Dudley's protégé, the occultist and friend of colonizers, John Dee. And let it be noted that Dee and others drew explicitly from Geoffrey of Monmouth, and in particular from the passage we have cited in which the Goddess promises the Britons "the round circle of the whole earth" for what Dee called the "incomparable BRYTISH IMPIRE." [12]

The old word "Briton," first invoked by one Lowland Scot and implemented by another, was on the surface a neutral geographical term. But it also carried a strong affective charge, a sense of something not only more general but more ancient than England, Wales, or Scotland—an identification with a more fundamental, underlying reality. James VI/I was the first "king of Britain" since his fictitious models in Geoffrey. Yet the new "Britain" was also an entity opposed to the truly archaic "British" or Atlantic reality still represented by the "barbarous" Gaels. Thus, as a hegemonic term, "Briton" constituted another false resolution. It called on resources of psychic energy which reached back both mentally and historically (at least on the conscious level) only to the edge of a great split, beyond which all identification with the "contemporary ancestor" was denied or demonized.

The English boasted of their high state of "civility" by pointing to the fact that they had virtually abolished serfdom to an extent unknown even on the Continent. The Irish, they asserted, could be raised to this "civil" condition if they were first subjected to the English, who would teach them "civil" responsibility and eventually set them free. Some English writers refined on this thesis precisely by noting the objectionable behavior of the old Anglo-Norman nobility toward the native Irish, as contrasted with that of the English lords in England. Rather than seeing this as an outgrowth of the colonial system, they viewed it as simply another proof of Irish barbarity. They recommended that the "degenerate English" lords be reformed so that the Gaelic Irish themselves could more effectively be subdued by that force which was all they could understand, and their pre-feudal law be extirpated in favor of English law, so that they could gradually be raised to accept English freedoms.[13] In fact, of course, no such raising took place, and its failure to do so over the next three hundred years simply spurred the English to redouble their efforts—or at least it so spurred those English who succeeded in ignoring the discrepancy between their idea of "civilization" and the savage effects of their policies to Ireland.

The main point to be noted is that the English conquest of Ireland, like the Spanish conquest of America, was no simple grab for power at the expense of a weaker nation. At any rate it was not that to its theoretical spokesmen, and their writings on the subject should not be taken as simple rationalizations of pillage. Invalid justifications for the illegitimate use of power they no doubt were, but in a more subtle and deep-structural sense than simple hypocrisy. Westerners, emerging from the largely ahistorical mentality of the Middle Ages, were beginning to put their new knowledge of other times and places within evolutionary and developmental schemes. Naturally they tended to put themselves at the top of any such; but a central point is that the mentality which led to the destruction of native Irish and American cultures was no "relic of medieval barbarism," as is often said, but rather an expression of the most "advanced" and "enlightened" thought of its time, conceived in deliberate *opposition* to "medieval barbarism," and having as its conscious goal to work for the "barbarians'" own good, and to "bring them into the present era." (Once again, this "humane" and "enlightened" emphasis on the subjects' "own good," combined with an essential denial of their own goodness and personal validity, reminds one strongly of what Fanon had to say about the *motherly* aspects of domination. The inability of the Western mentality to attain maturity without infantilizing others has to do with the imperfection of its rites of passage, in which patriarchal authoritarianism feeds and is fed by an unresolved mother-fixation.) The parallels between this Renaissance developmentalism and the mentality—and results—of modern "development theory" need not be spelled out at this point. As Sartre noted, "with us there is nothing more consistent than a racist humanism, since the European has only been able to become human through creating slaves and monsters." [14] Once again, "whoever is uprooted himself uproots others. Whoever is rooted in himself doesn't uproot others." [15]

Such was the origin of our concépt of "civilization," and such were the applications of that concept to Ireland. How was this concept put into practice to "civilize" that country?

It has been pointed out many times that the British colonization of Ireland—we here use the word "British" for the first time in its modern sense, popularized under James I—was a practice ground for the colonization of other non-"Western" countries. [16] And as in America, it was soon realized that the only effective way to subdue Ireland was the mass dispossession of the population in compact areas. The most appropriate place to start was Ulster, for three connected reasons.

In the first place, as we have seen, Ulster is so close to Scotland that it is really part of a bridge between the two countries. (Indeed, a geological formation on the Ulster coast called the "Giants' Causeway" is believed in folklore to be the remains of a literal bridge.) This transitional territory has been subject to population movements in both directions for millennia. In Irish legend dating from long before 1610, it is said that when the gods gave the provinces of Ireland their characteristics, they gave to Meath kingship and its attributes; to Munster music, chess-playing, and so on; to Leinster prosperity and its attributes; to Connacht learning and its attributes; and to Ulster they gave battle, contentions, hardihood, strife, haughtiness, pride, unprofitableness, conflicts, and war. [17] The Gaels invaded Scotland from Ulster, where it appears that a revolt of a pre-Gaelic British tribe had only recently been crushed, [18] and at first their chieftains ruled both sides of the channel. Scots also frequently washed back into Ulster, as it were. In 1315, a year after Robert the Bruce defeated the English at Bannockburn, his brother Edward landed at Larne in Ulster, with whose chiefs he had negotiated, and declared himself king of Ireland. He ravaged the country up and down for three years, for the glory of Scotland and to the detriment of English overlords and native Irish alike, until he was killed at Fochart. Later, in 1399, the Macdonald inherited part of Ulster, and Scottish Gaels from his Lordship of the Isles moved in, first as conquerors and then as refugees from

James IV. During the Elizabethan conquest, these Gaelic Islesmen, as anti-English as the Irish, waged a three-sided war which complicated and bloodied the situation to the point that much of Ulster was de-populated. Such English control as had existed nearly vanished; on the eve of James I's plantation of Ulster, Sir John Davies, using a sig-nificant analogy, described the interior of the province as "heretofore so obscure and unknown to the English here as the most inland part of Virginia is yet unknown to our English colony there." [19]

Such was the first reason for targeting Ulster as a "British" colony. For the second, Ulster was close to a depressed part of Scot-land, the western Lowlands. And for the third, Ulster was also very close to the Scottish Highlands and Isles, where the Reformation was not penetrating, and where the danger to the Lowlands from the "wild" Highlander was therefore redoubled. James pursued a deliber-ate, though unsuccessful, policy of outright extermination against some Highland clans; [20] but, England having abandoned the Highlan-ders' cause, the latter sought help, and got it, from their Irish cousins. Thus for these three reasons—the geopolitical ambiguity of Ulster, the depressed and "overpopulated" nature of the adjacent part of Brit-ain, and the dangerous connection between Ireland and the High-lands—an emigration of Protestant Lowland Scotsmen would have a high feasibility on both sides of the water and would drive an effective wedge between the two rebellious Gaelic nations of James' domain.

Such were the reasons of state; and for the populace involved, too, there were plenty of reasons for emigration. As the feudalization of Scotland had hit the western Lowlands with particular disadvan-tages, so did the first stirrings of capitalism. Under feudalism, a lord's tenants could at least manage the services they were assigned in re-turn for their tenancy. But the sixteenth-century substitution of cash payments for services—*de facto* capitalism, extended from the burghs to the countryside under the formal guise of feudalism—was now driving many of the poorer tenants off the land and into the burghs, where they began to form a depressed urban proletariat. (This is what historians usually call the "freeing" of the British serfs—or at any rate, this was the form which that "freeing" often took on the periph-ery.) Ulster offered land without noble lords—the declining feudal system was scrapped altogether. [21] In addition, Ireland was more re-mote than Scotland from the politico-religious seesawing that racked Britain and all northern Europe for most of the sixteenth and seven-teenth centuries; the Scots' Calvinism would at least be consistently tolerated, or so they thought.

And so, throughout the seventeenth century, Scottish emigrants by the thousands fled to Ulster. They came from every part of Scotland *except* the Gaelic Highlands and Isles, but especially from the southwest, from Strathclyde and Galloway—a fact easily supported, if it needs support, by comparing a map of Scottish family names with, say, a West Virginia telephone book.[22] The Galwegians were returning to a land many of their ancestors had left centuries before. The others were largely descendants of the Strathclyde Welsh, with some dollops of what had been Norse, Anglo-Saxon, and Pictish. In later stages, inland areas also received sizable numbers of English settlers, mostly from the semi-"Celtic" northwestern and southwestern counties. More Scotsmen fled their homeland in the 1640s and thereafter, when intransigent Presbyterians, especially in the southwest, subscribed to the Scottish Covenant. In the wars that racked Britain for a generation, the Covenanters fought bitterly under their motto "Jesus and no quarter!", switching sides more than once as English allies betrayed their cause. Pro- and anti-Covenanters alike fled to Ulster to escape the massacres perpetrated by each side in turn. Charles II's general, Lord Claverhouse, would be remembered centuries later in Appalachia: "Behave yourself," children would be told, "or Clavers will get you!"[23]

Whatever their origin, these poor townsmen and hard-pressed peasants had common characteristics which produced a common impression on their "betters." The Reverend Andrew Stewart, author of the previously quoted account of religious revivals in Ulster, characterized these "small colonizers" in the following way:

> From Scotland came many, and from England not a few, yet all of them generally the scum of both nations, who, for debt, or breaking and fleeing from justice, or seeking shelter, came hither, hoping to be without fear of man's justice in a land where there was nothing, or but little, as yet, of the fear of God.[24]

One of these "scum's" descendants was to speak thusly of his neighbors in Chicago (where there is little enough of the fear of God):

> Then they'll tell you they've driven through the mountains of Kentucky and West Virginia, and they thought it was pretty there, and they want to know if there wasn't *something* that I couldn't find back there. I tell them no, there just isn't. They don't understand, though. They think jobs are around, if you really look. They think we're lazy, or something, and we didn't have the brains to stay in school, and we're running away from some crime, you know, or we've done a bad deed—otherwise we'd be back there.[25]

North Britain, Political Units and Languages, AD 1630

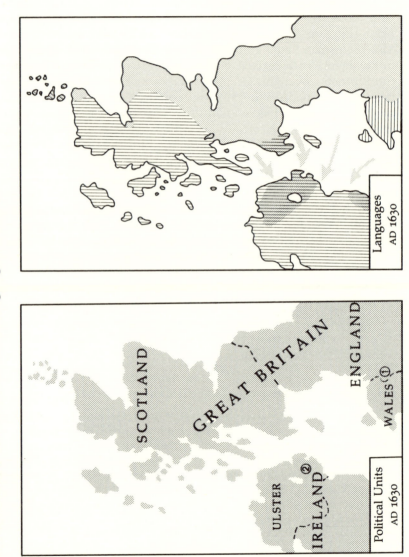

1. Wales to England
2. Ireland to England

KEY TO LANGUAGES

Welsh
Gaelic
English
Norse

Languages
AD 1630

SCOTLAND

GREAT BRITAIN

ENGLAND

WALES ①

ULSTER

IRELAND ②

Political Units
AD 1630

North Britain, Political Units and Languages, AD 1980

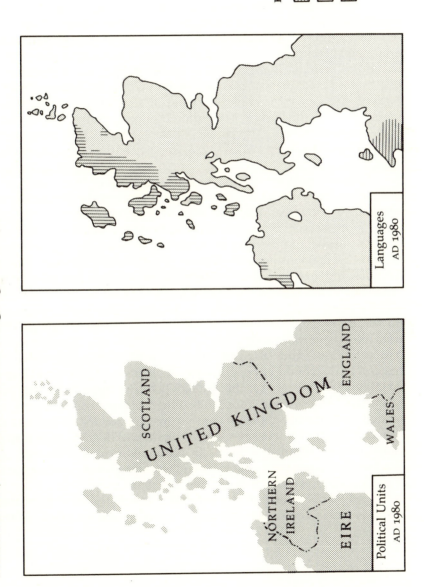

Political Units
AD 1980

EIRE

NORTHERN
IRELAND

SCOTLAND

UNITED KINGDOM

ENGLAND

WALES

Languages
AD 1980

KEY TO LANGUAGES

Welsh

Gaelic

English

The Reverend Mr. Stewart, three centuries ago, did not inquire as to whether the experience of constantly being seen in such a way might be connected with the lack of self-esteem that manifested itself in the hysterical revivalism he described, and in negative "unworldliness." And neither have most of his successors to this day, whether among those of the clergy who talk (or once did) of "yesterday's people," or among members of the clergy's daughter profession, academia.

Once in Ireland, the settlers seem to have converted and/or inter-married with the subject race to some appreciable degree. (Leyburn's negative judgment on this question,[26] based largely on commonsense arguments, contradicts the solidest piece of evidence, namely family names, as he himself admits.[27]) Nevertheless, the native Irish were a dispossessed race, who mounted constant terroristic raids against the settlers; the general Catholic uprising of 1641 brought widespread massacres, and the Puritan Revolution brought equally bloody attacks in the other direction. The parallel between "wild" Irish and "wild" Indians has often been made—even, in naïve enthusiasm, by modern Ulstermen.

Indeed, not only was this parallel drawn at the time, but it was not the only one of its kind. During the seventeenth century, the pe-ripheral "Celtic" areas of Britain itself were widely compared with the most "savage" parts of the Empire. What we have seen for Ireland was only one aspect of this. "We have Indians at home," Roger Williams quoted "an eminent person" in 1652—"Indians in Cornwall, Indians in Wales, Indians in Ireland."[28] The overt subject, though, was not the economic "development" that was going on at the time, but the spread of the Gospel in its Puritan form.[29] Sir Benjamin Rudyerd had noted in the House of Commons in 1628 that in some places in Britain, God was "little better known than amongst the Indians": namely "divers parts of Wales" and "the uttermost skirts of the North, where the prayers of the common people are more like spells and charms than devotions."[30] Once more, the analogy between the seventeenth and twentieth centuries is as important as the historical connection; since this concern for the "unchurched"—this missionary movement di-rected at Christians whose existing religion was deemed inauthentic, and occurring simultaneously with economic exploitation—had oc-curred more than once in the past, and was of course to repeat itself in another "discovery" of "a new pioneer region."

Connecting this with the psychohistorical thread of our fabric, one may note that Williams, commonly represented in American history as an unusually gentle and tolerant person, was a typical Englishman of his age with regard to Catholicism. "I cannot see," he proclaimed, "but that the first and present great design of the Lord Jesus is to destroy the Papacy. . . . Christ Jesus in His holy wrath and jealousy will burn and tear the bloody whore of Rome in pieces."[31] Thus Williams' anti-Catholicism, which in this pamphlet he connects with missionary work among pagan Indians and supposedly quasi-pagan "Celts," is informed with the imagery of extreme, exclusive and *ipso facto* insecure autonomy against the Bad Mother.[32] One can also connect this theme with the experience of separation from the land, in Williams' society and in his own exile from New Haven which led to the founding of Providence.

(And remarkably enough, the parallel between the missionary movement against Christians in the seventeenth and the nineteenth-twentieth centuries extends even to this detail of anti-Catholic motivation. In the same article in which W. G. Frost called for the "accelerated development" of the mountains, he proclaimed: "Protestant America needs numerical reinforcement. The sense of this need is forced upon us by the great increase of the foreign born and the hyphenated population."[33])

The settlers in Ulster had moved, essentially, in order to find a new life and to live it on their own terms. In the second hope they could only be disappointed, for Europe's power was expanding ever outward, and their own emigration had been a tool of that expansion, however little they may have realized it. By introducing into Ireland the Bolivian potato, the first crop able to produce high food value from the soil of the Atlantic Zone, they undermined the ancient stock-raising economy. (In parts of Ireland, the traditional evening meal is still called "boiled Protestants.") Cromwell's fanatical genocide campaigns finally broke the back of Iron Age civilization in Ireland, but the Scottish Ulstermen were also threatened, with forcible deportation at least, by Cromwell's plan to anglicize four-fifths of the island.[34] The worst crisis of the Ulster Protestants, however, came under the Catholic James II, when his commander in Ireland, the native Ulster Irishman Tyrconnell, announced his plan to drive the Ulster settlers back to Britain. His attempt to do so during the war between James and Parliament's choice for king, William of Orange, met such unexpectedly stiff resistance that it played a large part in James's defeat. James I's plan to drive a wedge between Ireland and the Scottish Highlands had succeeded—against his own grandson.

A century after the beginning of the Plantation, then, the worst seemed over for the Ulster Protestant. The Catholic Irish had been neutralized physically and politically; the settlers, free from both Scottish feudalism and Irish terrorism, were developing thriving industries; the stability of their new life, and of their newly recovering identity, seemed well assured.

But this situation could not last. The stability of Ulster depended on Ireland's being incorporated within the military frontier of England, and behind the military frontier inexorably marched the economic and social frontiers. Once more the people who were to become the "Scotch-Irish" had placed themselves, or allowed themselves to be placed, in an unstable, ambiguous position on the ever-shifting frontier. Indeed this may now be called one of their defining characteristics. The Ulster Protestants' ancestors had been traumatized at least five hundred years before by the forced, belated crash-program feudalization of the Lowlands and other "Celtic" fringes of Britain, and they had been subjected to a thwarted and repressive passage which tended to foster a distorted and ambivalent sense of identity. For centuries, their descendants would be encouraged to derive their sense of identity from outside sources (or to defend themselves from such pressures by isolation and projection). Thus they fit easily into—and indeed inaugurated—the classic patterns of what has been called "servitor-imperialism." Again, "whoever is uprooted himself uproots others. Whoever is rooted in himself doesn't uproot others."

The ambiguous nature of the Ulster Plantation had two intersecting dimensions. In the first place, Ireland was in an ambiguous legal position; it was neither part of England nor a colony; it had its own (all-Protestant) parliament but not its own "crown." Its legal status was in effect subject to whatever interpretation England wished to put on it. In the second place, though specifically subject to England and not "Britain," most of its Protestant settlers were of Scottish origin. We see here that the old "Atlantic" world was still feebly alive. To the Scots nothing was more natural than to follow the ancient routes down into Ulster, as so many (including many of their own ancestors) had gone in either direction before them. But the English, on the other hand, saw things exclusively in terms of the east-west axes of European expansion. With the consolidation of the English kingdom in Tudor times, the chief intersection of these two axes had shifted from Britain to Ireland. England and the Ulster Protestants were thus separated by a fundamental difference in outlook, a lack of understanding as great as that which stood between England and the Irish

Catholics. When the Belfast Presbytery protested the execution of Charles I, it was no less a person than Cromwell's Latin secretary, John Milton, who sniffed at the "blockish Presbyters" and the "barbarous nook of Ireland"[35] from which they dared to criticize English policy.

As soon as the economic interests of Ulster began to oppose those of England, the latter took harsh steps to protect itself. When Ulster industries became competitive with English ones, England enacted trade restrictions that crippled them. When Ulster responded by developing new industries, England enacted new restrictions. Furthermore, though conventional accounts speak of the "growing prosperity of Ulster"[36] during the post-Cromwellian period and though it is true that a good deal of capital accumulated among Ulstermen, it is equally true that only certain of them became prosperous. The Ulster landlords were not feudal noblemen but capitalist entrepreneurs; but in the growing new system their power was not less but greater than that of their predecessors. As many times before and since, a change in the system had betrayed wishful hopes that the basic facts of domination would disappear along with certain forms. Often absentees, and freed from even the nominal restraints of the Scottish feudal system, these landlords raised the rents as steeply as possible with the death of each successive tenant, driving poorer people into the urban proletariat just as had happened in Scotland, and often replacing one Protestant renter with several Catholics who had pooled their funds. Many renters marched on their landlords and were violently suppressed—an episode usually called the Ulster rent "riots." Among lesser landowners, the absence of primogeniture resulted in land being divided into smaller and smaller portions until self-support was impossible.[37] As in many "developing" countries today, the accumulation of capital simply widened the gap between rich and poor.

Then, when William of Orange was succeeded by Queen Anne, came the most serious religious persecution the Ulster Scots had experienced in their new land. Ireland was an English dominion, and the so-called Church of Ireland was (and is) Anglican, a church Catholic in structure and historical concern but heavily influenced by Protestant ideas. In 1704, the Irish Parliament was finagled into passing the Test Act, which made not only Protestantism but the reception of Anglican sacraments a prerequisite for holding office. The Ulster governments were thrown into confusion as dozens of officeholders were summarily dismissed or forced to take oaths and observe rites contrary to their consciences. The act was interpreted so harshly against

Presbyterians that even marriages performed by ministers outside the Apostolic Succession were declared invalid—a provision which actually favored Roman Catholics over Presbyterians, and which immediately reduced most of the population of Ulster to legal bastardy.[38]

In short, the Scots of Ulster found their whole way of life treacherously invalidated by their own authorities. In addition, wealthy Presbyterians, fearful of disruptions, threatened to withhold their church tithes if their synods opposed the act. Since London had already withdrawn the funding that it had provided to the Presbyterian synods in recognition of their opposition to Cromwell, the Presbyterian conscience found itself cruelly pressed from both directions.[39] When the effects of the Test Act, combined with the trade restrictions on Ulster industries, were compounded by a succession of drought years which shook the remaining props of the Ulstermen's security, many concluded that it was time to move again—this time to America, to the frontier, where the effective power of English interference would surely never penetrate.

The preceding discussion of the Ulster experience may seem brief and summary for a book on the "Scotch-Irish." This epoch, however, has already been well examined by students of American ethnicity and of Appalachia, often to the neglect of earlier and, I believe, more significantly formative periods. The fact that Appalachians' ancestors acquired their somewhat awkward name from that experience—and then only in retrospect—should not mislead us into thinking that this relatively brief episode is specially pivotal. I have also, perhaps, felt unenthusiastic toward going into detail about matters that have been caught up into two different sets of pernicious mythicizations which are still killing scores of innocents. I have, at any rate, been content here to place the Ulster experience within the context of this study by discussing it as a result of past experiences and a forerunner of later ones. I believe that in this way the discussion, brief as it has been, will suggest ways in which students of the Plantation and even of modern Ulster—to say nothing of students of "Scotch-Irish" experience in Appalachia and elsewhere—may see new dimensions in their own concerns.

What we have seen in this chapter, then, is a natural development, under the conditions of a still expanding economy, technology, and world of knowledge, of the basic pattern set out in the previous chapter. Economically, the development of early merchant capitalism intensified the objectification and commoditization of persons which had begun under feudalism. Intellectually, the old casual distinction which feudalism had introduced between "wild" and "tame" was ideologized under early capitalism into a dichotomy of "savagery" and "civility." Psychologically, these ideas involved complex projections arising from increasing repression and alienation. The reader will see that there is a complex interlocking relation among these factors, and may take his or her pick as to the most "basic" of them, if any.

Geopolitically, the fringes of the "Western" metropole became more and more a distinct peripheral zone with its own features over against the regions on either side—features not only economic but involving all the other spheres of life—a zone in which the factors I have outlined above had a particularly damaging impact, or rather, series of impacts. In particular I have wished to draw attention to how peripheral individuals identified with the core dweller, but in an insecure way which made them fiercely defensive (in more than one sense) against the "barbarians" with whom the core dweller identified *them*. This insecurity made their aggressiveness an excellent weapon for the core dweller to manipulate, while in fact the core dweller never forgot the peripheral dwellers' transitional status, and never let the latter truly forget it either. To the Gaelic "savage" the Lowlanders-turned-Ulstermen were *gaill*, quintessential foreigners; to the Englishman, they dwelt in a "barbarous nook" of the outer darkness. Finally we see how, in response to a combination of internal cultural, social, and psychological factors, and of external encouragement and manipulation, a part of this population began a pattern of moving along with the shifting economic zone in which they had been acculturated, thus insuring a repetition in different terms of their defining experiences. To the next stage of this process let us now turn.

4 The Red Rose and the Briar

We cannot say where the edges of Southern Appalachia are,
but we know very well the location of its center: the mountains.
—W. H. Ward

Yo que soy montañés sé lo que vale
La amistad de la piedra para el alma.
—Leopoldo Lugones

The Great Migration from Ulster to America took place in five
major waves between 1717 and 1775. A large proportion of these emigrants sold their services as indentured servants for a fixed period of a
few years, for much the same reasons (and perhaps better founded
ones) for which people in similar situations today join the army: to be
taken out of their situation, to be fed and housed, and to receive training, equipment, and their eventual freedom in a more hopeful situation than before. The earliest immigrants found English bigotry and
pro-Cromwellian sympathies too strong in New England; some went
north to what was to become Vermont, while most went to the more
tolerant province of Pennsylvania. Here their neighbors were Germans from the Rhineland whose recent experiences had been broadly
similar. Some of the latter were members of small sects who could find
no like-minded prince to shelter them during the Thirty Years' War
and the absolutist settlements of 1648; others were Lutherans who
preferred the risks of the American frontier to the risk of a revival of
deadly religious seesawing in Europe; many from both groups had
had their minds made up for them by the same climatic and economic
reverses of the 1710s which had triggered the first emigration from
Ulster. It was the Scotch-Irish, though, who settled closest to the frontier, and it was primarily the Scotch-Irish who moved in successive
waves down the Great Valley between the Blue Ridge and the Alle-
ghenies, spilling back eastward out of the gaps where the valley is

pinched behind Roanoke, and colonizing henceforward the Piedmont region of the Carolinas, so that their prolific increase and forward urge brought them to North Georgia at a time when there was still a sizable gap between them and the coastal settlers—whom, indeed, they considerably outnumbered.[1] And then, pressed once more by the coastal English, they started to move into the mountains.

This is the point at which to lay to rest the ghost of a suspicion that may have been nagging the reader's mind. Much ink has been spilled over whether the Appalachian people are predominantly "Scotch-Irish" or "Anglo-Saxon." But examination of the arguments on both sides shows clearly that the "Anglo-Saxon" theory, proposed by writers such as Harry Caudill[2] and the late Josiah Combs, rests on a false dichotomy, perceiving Scotland as a uniform nation of kilted Highlanders named Mac—the very people specifically excluded by law from the Ulster Plantation—and unaware of the tremendous amount of superficial anglicization in language and culture which the Scottish Lowlander had undergone even before the Plantation, a process which is of course one of the main points of this study. In particular, the argument from surnames is pointless, as Leyburn observes; for surnames were not widely adopted in Britain until the anglicization process was well under way, and this anglicizing of surnames was repeated both in Ireland and in the New World.[3] (A great deal of confusion has probably been generated simply by the awkward term "Scotch-Irish" itself, which seems to suggest "Scottish Gael" to those with some, but not a detailed, knowledge of the situation.) And insofar as English settlers participated in the emigration to the Appalachian Mountains (as to Ulster in the previous century), they seem largely to have been from those northern and western parts of England whose relevant history is broadly similar to that of lowland Scotland (and also from Wales, which is often obfuscatingly treated as part of England in studies of immigration, and whose experience is far more than broadly similar to lowland Scotland's for large stretches of its history).[4]

John C. Campbell held that the settlers of Appalachia were composed of Scotch-Irish, English, and Germans in approximately equal thirds; but his figures are based on surnames, and he states that "where an English name is common in both England and Ireland, it is assigned to England unless the family bearing it is definitely known to have come from Ireland."[5] We have just noted the flaw in this mode of argument; and recent research by Forrest McDonald and Ellen Shapiro McDonald implicitly overthrows Campbell's argument in the process of refuting the more elaborate form of it propounded by Howard F. Barker in 1931. The McDonalds conclude that Scotch-Irish and other "Celtic" settlers—including a hitherto underestimated number of Welsh settlers—were important in the colonies in general, in the southern colonies in particular, and on the western frontier in sizable preponderance.[6] Thus the colonial frontiersmen's difference from the coastal dwellers went a great deal deeper than the living circumstances of each on this continent; it went back to the Old World and, as we have seen, to great depths of both time and experience.

The land into which the Scotch-Irish pioneers were now pressing had also had a long human history, and one on which geography had already imposed patterns that were to be repeated later. A standard physical map of the United States, keyed to elevations, shows the range of the Appalachians and the smaller, lower one of the Ozarks on opposite sides of what seems to be a fairly even slope between the Gulf Coast and the Midwest. A map of surface irregularity, on the other hand—a map showing the proportion of land with a given slope, as distinct from height—reveals a quite different picture. A band of low but very roughly dissected country connects the two highland regions and divides the flat coastal and lower Mississippi plain from the nearly as flat Midwest, dipping and narrowing to a slender ridge (the so-called Illinois Ozarks) where the Ohio and Mississippi Rivers pierce it.[7] Thus Appalachia, which divides East from West, is only the most distinct part of a region which also divides North from South—and connects them—both geographically and culturally, and had done so for many centuries before European settlement.

(The name Appalachia dates from the first European exploration of the south under De Soto in 1539–43; but it originally referred to an area in northwest Florida, and it was the vague cartography of the sixteenth century which led to its drift northward into the mountains.[8] De Soto himself referred to these as the Mountains of Xuala, after a village in North Carolina where he first entered them. De Soto also entered the Ozarks and/or the Ouachitas, and for over one hundred years maps showed the "Xuala" or "Suala Mons" as a vague ridge enclosing the South and separating it from the then unknown lands to the north; in fact, in typical examples the name is applied to an area corresponding to the Ozarks.[9] If one were looking for a name for the geographical and cultural region comprising Southern Appalachia, the Ozarks, and the hilly country between—one less ambiguous than

"Upland South"—the name "Suala" might be thought both appropriate and authentic.)

As for the human history of Appalachia, we may start again with the supersession of hunter-gatherers by Neolithic peoples who left impressive monuments—in this case, the Adena culture of the middle Ohio Valley, the first of the so-called "Mound Builders." Arriving about 1000 B.C., they elaborated a culture featuring burial and effigy mounds, which was invaded from the north some five hundred years later by a nation or nations which blew up the mound idea into elaborate and spectacular forms. This culture, the Hopewell, covered the whole region enclosed by the Ohio, the Mississippi, and the Great Lakes, and possessed a trade network encompassing most of what was to be the United States. This was the classic "Mound Builder" culture. By the time of Christ, the Adena people had been conquered and scattered in refugee groups from Alabama to the St. Lawrence; by five hundred years later, the Hopewell culture too had collapsed for uncertain reasons. During all of this period and that which followed, parts of central Appalachia remained in the hands of simpler hunting-gathering cultures.[10] Parallels between American mound builders and European megalith builders have been drawn since the nineteenth century, and recent scholarship provides an odd such parallel. Until recently it was generally held that the Adena culture was derived from Mexico, as the megalith builders were thought to be from the Mediterranean; but in the past couple of decades, new dating has suggested that Adena and Hopewell developed locally, and that Mexican influence, probably indirect, occurred only in late stages.[11]

In the nineteenth century, when the mounds became well known, the idea became widespread that they were the work of some mysterious super-race, probably white, who must have had an advanced metal-using technology, and that the historic Indians were descended from their destroyers, members of a different and inferior race. Of course the mound builders were simply Indians themselves; this has been generally agreed on by scholarship since the 1880s.[12] But the old "Mound Builder" notion can still be found in popular journalistic accounts and even in some state history textbooks and other studies in Appalachia.[13] The appeal of this notion—in particular, its stubborn persistence in the popular mind after a hundred years of solid evidence to the contrary—is not hard to explain. It soothes the consciences of the race that exterminated the natives of America, by allowing it to imagine that those natives were themselves usurpers, who had wiped out a "civilized" nation with which white Americans

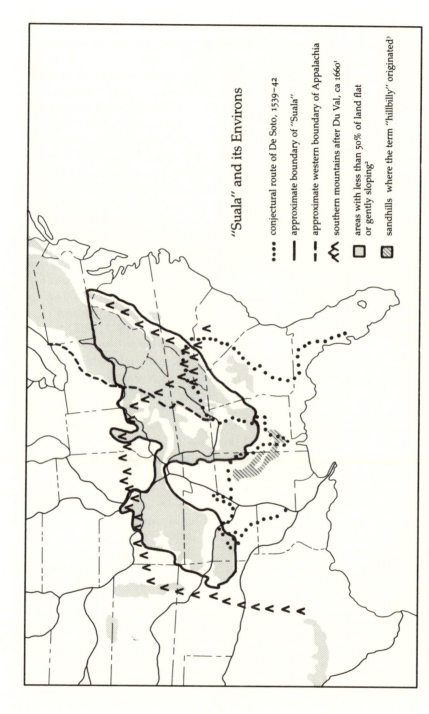

"Suala" and its Environs

- • • • • conjectural route of De Soto, 1539–42
- ⎮ approximate boundary of "Suala"
- ⎮ ⎮ approximate western boundary of Appalachia
- ⋀⋀ southern mountains after Du Val, ca 1660[1]
- ▨ areas with less than 50% of land flat or gently sloping[2]
- ▨ sandhills where the term "hillbilly" originated[3]

1. Johnson, *America Explored*, 174.   2. *National Atlas*, 63.   3. C. Williams, *Southern Mountaineer*, 3–4.

can identify. Thus the European conquest of America comes to seem like the restoration of an ancient, right scheme of things, a returning of the land to those who have a right to it. In this way the story parallels the mythos of the European settlers' own ancestors, which held that the pre-British inhabitants of Albion were African Hamites who had displaced a race descended, like the British themselves, from Japheth. Note, for example, the repeated pattern that exaggerates the achievements of the favored race (use of smelted metal)[14] while minimizing those of the unfavored one (ignoring their agriculture). As for more recent mystifications, let us note that Barry Fell's shifting speculations, to the effect that variously identified Celts colonized the East Coast,[15] are a wild mishmash of ignorance. Claims that one or another Old World nation "discovered" America before Columbus are, with the exception of the eleventh-century Norse coastings, almost totally unsupported. The constant stream of such claims represents, it would seem, a sort of collective American oedipal machismo, a need to jostle for prior possession of the motherland.

After the decline of Hopewell, other native cultures gradually took shape in eastern North America. By the time of first European contact, these were divided into two zones divided by the ridge country of "Suala." To the south, nations with a complex social and class structure built flat-topped temple mounds of distinctly Mexican inspiration. This culture penetrated Southern Appalachia in varying degrees, and a branch of it ascended the river valleys through the thin neck of "Suala" to produce great centers on the middle Mississippi and lower Ohio Rivers and fringe offshoots in Central Appalachia. By the eighteenth century, this Mississippian civilization was in an advanced state of decline on account of the ravages of De Soto and other Spanish gold-hunters, and more importantly due to the less violent but more profound stresses caused by the incorporation of the whole eastern U.S. into European-based trade networks long before most of the area was explored by Europeans. By the time of first European contact in the late seventeenth century, the Mississippian areas north of "Suala" had been abandoned to the simpler and less settled societies which prevailed in that area.[16]

And Appalachia, during this period, was already an area of transition, dispute and ambiguity between North and South. The main Indian nation of Southern Appalachia was the Cherokees, whose culture was that of the Southeast, but who had come from the north at a remote period, and whose language is related to Iroquois. Further north, in Central Appalachia, the first tribes to be contacted were members of the Siouan family. But very shortly thereafter the Iroquois, with European weapons and a sophisticated way of dealing with the balance of European powers, started building their empire down the Ohio and up the Great Lakes, and the Siouan tribes (with the Shawnees of the middle Ohio) were scattered or exterminated. By the beginning of European settlement, most of Central Appalachia was a hunting ground with no permanent villages, an area claimed by both the Iroquois from the north and the Cherokees from the south, and traversed by less settled Algonkian tribes moving in response to the dislocations of the times. This ambiguity between North and South was matched by an ambiguity between East and West, as evidenced by the early history of European exploration. The Ohio River, for example, was discovered twice in 1673, once by the French coming down from the Great Lakes, and again by the English coming over the mountains; these two nations disputed the area for another ninety years.

Such were the ambiguities of the land; and the Scotch-Irish pioneers who were starting to press into the area toward the end of that period of dispute shared in more than one way in the general ambiguity and disputedness. To begin with, although in Ireland they had been considered Scottish foreigners by both the native Irish and the English Ascendancy, Anglo-Americans now nearly always defined them as Irish. The term "Scotch-Irish" seems to have been originated or popularized by the immigrants themselves as a means of warding off confusion with the dispised "wild" Irish Catholics; it was widely current during the Great Migration of 1717–1775 and then fell out of use until massive Catholic Irish immigration in the 1840s and 1850s made the distinction useful again.[17] On the other hand, some Scotch-Irish, especially those who found themselves a minority in the English milieu of the coastal cities, also identified themselves with Ireland, joined in social events with their few Irish Catholic neighbors, and formed societies and lodges named after St. Patrick—a Northwest Briton, after all, who had done his main work in Ulster. And in the late eighteenth century, many Scotch-Irish American patriots joined the United Irishmen, a nationalist movement founded in Belfast by the Protestant Robert Emmet, designer of the present Irish flag.

Moreover, the frontiersmen, who were largely Scotch-Irish, were in an ambiguous position with regard to "civilization"—or more precisely, they were still, or once more, in such a position. Eighteenth-century observers frequently noted the roughness of the Scotch-Irish toward the native population;[18] they were not only prone to settle on

Indian lands illegally, but also apt to make overreactive or totally un-
provoked attacks on native villages. This was not simply "frontier behavior"; their aggressiveness conspicuously exceeded that of their
white neighbors, notably the Germans, many of whom accompanied
them southward along the Valley and Piedmont and, to a lesser extent
(because of this difference), into the mountains.

The basic reason for this aggressiveness is not far to seek, and
has been pointed out more than once: the Scotch-Irish were simply
transferring to the "wild" Indian the habits which they had formed in
a hundred or more years of combat with the "wild" Irishman, and in
centuries of combat with the "wild" Highlander before him. This
transference, however, was not simply a matter of distinctions being
"wilfully . . . ignored by the Scotch-Irish frontiersman in his Protestant fanaticism,"[19] in Toynbee's words. The analogy had been presented to them by the metropolitan authorities of England, and indeed by England's intellectual elite. We have already seen how these
men had compared the Irish with Indians and had advocated a policy
toward them based on Spanish policy in America, and how another
school of thought compared both Indians and Irish with pre-Roman
Britons. The two "savage" races were literally pictured the same; Piggott notes how "John White, who made brilliant drawings of Virginia
Indians while on Raleigh's 1585 expedition, used their distinctive
characteristics in portraying Britons and Picts, and through the engravings of these in de Bry's *America* of 1590 they found their way onto
the title page of John Speed's *Historie* of Britain in 1611."[20] Indeed,
long before the Scotch-Irish emigration to America, this analogy had
not only been formulated in thought and image but carried out in action: the Elizabethan campaign in Ireland was "a period of appren-
ticeship"[21] for many who later led colonizing ventures in Virginia,
such as Gilbert, Raleigh, and Frobisher.[22] Once colonization was actually under way in America, English attitudes toward and treatment of
the Indians followed in detail and in precise stages the corresponding
events in the Ireland of the previous century.[23] And James Logan, the
Scotch-Irish provincial secretary of Pennsylvania, proposed to his su-
periors that they encourage Scotch-Irish settlement on the frontier as
a conscious response to his cousins' behavior on the frontier of Britain
in Ireland.[24]

As for the psychodynamics of this process, Michael Rogin, in his
brilliant study *Fathers and Children*, has shown how the colonists projected onto native Americans the characteristics of children, thereby
investing them with the ambivalence and hostility the colonists felt to-

ward their own childhoods and their own unsublimated, rejected impulses, and making the native's replacement by the white man seem as
desirable and indeed as inevitable as individual growth from childhood to maturity—though of course such a projection process, with
such murderous results, was only a result, and a cause, of failure to
attain true maturity. Rogin, however, does not mention that this pathology had been rooted for hundreds or even thousands of years, as
an integral part of the dynamic not only of America, but of Western
civilization as a whole. Although he mentions that Andrew Jackson's
parents were such recent immigrants that his two slightly older brothers had been born in Ireland,[25] Rogin makes nothing of the Scotch-
Irish experience *in* Ireland, let alone Scotland, not even in his other
reference to the frontiersmen's background:

> Discussing his motives, Jackson accused the Indians of designs actually
> his own. . . . The expanding frontier invaded Indian boundaries, and
> whites wanted war as much as or more than Indians. Whites signed
> treaties only to move onto lands retained for Indians, and bought and
> sold land in Indian country. Was the "Savage Tribe that will neither ad-
> here to Treaties, nor the Law of Nations" the Cherokees or the Ameri-
> can Scotch-Irish? Jackson's language suggests a primitive identification
> with the Indians in which he ascribed to them characteristics of his own
> people. He was talking about himself.[26]

The point is well taken; but we can place this within the context
of the Scotch-Irish historical experience. We have seen how the larger
society had for centuries encouraged the forebears of the Scotch-Irish
to deal with their traumas by that false solution of projective identification which was always latent in the psyches of Europeans as a
whole: to become human, in Sartre's phrase, by making slaves and
monsters, golliwogs and Gogmagogs. Rogin points out how Southern
Indians were demoralized by the disruption of their native structures
of social control and were then stigmatized as "lawless" for behaving
in a demoralized manner.[27] But we have seen that the ancestors of the
Scotch-Irish had been through a similar process of invalidation some
seven hundred years earlier, when their traditional law was replaced
by feudal law. And we may surely suggest that the accommodations
which the western Lowlanders had been forced to make to this trauma
(and to repeated experiences of invalidation later in Scotland and
Ireland) might have affected their attitudes both toward the Indians'
law and toward that of the coastal authorities who made treaties.
Rogin quotes Jackson's mother: "Never tell a lie, nor take what is not
your own, nor sue anybody for slander or assault and battery. Always

settle them cases yourself!" [28] How easy it is to imagine an Appalachian parent saying this today. But Rogin comments on the passage with a purely psychological exposition which shows no awareness of the historical reasons for alienation from legal structures among Jackson's ancestors and neighbors—or among their descendants.

Rogin writes of the era of Indian removal: "White culture was deeply riven within. White men encountered not merely another culture in Indians but their own fantasies, longings, and fears. Self-proclaimed liberal values cracked under the pressure. . . . Whites experienced their own activities and desires as alien, external forces. Petrifaction of the self closed them to the Indians' fate." [29] As we have seen, we may expand this thesis from a two-layered scheme to a three-layered one, in which the pattern of attributions and injunctions imposed by the frontiersman on the Indian, by the coastal dweller on the Indian, and by the coastal dweller on the frontiersman all bear a close and interlocking relationship; and we may also extend this thesis in time both forward and backward over a span of centuries or more.

This peripheral and transitional status of the Scotch-Irish frontiersman as a figure between "civilization" and "barbarism" was noted at the time, unsympathetically, by outside observers. Francis Asbury, the energetic Methodist bishop who crossed the mountains twenty times, noted in 1790 of some mountaineers who were guarding him from Indian attack that the "poor creatures" were "but one remove from savages themselves," and that he felt more endangered by them than by the Indians. [30] A decade later, a traveler from England (one who got no closer to the frontier than New Jersey) wrote:

> None emigrate to the frontiers beyond the mountains, except culprits, or savage back-wood's men, chiefly of Irish descent. This line of frontier-men, a race possessing all the vices of civilized and savage life, without the virtues of either; affording the singular spectacle of a race, seeking, and voluntarily sinking into, barbarism, out of a state of civilized life; the outcasts of the world, and the disgrace of it; are to be met with, on the western frontiers, from Pennsylvania inclusive, to the farthest south. [31]

We note here how a group whose homeland had happened to become a periphery of another culture is described as an "outcast" of that culture (now identified with "the world")—as if the metropole had somehow created the periphery by expulsion of its own rejected contents ("Can ye nocht mak a Heilandman of this horss tord?"). The psychological truth of this is far greater than its historical truth; like all such projections, it tells much more about the speaker than about the subject. And the remark about "sinking into barbarism" anticipates a more famous later statement by Arnold Toynbee which we shall discuss in its turn. A few years after this, an American who at least had visited the frontier wrote that "the backwoodsmen . . . are very similar in their habits and manners to the aborigines, only perhaps more prodigal and more careless of life"[32]—a judgment against which even his anonymous editor protested.[33] In all this it must be acknowledged that life on the frontier was often violent and brutal; but the problem lies in the classification of this behavior within the framework "civilization/savagery." The distinction between the English coastal dweller and the Scotch-Irish frontiersman was noted even by the native Americans themselves; these "savages" were also appalled by their neighbors' "savagery," and the myth grew up that while the Tidewater people were simply human beings who had come from another land, the backwoodsmen "grew from the scum of the ocean while it was troubled with an evil spirit, and this scum was driven into the wilderness by a strong wind."[34] Scum of the earth as seen from one direction, scum of the sea from another: we run along like apples on the flood.

Thus the Scotch-Irish frontiersmen moved into the mountains. The Cherokees, and other people in the way, were not simply driven out of the settlers' vicinity as had so often been done before; they were herded west of the Mississippi by military force and with great loss of life. Nor were they simply driven due west from Southern Appalachia to what is now Oklahoma: their "Trail of Tears" ran in a great curve northward across the Ohio into southern Illinois, staying at all costs in the very roughest territory, the thin middle strip of the region I have called "Suala." A few Cherokees managed to stay behind in the fastnesses of the Smokies, and were granted a reservation there half a century later. Ironically, in 1750 the explorer Dr. Thomas Walker, perhaps aware of historical parallels, had named one of the mountains' main rivers after the Duke of Cumberland,[35] "the Butcher of Culloden," who had supervised the destruction of Scottish Highland culture after the Rebellion of 1745. *Ubi solitudinem faciunt, pacem appellant.*

But not only were the Scotch-Irish frontiersmen misunderstood, labeled, and depreciated: so was their new homeland, and so is it still. In his study of Jackson and the frontier experience, Rogin makes only five references to the Appalachian Mountains, all of them as to a "barrier" from which one is located either eastward or westward.[36] A similar mental picture can be discerned in Leyburn's writing and in that of almost all historians of the frontier, who follow in this respect nearly

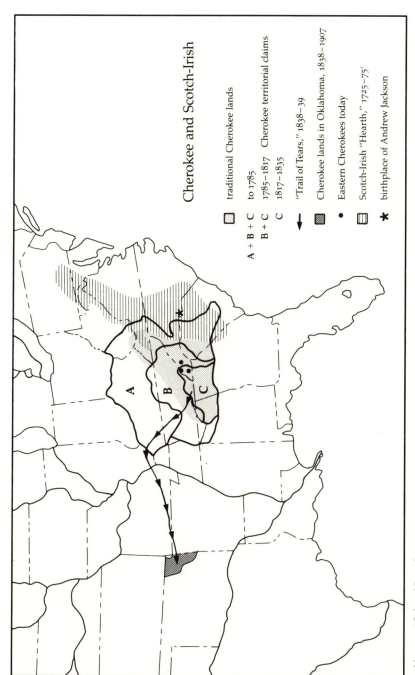

Cherokee and Scotch-Irish

☐	traditional Cherokee lands
A + B + C	to 1785
B + C	1785–1817 Cherokee territorial claims
C	1817–1835
↓	"Trail of Tears," 1838–39
▨	Cherokee lands in Oklahoma, 1838–1907
•	Eastern Cherokees today
▥	Scotch-Irish "Hearth," 1725–75'
✱	birthplace of Andrew Jackson

1. Newton, "Cultural Pre-adaptation," 149.

all thought and writing on westward expansion from the colonial period to the present. Leyburn, for example, writes as the last sentence
of his text: "If one wanted a representative American of the early nineteenth century, whether east of the mountains or in the great river valleys to the west, such a representative could be found very generally
among the descendants of the Scotch-Irish." [37] The mountains appear
here as a one-dimensional ridge where no one actually lives. And the
sentence also, not by chance, reflects a common attitude about the
Scotch-Irish relation to "general American" society. In an appendix,
Leyburn writes:

> In the history of immigration to this country, it is commonplace to ob-
> serve that each new group of arrivals, if in numbers great enough to be
> "visible," has had to endure a period of dislike from older Ameri-
> cans. . . . The advent of numerous "foreigners," with strange manners,
> ignorant of American ways and ideas, wearing curious clothes and
> speaking a gibberish, has repeatedly caused dislike, ridicule, and even
> hostility. . . . The Scotch-Irish also occasionally experienced this preju-
> dice, although, fortunately for themselves, they had to endure it for a
> very brief time. Upon their arrival in America they . . . went on imme-
> diately beyond the western fringe of settlement and took up frontier
> lands. By the time of the American Revolution, which they ardently
> supported, they had proved themselves good fighters against the In-
> dians and therefore good Americans. As they moved still farther west
> to the Ohio Valley frontier, they intermarried with pioneers of other
> stocks and so completely lost their identity as a separate people. [38]

What Leyburn says about the disappearance of a "Scotch-Irish"
ethnic group in America is in fact largely true of those Scotch-Irish
frontiersmen who joined the migration westward to the Ohio Valley
and beyond. It is less true of those of the Old Southwest, and much
less true of those east of the mountains, many of whose communities
retained their separate identification, along with characteristics distinctly visible to outside observers, into the late nineteenth century
and even later. The assertion that the Scotch-Irish lost their distinctive
identity as "they" moved west tends to confuse movement in space
with the passage of time in a distinctly American manner, as if the
eastern seaboard, let alone Europe, simply disappeared into the past
somehow. And once more, the mountains themselves are utterly
ignored.

The Scotch-Irish who remained in the mountains often tended
to stop thinking of themselves *as* Scotch-Irish, as they mingled with

the immigrants of German, Welsh, English, Highland Scottish, and other backgrounds (a minority in most mountain areas)[39] who settled the region with them. There are many exceptions; both my own parents remembered that they were mainly Scotch-Irish, and Robert Coles mentions distinct traditions of Scottish ancestry[40] and even, rather amazingly, Scotto-Norse.[41] But at any rate, "identification" is not the same as identity, as we have seen several times over; the very nature of the Scotch-Irish identity had been formed by repeated forced abandonments of identification. Now, however, within this "nonexistent" zone of the mountains, a new identity was being fostered as it had been in the "nonexistent" Atlantic Zone of Europe. Here, in this area ignored by the rhetoric and mentality of American expansion, having no "real" place in the American sense of identity, this new identity began to take shape. Though rooted largely in the collective experience of the Scotch-Irish, it was no more to remain confined to those of Scotch-Irish descent than the "general American" mentality has remained confined to Anglo-Americans.

People who prefer to live among mountains are distinctive to begin with, and for various reasons they were even more so at the time under discussion than they are now. In the first place, of course, communication through mountainous territory was much slower and more hazardous than it is today; settlers in mountains had to make a special effort to get into them, and once there they had to put up with difficulties in farming conditions and in other regards. But the physical barriers to mountain settlement were less important than (though largely a basis for) profound conceptual and symbolic barriers. Let us examine these barriers, and how mountaineers overcame them before—or rather instead of—"overcoming" the mountains themselves.

There was serious controversy in Judaeo-Christian thought as to whether the very existence of mountains was part of God's original plan for the world. According to some, mountains were like tumors and wens, and had come unto being at the Fall, when God had said, "Cursed be the ground for thy sake," or at the Flood, when the fountains of the great deep were opened and the earth's surface collapsed into ruins. Since Man (the restriction in gender is intended) was the lord and microcosm of the world, "Man's" sin had extended to the world, cutting it off from God's grace; the chief outward and visible sign of this fall of the macrocosm was the existence of mountains. Thus these rough, uncultivable areas, which were themselves "useless" and made communication difficult and dangerous, became external symbols of the subject's consciousness of his own divided selfhood and tumored soul.[42] The sixteenth-century Lowland Scottish poet Sir David Lyndsay wrote regarding the effects of the Deluge:

> The Erth, quhilk first wes so fair formit,
> Wes, be that furious Flude, deformit;
> Quhare umquhyle wer the plesand planis,
> Wer holkit glennis, and hie montanis;
> From clattryng cragis, gret and gray,
> The erth was weschin quyte away.[43]

(Here Lyndsay uses two Celtic words, *glen* and *crag*, in describing the "deformit" landscape of our world. Of course this was not a deliberate jab at "Celtic" culture; the words simply existed conveniently in the Scots vocabulary—and were later borrowed into standard English—having survived from pre-anglicization days to describe landforms unfamiliar to the colonizers. Nevertheless, this word usage reflects *structurally* the denigration of things "Celtic" which characterizes the period.)

Others, however, took a different view, saying that the external world was good and that only man was vile. One of this view's chief supporters was Calvin, who held staunchly that God's glory was manifest in the beauty of creation, and that the fault was not in any deterioration of the world itself, but in humanity's impaired capacity to relate to it properly.[44] The controversy of the "defense of mountains" was still going on at the time of the great Scotch-Irish migrations; and on the popular level in a fringe area, no doubt earlier and medieval attitudes were still strong. But the migration *into* the mountains, as opposed to passage through them, would have filtered out those with anti-mountain attitudes, and would have selected for those actively drawn to mountains: those, perhaps, who saw them not as inconveniences, much less as a jumbled pile of ruins which externalized humanity's own "deformit" condition—nor yet, by reaction, as a romantic Sublime, a different type of projection—but as a part of Creation to be enjoyed and dealt with like any other. And indeed, after a century of familiar but obfuscating missionary stereotypes about "unworldly fundamentalism," this positive attitude to Creation is being recognized as a prominent feature of the most traditional Appalachian spiritual current, the "Religion of Zion."[45]

The existence of such positive attitudes—not only toward mountains as such, but toward the whole social and cultural constellation which the Southern mountain situation fostered—is also shown by the fact that many who left the mountains have returned to them from pre-industrial times to the present, and that some of the most important strands of emigration from Appalachia traced the ridges of "Suala" westward to populate the Ozarks.[46] This latter fact in itself shows only that mountain-dwellers are like others in preferring familiar topography. But, as we have seen, the traditional Western attitude toward mountains makes this fact remarkable enough for Western Christians, and indeed for Western Christians from lowland areas— makes their very conformity to the pattern an exceptional fact, whether their attitudes emerged in direct engagement with the "controversy of mountains," or whether those attitudes simply arose from the same milieu as that controversy.

Leaving aside all definitional questions regarding an "Appalachian ethnic group," it thus seems defensible to say three things: that frontier mountain dwellers from the beginning had different tendencies from lowland dwellers in some fundamental attitudes; that this difference predated and underlay, though it was accentuated by, the differential effects of nineteenth-century "progress"; and that the post-Civil-War "discovery" of the mountains was therefore far from a sheer invention, as some seem to have claimed. To be sure, in Henry Shapiro's phrase, we must avoid replacing racism with "place-ism."[47] Traditional Appalachian culture(s) showed a spectrum of attitudes toward land and environment, attitudes which were and are affected by class and urbanity. Such differences are, for example, reflected spatially in the contrast between the hollows with their dendritic settlement structure of Atlantic-style dispersed farms, netted closely into the landscape, and the county towns centered on their town squares and plotted around them like *Roma quadrata* in a pattern with antecedents in Ulster and analogues in Spanish America.[48] It is important not only to avoid blanket generalizations on this score but also to recognize the importance of factors such as social class, the distinction between rural and urban, and in modern times the necessity of defense against forces which, in addition to being socially and culturally destructive, are physically destructive to the land itself. I have no intention of obfuscating or distracting from these considerations, though I think it would also be obfuscating and distracting to assume that their relation to forms of consciousness is all in one direction. My suggestions here, however, draw on materials and on modes of analysis which have not been commonly used in Appalachian studies, and I offer them for their relevance to the question of whether Appalachian culture(s) *simply* reflect rural cultural forms in general, especially regarding attitudes toward land and environment. I strongly suspect, however, that the idea of Appalachian "distinctiveness," hitherto controversial, is on the verge of being put on a sounder basis as sociologists and anthropologists move away from the concept of culture as a bagful of "traits" held together by an arbitrary "boundary" and toward the view of culture as a systematic structure of meanings, a framework of "common understandings concerning the meaning of a set of symbols." [49]

And as for the symbolic place of land in the Appalachian structure of meanings, we may turn (not for the last time) to Robert Coles, one of the few outside observers who has made a largely successful effort to observe mountain people with genuine imaginative sympathy. Coles notes:

> Indeed, from the first day of life many of the Appalachian children I have observed are almost [?] symbolically or ritualistically given over to the land. One morning I watched Mrs. Allen come out from the cabin in order, presumably, to enjoy the sun and the warm, clear air of a May day. Her boy had just been breast-fed and was in her arms. Suddenly the mother put the child down on the ground, and gently fondled him and moved him a bit with her feet, which are not usually covered with shoes or socks. The child did not cry. The mother seemed to have exquisite control over her toes. It all seemed very nice, but I had no idea what Mrs. Allen really had in mind until she leaned over and spoke very gravely to her child: "This is your land, and it's about time you started getting to know it." [50]

In this remarkable ritual, the child's most basic feelings of motherly support, of Eriksonian "basic trust," are deliberately and in the most literal way transferred to, or extended into, the land. "What she did and said one time she has done and said again and again in that way and in other ways. All of her children, as one might expect, come to regard the land near their cabin as something theirs, something also kind and generous and important." [51]

Cratis Williams reported that when he asked his fellow mountaineers about their ancestry, he was often told some version of a story to the effect that three brothers had come over "from the old countries before the old Revolutionary War." [52] One had settled in the mountains, one had gone west, "and we never knew what became of the other." [53] This story is so widespread that, as Williams said, it can hardly be historic; but its widespread occurrence itself bespeaks an appeal which demands an archetypal explanation. In part of himself, the mountaineer feels himself to be located where he is, in the center. In part, he feels himself to be located in the West, to be a member of a community at the world's edge. And this Westerner, in turn, feels with part of his being that he does not know what has become of himself—that he has passed the edge of the world and lost himself among the ghosts and demons outside the city wall. But the brother who stayed here is the one whom the mountaineer claims as his forebear; and it is in the center of his own world that he primarily feels himself to have his being.

This mountain experience is, I think, important to an understanding of some significant differences between Appalachian consciousness and that normally associated with "Americans." The critic Robert Scholes attributes traditional "American" expansiveness to a "prairie consciousness," a mentality conditioned by the absence of limits on the liberal horizon; while side by side with this exists a mountain consciousness, more aware of limitations.[54] This is, however, a negative (though not derogatory) way of putting it. A still more negative approach, and this time one plainly disapproving behind its mask of "objectivity," is the sociological commonplace that mainstream "Americans" perceive themselves in a dominant position vis-à-vis "nature," while mountain people feel themselves to be "subjected" or "submissive" to "nature." One sociologist half a century ago made this point in remarkably archetypal terms by saying that mountaineers' ancestors "represented genetic and cultural extraction from . . . a Celtic world which had not yet defined itself from its elemental womb of Nature."[55] The analysis of these contentions exposes fundamental flaws running through the whole body of the conventional wisdom they reflect, and reveals much about the mentality of domination in Appalachia, in America, and in the modern world. Let us explore, then, the meaning of "nature"—and the nature of meaning.

INCURSUS: *Children of Nature*

In discussing the mountaineer's relation to the environment, I have deliberately avoided using the word "nature" because our present common-sense idea of "nature" is a vacuous concept, or at least a highly changeable one, the result of a long historical process intimately connected with the themes of exploitation and dominance that run through our civilization. Like, indeed, the concept of "civilization," the concept of "nature" is not something given in the "objective" world but a cultural construct. And though the word "nature" is older than the word "civilization," the meaning we usually give it is even more recent.

The Latin *natura*, from *nasci* "to be born," is a translation of the Greek *physis*, from *phyein* "to grow, become," originally the same word as English *be*. It was Aristotle, the originator of our "commonsense" notion of "objectivity," who invented "physics" as a study of how things "were" in the "external world"; and Lucretius' *De Rerum Natura*, usually translated as "On the Nature of Things," is better rendered (as by Rolfe Humphries) "The Way Things Are."[56] This "way things are" was almost never personified; the invocation of Lucretius' poem is not to Mother Nature but to Mother Venus. It was in the Middle Ages that *natura* came to mean what we call the "natural" world, as distinct from the human soul, which belonged to the "supernatural" world. It is at this stage that Nature comes to be personified as a female allegorical figure, a mother who can have children; it, or she, is being seen for nearly the first time as a definable entity in contrast with something else.[57] But "nature" also included the observable regularities of "human nature," and even in the eighteenth century this is what was usually meant by the word in the writings of Neoclassicists who praised "fidelity to Nature." It was not until the Pre-Romantic period that the word came to be firmly fixed to the nonhuman environment, though older senses remained active behind this one, and particularly the identification of external "nature" with those aspects of the human organism that were seen as "physical," external to the self, and in need of subduing and domination. (From the Renaissance to the eighteenth century, one common use of the word "nature" was as a synonym for "genitals," especially female.[58])

Thus the common idea that mountain people are "submissive" or "subjected" to "nature"[59]—a concept often condensed into the single word "fatalism"—is, first of all, based on a false dichotomy; it is assumed that any attitude not "dominating" must be "submissive." At least, as the statement is generally presented, it does not suggest that any other possibility was taken into account in interpreting the data. (The same formula of "submissive" versus "dominant" is often used by historians of science to describe Western attitudes toward "nature" before and after the twelfth-century revival of Aristotle.) The better-phrased formula "fitting into" nature is sometimes used, but even so it tends to be interpreted in a covertly disapproving way. Regardless of what vocabulary is used, however, this value-judgment tends to creep in, since the modern concept of "nature" is conditioned from the out-set by the dialectic of dominance and submission. Nature is, by im-plicit definition, that which is or should be subject to Man (*sic*), who stands outside its mother-world and must not "regress" to "fit into" its "elemental womb." Hence environmentalists are abandoning the word "nature." And, significantly, the word in this sense is not found at all in traditional mountain speech, which tends to use "nature" in reference only to human beings or other living things and in senses derived from classical Protestant theological discourse. What "main-stream" Americans call "nature" is, to mountaineers, "the Creation."

Robert Coles notes repeatedly that Appalachian children's draw-ings of "their homes" differ sharply both from those of middle-class "American" children and from those of other low-income children. They are full of the hills, of water, of the sun, but people and their works are inconspicuous or absent.[60] From the examples Coles re-produces, it is apparent that the "natural" features "dominate" the composition, but not in an overbearing way. They are simiply there, their quiddity noted and enjoyed. Coles compares the approach to that of Chinese and Japanese painting;[61] we may also compare it to the poetry of the T'ang Dynasty, and to the poetry, similar in many ways, which was being written contemporaneously at the opposite end of the Old World in Irish and Welsh—poetry which contrasts sharply with other Western literature of the so-called "Dark Ages."[62]

Furthermore, in one case (evidently meant as exemplary), Coles connects this feature with a child's inability to draw a picture of himself as an adult. Children from other backgrounds—again, both middle-class and poor—"can be this or that, live here or there, realize one or another dream or fantasy. But Billy knows exactly where he is and where he will most likely be (if *he* has anything to say about it) and he also knows why his future seems so assured, so concretely before him, so definite."[63] That is, his sense of identity *is not located inside his skin;* in many ways, and especially in the time dimension, *it is located in the world with which he shares his being.* It is "part of something well nigh everlasting, something that continues, goes on, stays, *is there,* however hard and difficult and miserably unfair 'life' can get to be."[64] None of this is surprising if his mother is like Mrs. Allen above; she will have assured that his primal bond with his mother—the founda-tion of his identity—is not simply located inside his skin (or hers) either.

It is instructive to reflect that an observer less sympathetic and imaginative than Coles would probably interpret this boy's picture-drawing "deficiency" as a defect in "self-image," a "poverty trait" to be "cured." Such an observer would want to remove the boy from a "neurotic dependency relationship" which does not exist, as he would want to remove the boy's culture from the "elemental womb" of a "Nature" which exists only in the observer's mind. For the mountaineer, however, it is not a matter of deficiency but of fullness; it is not a question of depending submissively on "Nature" but of participating solemnly and joyfully in Creation.

Such is the mountaineer's relation to "nature," or rather to land, environment, and Creation. And thus we see that the other sociological cliché, that Appalachia represents a "retarded frontier,"[65] is virtually the opposite of the truth. In fact mountaineers, whether consciously or not, opted out of the true frontier mentality of domination and submission when they chose to stay in the mountains, an area literally damned by much established theology and ignored by the rhetoric of American expansionism from that day to this, and when they chose to participate only selectively in the broader economic system of America that included the metropole and the frontier as symbionts,[66] and to ignore the sign-system which opposed "civilization" and "nature" as contraries. After all, as we have seen, the fundamental characteristic of the frontier—one which Turner downplayed almost to the vanishing point—was the presence of the native American as a creature to be projected upon, demonized, subjugated, and driven out. And it was precisely with the final effective removal of that presence (though this was heartily collaborated in by the mountaineers themselves) that Appalachian identity as such began to take shape.

For the first time in thirteen hundred years, the bulk of these people were not located between Anglo-Saxon culture to the east and another culture to the west. For the first time in seven hundred, they were not subsidiaries within the Anglo-Saxon and "Western" orbit, despised advance men in the battle against those whom the "West" chose to call barbarians. No longer sandwiched between "civilization" and "barbarism," and to a large extent removed from the larger economic and social network of the country, they could begin to free themselves from these dichotomies, and their collective selfhood could begin to heal itself. The filter of "mountain consciousness" aided the revival or reassertion of a sense of connectedness with the land, while the terrain encouraged the retention and reinforcement of Atlantic land-use patterns,[67] in contrast with the continental and English patterns of many other areas. The destinies of the Scotch-Irish had in fact once more forked into two paths: one to follow the frontier westward, to become not only "Americans" but Americans with a vengeance, and the other to build a valid identity of its own. To be sure, at this period, the people of the Appalachian region had no need to articulate a self-definition as "Appalachians" or even "mountaineers," since their mutual self-identification as individuals in their own communities had no need of a generalized articulation. Their way of life needed no such relation to consciousness while "outside contacts . . . occurred *on the highlander's own terms* and had only marginal influence on the quality and direction of mountain life."[68] "Appalachia" was a definition imposed from outside; but it is important to realize that it was imposed (in whatever distorting and damaging terms) on a pre-existing reality.

But, as hardly need be pointed out, the newly forming mountain culture was not through with difficulties. One serious blow occurred only a generation or two after its formation. Although no longer sandwiched between the "civilization" of the East and the "barbarism" of the West, it now found itself between the twin lowland "civilizations" of North and South. And twins they were in the reduction of human beings to commodities, whether as slaves or as factory workers; on that score, as Joel Kovel points out, Southerners simply "attacked the North for pushing wider what [Southerners themselves] had already pushed deeper."[69] Although the Appalachians were politically part of Southern states, their population had come mainly from the middle colonies, spoke a dialect with both Midland and Southern features, and essentially lacked the slave system and, for the most part, the virulent racial mythology which went along with it. (As the formidable Don West has pointed out, the first abolitionist periodical in the United States was not William Lloyd Garrison's *Liberator* but Elihu Embree's *Emancipator*, published in East Tennessee.[70] Of course the mountains were largely free of slavery "only" because their climate, terrain, and soil were mostly unsuited to crops and plantation sizes for which slave labor was profitable. But this was also the reason the North had no slaves, and when the Industrial Revolution occurred, the North did its best to remedy the defect with what it had available.) In addition to these differences between highland and lowland South, the lowland majorities in the mountaineers' state legislatures tended to treat the latter's land as a row of insignificant hinterlands, as that dimensionless and inconvenient ridge which they have always been in the American imagination.

Thus it was not surprising that, when the Civil War came, most mountaineers sided with the Union. The Union loyalty of the region was in fact decisive in the war's outcome, and Lincoln (who recognized the new state of West Virginia over serious constitutional objections) was inclined toward a generous program of postwar help toward the mountains. But the Radical Republicans scrapped this plan and basically ignored any program of rewards for loyalty in favor of punitive measures aimed at the entire South. The South responded, as soon as Reconstruction was over, with retaliation toward those representatives of Republicanism and loyalism who lay within its grasp—blacks and mountaineers. In the mountain sections of all states, roads deteriorated and literacy rates plummeted. The mountains had not been conspicuously poorer than the rest of the South—indeed, Frederick Law Olmsted in 1853 had found them noticeably less so[71]—but now they fell rapidly behind both relatively and absolutely. It was at this time that most of the region fell into that state of wholesale, involuntary isolation which outsiders later mistakenly presumed to have been inherent in the mountains from the beginning.[72] Deteriorating conditions and the social fractures caused by the war set the stage for the infamous feuds which raged for the rest of the century and beyond. Under these pressures and those which followed, the Creation-affirming Calvinism of the "Religion of Zion" was largely superseded by the "Evangelical" Christianity more familiar today.[73] The latter is a religion which tends to accept the modern meaning of the word "nature" and project it upon Scripture and theology in a Creation-denying, life-denying way.[74] The results for the human psyche can be seen in the hysteroid "revivalism" that returned in this period to the prominence it had enjoyed in socially and culturally shattered Scotland and Ulster two centuries earlier. Thus, punished by the South as "traitors" and with their loyalty forgotten by the North, mountaineers were once more like apples on the flood.

Nevertheless mountain culture and society not only survived but became more deeply rooted. Indeed, the two generations after the Civil War are often designated Appalachia's "classic" period. The region's isolation, originally imposed from without, became to some degree self-chosen as a survival tactic—a choice which brought both gains and losses, as we shall see. It was in this period that outside literary and sub-literary observers began to be aware of mountain people as such, though their primitivism both hard and soft was essentially stereotypical and external.[75] But in the last decade of the nineteenth century, several linked events in the world outside the mountains converged to affect the region deeply. The western frontier of settlement closed in upon itself and disappeared; metropolitan industrial interests began to seek out the mountains' resources; and there emerged a growing awareness of mountain people as a distinct group. As need hardly be pointed out, that awareness was not to bring unmixed benefits. Such a mixed result was inherent in the nature of that awareness—an awareness conditioned by the same patterns of misperception which we have traced back to the Roman Empire, and which we shall now trace forward into the present.

5 *Writing and Difference, or, Some Versions of Pastoral*

I wonder how much more they can get out of Appalachia.
—Store clerk in California,
to the author buying *Foxfire 7*

It would be pointless to recount once more the history of industrialization and its effects in the mountains, especially when the task has recently been done magistrally and definitively by Ronald Eller in *Miners, Millhands, and Mountaineers.* Eller has concentrated on the economic and political effects of industrialization in such a way as to demonstrate irrefutably that Appalachia has been "modernized" as thoroughly as any other part of the country, but "modernized" in a way which embodies the inseparable (if still widely unacknowledged) underside of the modernization process. Here I wish to explore other aspects of Appalachian modernity, and especially to examine other aspects of its negative manifestations as they victimize mountain people.

The pivotal years in the beginning of this process are the 1890s. The 1890 census was the first to show the disappearance of the western "frontier of settlement" as a distinct entity. And it was precisely after that year, as Henry Shapiro points out, that the missionaries "became the experts on mountain life which the local colorists had been in earlier decades,"[1] and inaugurated the distinct shift toward the perception of mountain life as "squalid and degenerate,"[2] and of "the existence of Appalachia itself . . . as a problem to be solved."[3] What is the connection between these two facts? The key lies in the phrases with which in 1895 W. G. Frost, the new president of Berea College, announced his "discovery" of Appalachia—"a new world," "a new pioneer region."[4] Appalachia has often since then been described in terms of "pioneer" or "frontier" life, and quite inaccurately. The mountaineers of Frost's time were hardly "pioneers" on the land they had farmed for three or four generations, and their society, whatever its human defects, was as mature as any other regional society of comparable age. But here, at the image's point of origin, we see its fundamental purport: Frost's phrase "a new pioneer region" refers explicitly to his *own* urge to "pioneer" missionary activity in the area. Indeed, he rejoices that the region had been "discovered . . . just as our western frontier has been lost in the Pacific ocean."[5] In the secular sphere, too, we see the same imagery; thus in John Fox, Jr.'s *The Trail of the Lonesome Pine*, it is the Lowland geologist Jack Hale, scouting for coal seams in Eastern Kentucky, who is proclaimed as "by instinct, inheritance, blood and tradition—pioneer."[6]

What had happened was this. The western frontier having closed, the dynamic of the "American" character demanded that another frontier be found, another pioneering wave be launched, another "nature" be subdued. And why was that wave launched against Appalachia? The strictly economic reasons are plain enough. Appalachia was a land rich in timber and mineral wealth, lying amidst the economic centers of the East. But this economic process coexisted with a process involving projective identification with mountain life on the part of the "wider" culture. Shapiro and the late Cratis Williams have shown that as the closing of the frontier coincided with the inauguration of the Appalachian missionary period, so the preceding period of the Western Indian wars had coincided with the Appalachian tourist period, in which the local-color writers had described Appalachia in terms emphasizing "natural" features and describing human relations basically as romantic outgrowths of that "nature."[7] The attitudes toward the region which were being prepared in the "American" mind had their parallels in the history of those "Americans'" ancestors. Writing of the early Virginia settlers, Bernard Sheehan notes:

> In one mood Europeans sought a return to original innocence. In another they were convinced that they had once been mired in savagism and had managed by dint of hard work and the blessings of Providence to reach the civil stage of life. Ignoble savagism conveyed the impression of childishness and immaturity, of stunted growth; civility assured European society that it had achieved adulthood. This assurance, however, did not obviate the possibility of a slide back into the savage state. The ignoble savage always loomed as an external threat to Europeans and as an internal danger because he represented primal urges that, although subdued, remained part of the human condition.[8]

The earliest impressions transmitted from America were paradisaic. The new continent stimulated prelapsarian yearnings for a haven from the insecurities and distractions of European life. . . . Treatment of the Indians through the paradisaic formula turned them into an ideal to which Europeans appealed in their chagrin at the shortcomings of their own way of life. The paradisaic formula left the Indians in a curiously insubstantial state. Not only was their way of life seen from the perspective of the white man's world, but it lacked the particularities of a real social order. And yet native Americans were real enough to make a distinctive mark on the history of English colonization in the New World. When they resisted the invasion of their territory or asserted the strength and integrity of their society, Englishmen tended to stress the ignoble side of the doctrine of savagism.[9]

Indians, that is, were assumed, for good or ill, to be children; and when they nevertheless persisted in acting like the adults they were, they were seen not as adults but, for ill, as bad children. Their real adulthood was then ignored and undermined in the attempt to "raise" them to a different concept of adulthood, perceived as the only real one. The result, even when the Indians survived physical assault, was deadly: "Needless to say, no Indians gained admission to colonial society. They tended to become disintegrated Indians rather than Englishmen."[10]

Much the same process which Sheehan documents for the Virginia Indians of the seventeenth and eighteenth centuries had happened to the Irish in the sixteenth and seventeenth, to the Lowland Scots in the twelfth through fifteenth, and to the continental Celts at the hands of the Romans. The metropolitan's conception of the "barbarian" was split into the two images of soft and hard primitivism, noble and ignoble savagism; and the shift from one to the other occurred *within* the paradigm of primitivist assumptions as the result of failure or refusal to *abandon* it altogether. The Lowland Scots had survived physically, though at great psychological and cultural cost, by acquiescing in those assumptions and allowing themselves to be "raised" to European "adulthood"; as a result, their forced internalization of that paradigm, an internalization peculiarly fierce as it rested on continual repressive denial of the truth of the matter, had made them the fanatical but despised advance-men of "civilization" in Scotland, Ireland, and America. Now, though, as the people of Appalachia began to extricate themselves from that paradigm, its bearers confronted them once again, reminding them (if they had ever forgotten) that they had never been fully accepted into "civilization," and that the conditional acceptance which "civilization" had extended—on the condition that they continue their despised but necessary function—could be withdrawn at any sign that they were prepared to reappropriate their own identity on the basis of their sense of their own selfhood.

Furthermore, the very meaning of the word "civilization" was changing to mountaineers' great disadvantage. Indeed, an important factor in the denigration of mountain culture after the Civil War was supplied by the invention, in 1866, of the Gatling gun. It was not that automatic weapons were then used against mountaineers—though eventually, indeed inevitably, they were. Rather, this development and others like it fueled a shift in attitudes. In the early modern period, when Westerners had imposed their rule over most of the nonliterate world, "civilization" had been defined to include the remaining elaborate cultures which could adopt key innovations such as gunsmithing, and do so rapidly and thoroughly enough to retain their independence. Under industrial capitalism, by contrast, mass production and automatic weaponry (the first mass-produced items had been rifles) allowed the Western takeover of the great Asian "civilizations." So, given that "civilization," as we saw in Chapter 3, essentially means "ability to fend off Western assault," *the word "civilized" now came for many to mean "industrialized."* Thus the mountaineer was no longer on the edge of "civilization," no longer "something close to barbarism"; by the new definition, mountain society was unmistakably beyond the pale.

The mountaineer's new "savage" status quickly found widespread expression in print—an expression that has continued to this day. In 1899 appeared W. G. Frost's well-known article, "Our Contemporary Ancestors in the Southern Mountains." (How ironic that it appeared in the *Atlantic* two years after W. E. B. DuBois' seminal essay on Black consciousness.) Frost's successors have approached the mountains with varying degrees and mixtures of contempt and patronizing "sympathy," but they all exhibit a blindness to the essential integrity of Appalachian selfhood. And the key to this blindness lies in Frost's seemingly innocuous catchphrase, "our contemporary ancestors." The phrase indicates that, no matter how "sympathetically" mountain people are to be perceived, they are to be seen as a version of the observer, as a projection of parts of the latter's own self-image, and as implicitly deprived of an inner selfhood independent of the observer. Further, the phrase implies that the mountaineer is somehow arrested in time, deprived of some essential maturing process or rite of passage—is, in Shapiro's words, "an incomplete version"[11] of his or her own self; and, finally, that mountaineers can fulfill their destiny only by becoming essentially like the observer. The latter may sentimentally acknowledge the mountaineer's superiority in many ways, just as one may sentimentalize the analogous qualities of children—indeed, the particular qualities attributed to each show a striking resemblance. But this is the sort of sentimentalism which exists only to reinforce a sense of resignation, to anesthetize the pain of seeing the admired thing disappear.[12]

This process of projective identification is clearly reflected in the repeated use of the words "pioneer" and "frontier" to describe mountain life. We have seen above that at the inception of this image, it was the outsider who designated himself the "pioneer" in this "frontier" region—leaving the mountaineer as the "savage." But if, to some, white "Anglo-Saxons" could not be "savages," nevertheless their land was still seen as a "frontier," and so they must be "pioneers." The mountaineers of Frost's day were of course neither pioneers nor savages. But the general American could see mountain culture only as some version of that "American's" own. If mountaineers looked like America's idea of its frontiersmen, then Appalachia must be some kind of frontier—even if an arrested or retarded one, a phrase implying fixation and failure to develop, and precluding the imagination of alternatives to "development" in one particular direction. And if mountaineers resisted being seen as "pioneers," then once more, the only alternative was to see them as "savages."

Thus, as "the West" literally closed in on them, Appalachians began falling prey to the fate they had helped impose on their Indian predecessors. Like the latter, they became stigmatized or sentimentalized as "children of Nature."[13] The word "children" is of course significant, but so, as we have seen, is the word "Nature." This slippery word acquired meaning primarily in opposition to others: as, Nature versus Man, or Nature versus Civilization. In the first opposition, Appalachians have been dehumanized, looked on as a part of the environment on much the same level as the snail darter, to be "preserved" for much the same reasons, or else shoved aside in much the same way. As for the opposition Nature/Civilization, it is a dialectic of two equally slippery constructs, each of which indeed has meaning only in terms of the other. And note, in view of what we have said above, that in Appalachia the phrase "the coming of Civilization" has often been used to mean, not the arrival of white settlers in the mountains, but those mountains' belated penetration by the Industrial Revolution at the turn of this century. The Indian "threat," physical and psychological, to "America" having finally been neutralized at Wounded Knee in the final days of 1890, "America" was on the lookout for another barbarism to subdue.

Thus it was precisely when Appalachians achieved an identity *as* "Mountain People" that they became stigmatized (or sentimentalized) as "barbarians." It was precisely when they acquired the basis for an autonomous collective identity of their own, that they were attacked in terms applicable to upstart children by a culture incapable of achieving a settled maturity of its own, and therefore in constant need of imposing such projections on others in order to bolster its own hollow identity. Imposing inappropriate concepts of "frontier" onto mountain people had the ultimate effect, in the American consciousness, of assimilating them not to the frontiersman but to his dark twin the Indian—of equating them with that person from whom "civilization" had provoked violence, and against whom "civilization" had then set up the frontiersman's violence as a mirror, but a mirror in which each society—"civilized" and "savage"—saw the other. Now, with the Indian "vanishing" or invisible, the opposition Indian/frontiersman broke down, and industrial America "discovered" in its own "contemporary ancestors" a new race of "children of nature" to practice its civilizing mission upon. *Ubi solitudinem faciunt, progressum appellant.*

Thus one thinks, of course, of world-class scholarship's most famous acknowledgment of the existence of Appalachian mountain people: that by the late Arnold Toynbee in his *Study of History*. Toynbee attempts to show how a moderate challenge to a group may provoke a highly creative response, but that the challenge must not prove too great or it will be counterproductive. One of his examples is that of the movement of people from Scotland to Ulster and thence to Appalachia. His remarks, often quoted in fragments, deserve to be cited at length and subjected to a close reading.

The Lowland Scots, living (Toynbee asserts) under no particular stimulus, are in "relatively modest circumstances";[14] the Ulsterman, faced with the challenge of crossing the sea and battling the native Irishman, has made his province "one of the busiest work-shops in the modern Western World,"[15] apparently for reasons having nothing to do with geography, politics, or economics; while in Appalachia:

> In the human sphere, the "Red Indian" heathen was . . . a more savage adversary than the "Wild Irish" Catholic (however wilfully the difference might have been ignored by the Scotch-Irish frontiersman in his

Protestant fanaticism). In the physical sphere, . . . the Scotch-Irish immigrants who have forced their way into these natural fastnesses have
come to be isolated . . . from the rest of the World. . . .

[T]he Appalachian "Mountain People" at this day are no better than
barbarians. They are the American counterparts of the latter-day White
barbarians of the Old World: . . . the Kurds and the Pathans and the
Hairy Ainu. . . . [But t]hrough one of several alternative processes—
extermination or subjection or assimilation—these last lingering survivals will assuredly disappear within the next few generations. . . . It
is possible . . . that barbarism will disappear in Appalachia likewise. Indeed, the process of assimilation is already at work among a considerable number of Appalachians who have descended from their mountains and changed their way of life in order to earn wages in the North
Carolinian cotton mills. In this case, however, there is no corresponding
assurance: for the White barbarism of the New World differs from that
of the Old World in being not a survival but a reversion.

. . . [These] heirs of the Western Civilization . . . have relapsed into
barbarism under the depressing effect of a challenge which has been
inordinately severe. . . . In part, they have taken the impress of the
local Red Indians whom they have exterminated. Indeed, this impress
of Red Indian savagery . . . is the only social trace that has been left
behind by these vanquished and vanished Redskins. For the rest, the
neo-barbarism of Appalachia may be traced back to a ruthless tradition
of frontier-warfare along the border between Western Christendom and
the "Celtic Fringe" . . . which has been revived, among these Scotch-
Irish settlers in North America, by the barbarizing severity of their Appalachian environment.[16]

The unspoken assumptions behind this passage, as in all Toynbee's works, are breathtaking in their naïveté. One notes in particular
the constant shift between the literal and the extended senses of the
words "savagery" and "barbarism," with all the insupportable assumptions which this wordplay drags in. Toynbee notes correctly that
the Appalachian character was conditioned by the "barbarizing" effect of the battle against "Celts," "a ruthless tradition . . . handed
down unmitigated from an age when their [supposed Anglo-Saxon]
forefathers had been no better than Red Indians themselves";[17] but he
fails to see that this "barbarity" was picked up, not from the "Celts,"
but from the "civilized" peoples of the "Anglo-Saxon" lowlands. The
militant frontier openly expressed this denied aggressive component
of the Western "civilized" psyche.[18] The conflict itself, and therefore the "savagery" both of the dispossessed "barbarian" and of the
frontier-fighter, was created by the metropole as an expression of its

own aggressiveness. This interpretation is supported by the revival of such behavior in Appalachia in the absence of a "savage" foe and in the presence of renewed pressure from the metropole in the form of "civilization," i.e. war and industry. Even the "local Red Indians" had by and large not been "exterminated" by the "barbarous" mountaineers but had been driven out by the "civilized" U.S. Army, later to distinguish itself against the Indians' successsors at Blair Mountain and other sites of the mine wars.[19]

But was all this *merely* a matter of outsiders' perception and of imposition from without? Is the Appalachian environment itself entirely guiltless of its inhabitants' condition? What has happened in similar environments elsewhere? Comparing maps of temperature, rainfall, elevation, and the like, one finds two areas of the Old World which closely resemble Appalachia in their physical setting: the province of Auvergne in south central France, and the highlands of Shantung ("Mountain East") in China. The inhabitants of both Auvergne and Shantung are poor, "backward," and despised by their surrounding neighbors. For a moment it seems that Toynbee may have been right about the physical severity of Appalachia. Climate and terrain, however, make for more than one parallel in these regions. Auvergne lies between the great metropolis of Paris, the cultural and political capital of Western Europe, and the port city of Marseilles; and Shantung lies between the great metropolis of Peking, cultural and political capital of East Asia, and the port city of Shanghai. One begins to see that the "barbarizing severity" of Appalachia's environment may lie not within it, but around it. And note that Toynbee's remark that the mountaineer was becoming "civilized" in the North Carolina cotton mills was written a few years *after* October 2, 1929, when six striking textile workers from the mountains were massacred in Marion, North Carolina. Thus the face which capital shows to labor in "developing" conditions coincides with the face which "civilization" shows to "barbarism" under frontier conditions—and the creator of the frontier is not the "savage," nor yet the frontiersman, but the enforcer of "civilization."

Further, Toynbee's cool remark that "barbarian" minorities in the modern world must disappear by "extermination or subjection or assimilation" brings to mind two remarkably parallel statements made in the course of American history concerning inhabitants of Appalachia. In 1818, the House Committee on Indian Affairs reported: "In the present state of our country one of two things seems to be necessary, either that these sons of the forest should be moralized or exterminated."[20] Almost exactly a century later a metropolitan newspaper, editorializing on the Allen feud in Virginia, declared: "The majority of mountain people are unprincipled ruffians. . . . There are two remedies only—education or extermination. Mountaineers, like the red Indian, must learn this lesson."[21]

The "savagery" of the native Highlander, Irishman, and American had been perceived in terms of violence in order to justify their violent dispossession. Here, then, we are privileged to watch at the very moment that this rhetoric is transferred to their one-time foe. Mountaineers' "lapse into barbarism" consisted in the success of their never-crushed resistance to being seen entirely in terms of others. What Toynbee said about their learning their "barbarism" from their Indian predecessors is once more the opposite of the case. Appalachians had in fact attained their identity by abandoning the millennial struggle on the edge of "the West"—yet without submitting to total absorption into the dominant culture of the metropole. In this sense it is true, but not lamentable, that (in Jack Weller's words) "the mountaineer still lives on his frontier without having conquered it."[22] All of this was shocking treason against the spirit of the West; it threatened the very basis of that civilization's self-image that such a thing could happen, and in America of all places. That civilization proceeded to defend its self-image by projecting its own repressed and denied ferocity upon the mountaineer, urging the latter to join "the World" again by continuing to pass the results of this violence on to others rather than facing it on its own ground. (This process has not ended: the nation's highest proportion of Vietnam combat casualties was among West Virginians.)

The West's "heirs"—its children, those who were to inherit its property(ies) upon reaching maturity—had "relapsed," fallen back into a state of childish immaturity and incompetence. They had suffered that "slide back into the savage state" which, as Sheehan notes, had always threatened Europeans with "internal danger" from their "primal urges."[23] Now, in order to remove that internal threat, these "heirs" must be reclaimed or else disinherited. (Why, incidentally, does Toynbee suppose that this "reclamation" is made doubtful by the fact of the "reversion"? Had the "lapse" caused or demonstrated some essential lack or defect in Appalachians, separating them irrecoverably from the human race, or at least the "White" race? Having "forced their way into these natural fastnesses," gone where human beings do not belong, had mountaineers therefore forfeited part of their personhood? "The Appalachian Mountains may be high," said Robert Coles, "but they are not high enough to have cut off those who live near them from their very humanity."[24])

It is true that, as Bob Snyder said, "the duality of Appalachian/American exhibits a curious inner division of the WASP identity, of which the ideological maneuvers described by Henry Shapiro are an example."[25] But the Indian, *qua* Indian, had also always been defined by "WASPs" in projective terms, and the close relation (amounting in some ways to identity) between "WASPs" and Appalachians served only to strengthen the same projective process on the part of a civilization of which inner division was, and is, a central trait. Indeed, it is arguable, I think, that as early medieval Westerners were goaded to fury by the psychic threat of "Celtic" Christian civilization and the alternative it presented, so our own dominant culture is similarly threatened by the existence of an alternative "White Protestant" civilization in the South in general and in Appalachia in particular. Mountain religion especially, like its forerunners in the "Celtic" Church and in the later popular religion of "Celtic" countries, has borne the brunt of the modern world's civilizing mission since the days of early missionaries such as Edward O. Guerrant, whose *The Galax Gatherers: The Gospel among the Highlanders* is a series of glowingly romantic travel sketches (confusing Scotch-Irish with Scottish Highlanders, incidentally) by a man who unabashedly expressed his attitude toward missionizing these "untutored and un-Christianized people"[26] with a quotation from Cecil Rhodes: "So much to do, so little done."[27] Roger Williams, outcast ideologue of Old and New England, could hardly have said it better. Nor could Jack Weller, who parlayed an attempt to "Christianize" mountain Christians into a general attack on the culture—one whose popularity and influence have long outlasted the illusions of its now-dismayed author, who has reportedly said, "I'd burn every copy of that thing if I could."[28] But the essentials of this genre are perhaps best reflected in a "classic" sixties' article on mountain churches by Weller's admirer Nathan L. Gerrard, not an ordained cleric but a sociological one, who derived part of his framework from a study of violent criminal gangs[29] and was actually incapable of distinguishing between figures of speech and hallucinations.[30] Most significantly of all, Gerrard denies that the churches he treats of deserve to be called churches at all[31]—and thus, without knowing it, he echoes a rhetoric of thirteen hundred years' pedigree.

And in fact, if the word "Protestant" implies "WASP" characteristics, then it might be best to call mountain Christians something else. The experience of most Appalachians, Southerners and/or blacks in the Sunday-schools of our childhoods—the attitudes learned there toward material possession and competition—fly in the face of the Weberian thesis on "the Protestant ethic and the spirit of capitalism,"[32] as Weber himself noted. The mountaineer's traditional attitude toward the environment derives from or parallels, as we have seen, Calvin's stoutly maintained positive view of the nonhuman creation. And in wider cultural terms, when anthropologists and sociologists speak of "Western" habits of bodily distance, eye contact, greeting on the street (or lack of it), and so forth, any southerner will know that he or she is being read out of "Western civilization"—in fact, that "civilization" is here being implicitly defined as technological industrialism, or, as C. S. Lewis described it, "barbarism made strong and luxurious by mechanical power."[33]

Toynbee's mention of the war between Anglo-Saxon and Celt, and his simple placing of the Lowlander/Ulsterman/Appalachian in the former category, invokes yet another aspect of the mystification surrounding Appalachian identity—an aspect closely connected with that "curious inner division of the WASP identity" which Snyder mentions. In the 1890s, again, with the closing of the frontier, there was mounting concern about America's ability to deal with the floodtide of immigration from Europe, and especially about that immigration's predominantly Mediterranean, Slavic, and Jewish character. A great deal of soul-searching ensued concerning American identity and its relation to its European roots. In no time at all, a school of thought arose to contend that since the original "frontier" culture of Americans was "Anglo-Saxon," and since Appalachians were quintessentially "frontier" and "American," therefore Appalachians specially exemplified "pure Anglo-Saxon" characteristics.[34] The well-known existence of the "Scotch-Irish" element did little to counter this notion, given the belief, general then even among scholars, that the Lowland Scots and their Ulster cousins were "Anglo-Saxons" who had simply overrun and displaced a "Celtic" population.[35] Another manifestation of this "Anglo-Saxon" idea is the cliché use of the word "Elizabethan" for people whose ancestors for the most part were never subjects of Elizabeth I, and who came to America over a hundred years after her death.

Thus an image of Appalachian culture became appropriated as a counter in nativist opposition to "inferior" European immigrant cultures. (And these cultures, ironically, derived their perceived "inferiority" from the same seven-centuries-old economic relationships that had shaped Scotch-Irish and Appalachian "inferiority.") For some time, Appalachian culture could hardly be mentioned without invidious comparisons of these "Anglo-Saxons" with non-"Nordic" immigrants. Some such comments were relatively innocuous, such as Frost's invocation of "the great increase of the foreign born and the hyphenated population"[36] as something to counterbalance by dragooning mountaineers into mainline Protestant churches. Others, though, were frankly racist, notably as embodied in the views of the Virginia pseudo-aristocrat John Powell, organizer of the Anglo-Saxon Clubs of America and sponsor of the White Top Folk Festival[37]— though Powell's fellow racist, the eugenicist Madison Grant, took a less rosy view of mountain life and wondered how "Nordics" had managed to fall so low in such an apparently favorable environment.[38]

But this process had still more complex connections with the ambivalent nature of "Western civilization" as a whole. We have seen how the real Anglo-Saxons—and their Norman conquerors, the original bigots—had been both the bearers of that civilization and the invading horde from outside it; and we have seen that this paradox had worked to their descendants' material advantage for over a millennium. It had never been forgotten that the word "Anglo-Saxon" (in contrast with "English") connoted a sort of European frontiersman. Now this ambiguity came to work to mountaineers' disadvantage, as the double nature of the "Anglo-Saxon" tied in with the double valuation—noble and ignoble—of the American "son of the forest." Since the term "Anglo-Saxon" had been popularized by bigots, the notion became widespread that bigotry was endemic to "Anglo-Saxons," and that bigoted attitudes must be especially rife among these "isolated" remnants of "pure" Anglo-Saxon "stock"—people who were "southerners" to boot. This idea gained currency especially as those groups which were being insulted and injured by "Anglo-Saxonism" developed their own "americanized" intelligentsias. "Anglo-Saxonism" had been put forward by its inventors as the civilization to be defended; now it was proclaimed by others as the barbarism to be done away with.

Thus, to those inclined to think so, the very "Anglo-Saxonness" of the mountaineer became a mark of ignoble savagism. The people we now call "WASPs" were, after all, referred to by earlier sociologists as "native Americans"; and native was definitely not fine to those "WASPs" and others who saw their "contemporary ancestors," both strangers and kin, as once more "no better than Red Indians themselves." The "pure Anglo-Saxon yeoman" became the "white bigot," as the racism once foisted on Appalachians from without came to be attributed *to* them from without.

This misperception continues to the present day and works ongoing damage. It has been pointed out frequently and with exasperation that the lukewarmness of northern liberal support of Appalachian struggles in the sixties, in contrast to enthusiastic support of other groups, was largely due to liberals' perception of Appalachians as "white southerners," therefore "bigots," therefore somehow deserving of their own plight.[39] Of course racism is as endemic in Appalachia as in other parts of America—including the Northeast and including the middle class—but it is rarely of the complicated aversive type found in the South proper. Yet Appalachian groups in northern cities, the equivalent of black or Hispanic groups, have sometimes been mistaken for "white power" groups precisely by the others' "liberal" supporters. The latter project their own denied anti-black racism onto Appalachians, and southern whites in general—the dialectic reverse of the romantic "Anglo-Saxon" myth—while simultaneously attacking southern whites for many of the qualities they share with blacks. The process is so overdetermined—so many factors are working in the same direction—that the resultant attitude is extremely resistant to reason, and attempts to change it are often met with a startlingly angry defensiveness. The intensity of this denial measures the depth of the threat which such criticism poses to the "civilized" metropolitan's very ego-structure—as if this "curious inner division" threatened the mainstream "American's" identity individually as well as collectively. As R. D. Laing says, "The more one attempts to preserve one's autonomy and identity by nullifying the specific human individuality of the other, the more it is felt to be necessary to continue to do so, because with each denial of the other person's ontological status, one's own ontological security is decreased, the threat to the self from the other is potentiated and hence has to be even more desperately negated."[40]

Mainstream "America's" urge to heal its "curious inner division" by the brute force of denial gives mountaineers an exceptional relation to our society's oft-proclaimed "pluralism." The rise of black, Hispanic, native American, and to some extent white "ethnic" (Catholic) self-assertion has forced lip service, at least, to "pluralistic" concepts. But for many this is a superficial adjustment, a set of isolated concessions tacked as ornaments onto the basic assumptions of a consumption-oriented rationality. "Those people" are "validated"—

though only by essentially defining them out of the question, since taking them properly into account would mean the transformation of a whole mentality. But Appalachian mountain people cannot be so easily defined out of the question, since they are perceived as "Americans" of "Anglo-Saxon stock." Their "deviance" is perceived as "not a survival but a reversion." Thus the dominant culture must cling all the more tightly to its image of "yahoos" in the South and Appalachia. (This oft-heard epithet "yahoo" is significant: Swift's original Yahoos were an Enlightenment rationalist's paranoid nightmare of the "irrational" element in human nature—the nightmare, moreover, of a highly-placed Anglo-Irish Protestant.) Mountaineers' identification as "contemporary ancestors," as somehow "really" part of "us," makes attitudes toward them the last essentially unchallenged stronghold of the mentality, "Why can't they be like us?"[41] And this attitude's fundamental premise—that "we are the real adult persons, whose rationality sees things as they are"—is the mainstay of domination.

This process reflects, on one level, a familiar inability to deal with class as anything other than "income-grouping," or with culture as anything but a set of formulae for connecting "deviance" from the dominant culture with "deficiencies" in income and "education." Such ways of thinking have largely fallen out of favor among academics in the relevant fields, but they are still rife in vast sections of the "enlightened" population as a whole. But there are particular reasons why this blindness specially affects perceptions of mountain people. One reason for the widespread exclusion of Appalachians from "pluralist" attitudes may well be that, as Curtis Seltzer points out, "there is no organized mountaineer constituency in Manhattan."[42] But how many Indians are there in Manhattan? The crux of the matter is precisely that the mountaineer is now the stereotypic *substitute* for the Indian in "enlightened" consciousness. It is precisely mountaineers' perceived identity with the dominator which masks the fact that their "survival" of barbarity had been in the mind of that dominator, and their "reversion," after eight centuries, has been in the latter's own perceptions. As Christians project their hatred of the Gospel onto Jews, so "Americans" project their hatred of civilization onto Appalachians. If "entertainments" such as the *Beverly Hillbillies,* or Disney World's Hillbilly Bears (shades of the Hairy Ainu indeed!), were offered for national consumption at the expense of any other "ethnic" group—including, by now, any other white group—they could hardly survive the storm of "enlightened" protest. Yet as recently as 1981, CBS aired (and in 1984 replayed) a movie-length reprise of the Clampett family's capers. In the lumbering, subhuman forms of these boors, clowns, villains, and "rurall raskells" with "their beastlie kind of life," Albion's giant children of Ham are born anew.[43]

Some readers with doubts about my line of argument may have had them focused sharply by this last remark. Even if Appalachians are an oppresed group, may it not be arrogant to call them children of Ham? That particular mystification, after all, has had effects in "the West" which are much more direct and literal—and much more vicious and destructive—than with mountain people. And nowhere, of course, has this been truer than in America. Thus a black scholar, criticizing white ethnicists, has noted that "Blacks in our society symbolize all other nonwhites because Blacks represent to whites *the extremity of otherness.*"[44] This is precisely true, and no one can seriously dispute that blacks are in multiple dimensions the supreme victim in and of our society.

But white Appalachians have been victims of a different kind of game with shifting mirrors, of seeing in a glass darkly. As a "contemporary ancestor," the mountaineer has been subjected to an identity-robbing process as deadly in its effects as any other form of prejudice. This fact is perhaps most apparent where blacks and Appalachians live side by side in northern industrial centers, and occupy niches side by side in the minds of the "natives." Hence the northern city joke: "Why don't niggers let their kids listen to hillbilly music? They don't want 'em to grow up too lazy to steal."[45]

And what of the reverse situation—that of the black inhabitants of the Appalachian region, some of whom migrated there to escape Deep South racial practices? This study has so far omitted to mention them, and the preceding discussion has excluded them entirely. Black Appalachians have often enough been utterly ignored both in Appalachian studies and in black studies. I myself cannot speak for the latter; and in the former case, it indeed seems to me that many of the factors I have discussed for white Appalachians are not operative, or not in the same way, for blacks.

Many, but not all. Although here I must speak from the outside, it seems to me that Appalachian blacks are not simply *residents* but *natives* of the region. That is, they share in its features, and in particular they share in those featues for which the region *as a region* has been derogated. Here, too, the fact is most clearly seen in contact situations illustrating outsiders' perceptions. Thus, for example, to speak only of what I know myself: one day a lady strode into the library where

I worked in Huntington, West Virginia, and demanded that a co-worker of mine, a black woman from a Logan County family of long standing, give her an envelope which had been left at the desk for her. My co-worker had not been told of this envelope and asked where it was. The lady sharply insisted that my colleague was "supposed to know that." My colleague gently explained that she would try to find it. The lady fixed her with a withering gaze. "You're *from* West Virginia, aren't you?" she asked; and when my colleague admitted as much, the lady stalked off to report her incompetence. It is easy to imagine the reaction among this lady's "enlightened" neighbors if she had audibly made such a reference to my colleague's *race*. But I can vouch for the fact that what she actually said is perfectly acceptable among many belonging to her class in the "growth center," or royal burgh, near which I grew up.

This is all a matter about which a great deal more can and should be said, but my own knowledge and experience enable me to do no more than point at the fact for others. Plainly, though, the above anecdote and the preceding "joke" reflect different aspects of a single very complex nexus of regional, class, and "ethnic" matters. Furthermore, they both have to do with outsiders' perceptions of mountain people—perceptions whose relation to "reality," whatever that is, adds another dimension of complexity and controversy to the whole phenomenon. We have here a complex solid with a complex shape, so to speak. But that is just what we should expect with a living organism.

Thus mountaineers have been categorized by the dominant culture as "contemporary ancestors," as noble or ignoble savages. Examining this point further, what exactly does this categorization amount to in terms of interpersonal perception?

R. D. Laing, whom we have already cited, distinguishes two aspects of full human identity: identity-for-others and identity-for-oneself. If these do not coincide, identity is impaired. If one tries to get along only with identity-for-oneself, the result is the unreality of inauthentic existence.[46] He states: *"The sense of identity requires the existence of another by whom one is known;* and a conjunction of this other person's recognition of one's self with self-recognition."[47] Expanding this insight into the sociopolitical sphere, we see that a person's identity is violated by dominators, who could not preserve a power relation with the dominated if they saw the latter—or themselves—as they really are. Hence the relation I have called "sign-appropriation," summed up in Albert Memmi's definition of racism: "the substantive expression, to the accuser's benefit, of a real or imaginary trait of the accused."[48] To "real or imaginary" we may add "positive or negative"; for, as David Walls pointed out with regard to Appalachia itself, the positive and negative stereotypes are "contending on the same turf"[49] of a fixed image which implicitly excludes power competency and the ability to confront the dominator on one's own terms.

I have already described a repeated process involving infantilization on the developmental plane. On the existential plane, this process involves what Laing calls "disconfirmation of agency."[50] In this disconfirmation, the dominator implicitly denies the dominated an inner self and an ability to think and act on one's own behalf. Such disconfirmation can take "benevolent," patronizing forms, which are perhaps the most damaging—for example, the attitude expressed in Jack Weller's injunction, "Let us begin to guide the mountain man toward wholeness."[51] The attitude behind such a statement was laid bare by Rupert Vance when he wrote that Weller, "because he came as a missionary, . . . brought the objectivity of the stranger. Finally, he came to know these people better than they know themselves."[52] Here the positivist ideal of "objectivity" is explicitly invoked as a means of gaining a knowledge of the other which is superior to that one's own knowledge of who he or she is. Truly, "violence cannot be seen through the sights of positivism."[53] To connect this with our earlier themes, let us note that addressed to an adult, the call to "grow up" (in social terms, to attain "wholeness") is by implication just as infantilizing as the command to remain a child.[54] Just so, the call to "us" outsiders to "guide the mountain man toward wholeness" disconfirms the real agency of the mountaineer, refuses to recognize his or her real existence, and thus defeats its stated goal.

Some of the best intentioned people have fallen into such disconfirming attitudes. For example, Michael Harrington, in his classic *The Other America*, wrote of Appalachians and other southern whites that "the backwoods has [sic] completely unfitted them for urban life."[55] The word "backwoods" clearly conveys the image of a periphery, a hinterland, a part "behind" some ideal or rightful head—and in addition a forest, an area characterized by "nature" and animals, not human beings. And the word "unfitted"—especially as an active verb—seems to imply that the condition of living in the "backwoods" has somehow done something *to* their inhabitants to warp them from some correct state of "fitness" for "urban life," presumably to be identified with reality.

Thus agency, and identity itself—the ability to act, and the very ability to be—can be disconfirmed by the dominator, with the result that the discourse of the dominated comes to be centered elsewhere just as their economy and politics are. Memmi noted of the colonial schoolchild: "The memory which is assigned him is certainly not that of his people. The history which is taught him is not his own. . . . Everything seems to have taken place out of his country. He and his land are nonentities or exist only with reference . . . to what he is not."[56] He is not fitted for his own life, only "unfitted" for someone else's. This situation can exist even in the context of study of one's own land, and is perhaps deadliest then, since that which was implicit is now explicit. Thus a junior high-school student of my acquaintance explained to me why his least favorite class was "West Virginia Studies": "Nothing ever happened anywhere in the state till people came from the North, and then it's all chemicals and production figures." He intends to leave the state for good as soon as he can. His natural desire for enlargement of being has been channeled into a discourse in which being is bestowed only by the other, and even then is defined only in the other's terms, reduced to the numerically expressible mechanical process which feeds a real life in some other place. Having been assigned another's memory, his own identity is falsified. And of course his complaint simply puts into words something which happens all over Appalachia, and not only to schoolchildren.

Thus mountain culture has been perceived negatively, as an "unfitted" form of the dominant culture. But this categorization of minority culture as an aspect or mode of the "majority's" can be expressed in still another way. This way is a bit more complex and subtle but for that very reason all the more dangerous; for, although rising one step within the system, it does nothing to break out of it. This is the attitude of the "positive" sentimentalist who, instead of welcoming or lamenting the disappearance of the minority culture, clings to it uncritically, and objects to any change in it—on the part of others, of course. Like the others we have discussed, these persons accept an image that is essentially constituted by the discourse of the dominant culture, and insist on treating that image as a fixed quantity. Their view of it may (or may not) be more accurate, but it is still external, and thus has no place for internal processes of growth and change. And since this mode of thinking equates minorities with children, this approach is analogous to parental reluctance to let a child grow up and lose its "innocence"—and it has, therefore, the comforting effect of excluding the dominated from any effective participation in the world of power relations, and of precluding any threat that the object of the idealization will confront the subject on the former's own terms.[57] That all these "positive" stereotypes are of a piece with the negative is well put by Horace Newcomb in his discussion of the backhandedly "positive" aspects of *The Beverly Hillbillies* and the like:

> These Southerners are children, and their goodness is the simple good-ness of children. . . . The real viciousness of these views is not that hill-billies and Southerners are made fun of. It is that mountain people and Southerners are not considered part of the adult population of the country or of the culture. Programs about the South admit that the vir-tues presented there are the important ones, the ones best for life. But they simultaneously suggest that they are not available to those of us who live in the "real" world of adult interaction. Such a perspective is familiar to anthropologists. The native culture becomes the screen on which we project our own desires for innocence, for noble savages, for happy natives and for paradises before the introduction of evil.[58]

This paradisal projection is of course a sheer illusion; primitive people are as alienated from "natural" innocence, and as sadly con-scious of the fact, as the rest of us—and also as given to projections about the fact. As Eliade notes, "the 'good savage' . . . already knew the myth of the Good Savage; he was their own ancestor."[59] In the same way, modern humanity projects noble savagism upon its own "contemporary ancestor." Rich Kirby noted in the seventies: "A fair number of kids have decided (not unreasonably) that the Appalachian Region is Paradise Lost; this fact has given West Virginia a fair number of communes and short-lived organic restaurants. The same feeling among their elders leads to long-lived developments and National Forest land grabs."[60]

We have seen, through the examples of Sheehan and others, the destructive effects of such projections when their expectations are in-evitably disappointed. But the projection itself—as the last quotation illustrates in its way—is inherently destructive. The hallmark of living cultures is that they can undergo adaptive and creative changes from within, and adopt features from without, while not only refusing to be overwhelmed by the latter but making them uniquely characteristic of such a living culture of such an "enduring people."[61] Hence Celtic culture at its La Tène zenith reworked Central Asian art motifs into what everyone knows as "Celtic art"; early Christian Ireland reworked that art with Coptic, Byzantine, and Germanic motifs; and "classic" Appalachia developed its characteristic musical styles by adding to the fiddle the African banjo, the German dulcimer, and the Spanish guitar. Thus cultures, like mature individuals, adapt without self-destruction. But to see a sentimentalized culture in terms of child-hood, whether as childish or as childlike, is to see it as something which cannot change without ceasing altogether to be what it was. This sentimentalism only replaces the injunction "Grow up!" with the injunction "Do not grow up!"—and both injunctions are equally false to the subject's real maturity and integrity. Speaking of a case similar and related to Appalachia's, the Scottish Highland poet Donald Mac-aulay writes:

> Tha
> fhios agamsa: . . .
> mur tuig sinn
> nach eil fiar-ghràdh is fìor-ghràdh
> mar thionntadh an t-sìoda,
> gu bheil sinn aig ìre dìol-déirce. . . .
>
> (I do / know this: . . . / that if we cannot understand / that false and genuine love / are not facets of the same thing / we are in a beggarly state.)[62]

Fiar-ghràdh is fìor-ghràdh, false love and true love, are not facets of the same thing: the second wills the good of the self, the first to en-gulf it.

> Vala would never have sought & loved Albion
> If she had not sought to destroy Jerusalem: such is that false
> And Generating Love: a pretence of love to destroy love: . . .
> Calling that Holy Love: which is Envy Revenge & Cruelty
> Which separated the stars from the mountains:
>   the mountains from Man
> And left Man, a little grovelling Root, outside of Himself.[63]

The whole concept of "folk-culture," indeed, suffers from this inherent destructiveness, since its image is constituted in the domi-nant, modernized, rationalized culture out of precisely those ele-ments which that dominant culture has consigned to destruction.[64] Thus, whether simplistic "folk-culture" advocates realize it or not, "folk-culture" is doomed, *is* that which is doomed. And the bearers of a subordinated culture can only escape that doom by refusing to see themselves in the observer's parental terms, negative or quasi-positive, and by acting from the wholeness of their existence rather than from the dichotomous partialities, the "cloven fictions," of their essences.

INCURSUS: *Crimes Against Nature*

These numberless exhibitions of stereotypical attitudes toward mountaineers are lamentable enough in popular entertainment, particularly when they are not only continued into the present but (as with *The Beverly Hillbillies*) revived. But of course such attitudes also infest "higher" spheres, and this fact is nowhere more clearly reflected than in the creation and reception of James Dickey's novel *Deliverance* and of John Boorman's film from Dickey's screenplay. Nevertheless, it would be wrong to dismiss *Deliverance*, as most have, simply as a vulgar perpetuator of stereotypes. This would be to read on the surface level, as many readers and most moviegoers (including major figures in each case) have done.[65] But in fact *Deliverance*, in both forms, is a complex work which rewards a close examination, and does so in unexpected ways. Therefore I wish to examine in detail this particular use of images of Appalachia, in the hope that I may clarify some of the points I have raised.

Deliverance has been both praised and condemned as a celebration of the man-against-the-wilderness machismo incarnated in Lewis, the expedition leader (played in the film by Burt Reynolds). In fact, though, both the book and the film are deeply ironic and satirical works, multi-leveled and profoundly subversive of the attitudes of all their characters, not least the narrator's. Their chief flaw, and one which looms large from our standpoint, is that they adopt the use of mountain people—or of the images of mountain people as "children of Nature"—as symbols for the evil in "nature," or in "man's" relation to it, much as T. S. Eliot used Jews as symbols of the modern separate, rootless selfhood—a selfhood that Eliot both shared and hated.[66] Such a projective attitude surfaces in *Deliverance* as well. Dickey's mountaineers, like the Indians of classic American literature, are, in Leslie Fiedler's words, "living extensions of the threat of the wilderness"[67]—both the external wilderness and, as we shall see, the inner wilderness of the psyche. But both Dickey and Boorman are artists of genius, and their works are capable of conveying meanings that lie not only below the level of surface story, but even perhaps below that of conscious intention, yet of doing so without losing artistic coherence.

The mode of *Deliverance* is gothic. Fiedler has pointed out how, in America, the stereotyped gothic menace of the castle on the hill was replaced by the menace lurking in the dark gloom of the forest. The threat to the American psyche comes no longer from the harsh, forbidding world of the superego, which had lost its supremacy in the American republic, but rather from the chaotic, impulse-ridden id, now freed from its former restraints without true autonomy having been achieved in the process.[68] This is an acute analysis within its framework. But Superego and Id are themselves historically conditioned categories; they are, in fact, Freud's internalized reworking of the concepts of Civilization and Nature, which he took for granted as objectively "given" in the "external" world. Thus rather than saying that the forest symbolizes the id, it is perhaps better to say that the forest and the id are parallel constructs, both standing for a deeper universal reality. Indeed, in terms of the historical development of ideas, one may say that it is the id that symbolizes the forest.

Dickey prefaces *Deliverance* with a quotation from Georges Bataille: *"Il existe à base de la vie humaine un principe d'insuffisance"*[69] (there exists at the base of human life a principle of insufficiency). This insufficiency has been felt in all stages of culture, ever since the shamans told men and women how they had been tricked into dying. This sense of insufficiency lies behind all cultural definitions, for *omnis determinatio est negatio*, every definition is a denial; *différence* equals *différance*. Thus humanity comes to see things in terms of purity and impurity, innocence and guilt, sin and deliverance, civilization and nature. The party of hunters in *Deliverance* sets out for a weekend of bowhunting and whitewater canoeing—instructed by "movies and pictures of Indians on calendars"[70]—along a North Georgia "wild" river soon to be flooded for a reservoir. Their boyhood vanishing, their bodies beset by hints of mortality in paunch and hairline, they seek to confront a vanishing "nature" in order to fill out the insufficiency of their own "civilized" lives, but they find that they cannot escape the terms of the definition by choosing one side over the other; they take their insufficiency with them and find it waiting for them.

The three protagonists besides Ed, the narrator, represent facets of this consciousness. Lewis, the leader, is the pure disciple of Man (not humanity) in confrontation, "respectful" but ultimately dominating, with Nature. Drew approaches Nature with innocent enthusiasm, seemingly unaware of anything that could happen, while Bobby approaches it with ignorant contempt. And Lewis' approach is in fact a combination of this smiling innocence and this patronizing ignorance, as regards the reality of what he imagines he has confronted. These attitudes toward "Nature" are the same as those which the campers display toward the mountains' inhabitants. (It is a supreme irony that the film was made in Rabun County, Georgia, where *Foxfire* is edited, and that the building up of a gothic image of "squalid and degenerate" mountain life includes a horror-movie glimpse of an aged woman with a retarded child, who are in fact Mrs. Andy Webb, a noted midwife and healer featured in *The Foxfire Book* and *Foxfire 2*, and a grandson for whom she cared even in advanced old age.[71] Ed discovers the pair while he is wandering around peering into people's windows; one wonders if Boorman intends this comment on his own enterprise.)

The first mountaineer seen in the film appears in classic gothic style, a shadowy slouch-hatted scarecrow looming around the side of a building we have not been sure was still occupied; he is something, that is, that ought to be gone by now. The mountaineers in this scene are presented at times with a certain distant, stony dignity, like natural objects or cliché Indians, but they are not conveyed as human beings. Here, in the "Dueling Banjos" sequence, Drew plays a musical duet (actually guitar and banjo) with a retarded boy. The latter seems unable to talk, but he has abundant natural rhythm; being mentally retarded and thus dehumanized in a different way, this boor is permitted to be neither a clown nor a villain. When the aforementioned man starts clogging during this sequence, he seems an automaton, started up by the music, like a limberjack.

In the film, though, significant divergences from the book emphasize that the work is not on the side of "civilization" either. Bobby is much more openly dislikable and obnoxious than in the book; and at the end of the musical duel, the boy refuses to be friendly with Drew. Later we see this boy, the last person the party sees as they set out on the river, standing on a bridge above them like a presence, refusing their greeting as he stares after them, swinging his banjo like the pendulum of the human time the campers are leaving behind.

The next day, the campers' illusions about "nature" are shattered in the infamous rape scene. A pair of toothless bootleggers encounter Ed and Bobby resting on the bank. One of them holds a gun on Ed while the other sodomizes Bobby. As they are about to switch victims,

Lewis comes on the scene and shoots one rapist, but the other escapes. (How ironic, incidentally, that the mountaineers use guns while the city men use bows and arrows: the latter are assimilating themselves to their own image of "nature," while the former have no such category.) The rape is a visible expression of what is implied in the undertones of the banter the night before around the campfire in the spot the campers had "colonized"[72]—the infantile narcissism the campers have come out here to share, with what they call "nature" as an inert background against which to project their fantasies.[73] Here, the campers' projections come to life and trap them in a situation they cannot control. (In the film the campers, and Lewis in particular, are generally shot in front of the green of the forest, standing out against it. In contrast, the first rapist is initially seen moving *within* a wall of green, as if belonging to it, a "living extension" of its threat; and the rape scene itself is played with the campers in long shots, surrounded by the entangling viny, loamy gloom.) Ed has longed for, "not . . . the practicality of sex, . . . but the promise of it that promises other things, another life, deliverance";[74] what he gets is a hideous parody of this promise—polymorphous perversity collapsed into the ordinary kind. (The rapists' toothlessness—partial in the film, total in the book—is a sign of degeneration toward a parody of infancy; the oral stage is also suggested by their connection with moonshining.)[75]

And the violence of these men "who have forced their way into these natural fastnesses"—both the rapists and the "colonizers"—is a reflection of the violence of their whole society against "nature." This fact, which many have urged against the popular interpretation of *Deliverance,* is in fact implicit in the book and made explicit in the film by foreshadowing. The opening sequence consists of shots of blasting and bulldozing, with a voice-over of the four campers discussing their trip. Lewis, speaking of what is being done, remarks, "We gonna rape their whole landscape!" It is Bobby who laughingly calls him an "extremist." The same motif is conveyed more subtly in the opening passage of the book, as the campers examine a topographic map: "It unrolled slowly, forced to show its colors, curling and snapping back whenever one of us turned loose. The whole land was very tense until we put our four steins on its corners and laid the region out to run for us through the mountains 150 miles north."[76]

As the four escape down the river, Drew suddenly falls into the water as if shot, and the canoes wreck in the rapids. It is even less clear in the film than in the book whether Drew is actually shot. He seems to fall from the canoe in a sort of suicidal trance brought on by his guilt—though he is the only one with no direct part in the rape and murder. He, who showed súch rapport with the happy side of "nature," is the least able to deal by confrontation with the human evil that the campers have unleashed upon themselves—or perhaps, rather, he is most sensitive to the death around him, and is compelled to become a part of it. After the disaster, with Drew gone, Bobby useless from shock and general incompetence, and Lewis helpless with a broken thighbone, reduced to a swaddled infant—stripped down further than he had ever intended or thought possible, exposing at his core the terrified baby who has built up the armor of toughness around himself[77]—it is Ed who must climb out of the gorge and kill the other rapist. He succeeds, carries the body on his back to the cliffedge, and lowers it over so that Bobby can make sure it is the right man; but the rope breaks and they both fall. The mountaineer lands on the rocks, his face smashed beyond recognition; now no one can ever know whether Ed has killed an innocent man.

There is an echo here of a story eight hundred years older, and perhaps much older still. Let us recall Geoffrey of Monmouth's story of the foundation of the British nation by Brutus and Corineus. The latter, we are told,

> delighted in wrestling with the giants, of whom there were far more there than in any of the provinces that had been handed out to his companions. There was, among others, a detestable one named Goemagog, twelve cubits tall, who had such strength that with one shake he could pull up an oak tree as if it were a hazel seedling. On this day, when Brutus was at the harbor where they had landed, celebrating a feast-day of the gods, the giant came down on them with twenty others and did the Britons terrible damage. But the Britons, gathering together from all around, prevailed over them, and killed them all except Goemagog, whom Brutus ordered to be taken alive; for he wished to see a wrestling match between him and Corineus, who was eager beyond measure to match himself against such creatures. So then, Corineus, jumping for joy, girded himself, threw off his armor, and challenged the giant to wrestle. Then the contest began. In moved Corineus; in moved the giant; and they grappled each other with their arms, and troubled the air with their gasping breath. Soon Goemagog, squeezing Corineus with all his might, broke three of his ribs, two on the right side and one on the left. Then Corineus, goaded to fury, called up all his strength, heaved the giant onto his shoulders, and with as much speed as he could manage for the weight, he ran to the nearby coast. Then he climbed to the top of the highest cliff and shook himself loose; and that deadly monster, whom he had carried on his shoulders, he flung into

the sea. And the giant fell on a reef of rocks, and was smashed into a thousand smithereens, and stained the waves with his blood. And the place took its name from the giant's fall, and is called the Leap of Goemagog to this day.

Then, the kingdom being divided, Brutus set out to build a city.[78]

This story has very archaic roots, but in this form it dates from the twelfth century, the great age of the "taming" of "Celtic" countries. The stories, Geoffrey's and Dickey's, correspond so strikingly in motifs because they express analogous moments at different stages of the same process. The monstrous, Titanic children of Ham who had raped his father, and of Neptune the ruler of the dark waters and the shaker of the earth, are driven into the hills by new masters of the waves. They attack the newcomers, the bringers of civility and order, and their chief representative is bested in a mighty struggle and flung back into the element of his father from whence he came; he is smashed to pieces, losing his identity and becoming only a momentary stain on the dark chaos from which Creation rose. Later even than this version, his very name is distorted into a reminder of the Great Beast and the Old Serpent, who shall be cast into the lake of fire, and there shall be no more sea.

But the fundamental fact of this myth, layered over and repressed almost to invisibility in Geoffrey's version, is laid bare and brought to light by Dickey: The slain enemy is his slayer's own double in "nature," his own "body," his own repressed and denied self, whose crime and whose punishment enact in drama the daily situation of "civilization" and its discontents, and of human life in general and its insufficiencies. The fall of Goemagog represents the creation of "nature" from the rejected parts of the self, a rejection necessary for self-definition (*différence* as *différance*, the kingdom divided and the city built). His blood becomes the waves that surround and define Britain, as the blood of Blake's dismembered Albion becomes the waves that drown Atlantis. Just so, the slain mountaineer in *Deliverance* is both the part of Ed which is split off by the false dichotomy Humanity/Nature, and also the totemic animal, the antithetical ideal, identification with which is an attempt to heal the real primary split between mortal humanity and the mortality-less living creation. Thus, once more, the mountaineer is a middle term between humanity/civilization and nature/savagery.

In the scenes of the showdown between Ed and the mountaineer, the latter is clearly identified with "nature" several times. Before the mountaineer is shot, Ed sees "something relaxed and enjoying in his body position, something primally graceful; I had never seen a more beautiful or convincing element of a design."[79] After lethally wounding him, Ed tracks him just as he would a deer. And after he is dead, his body seems "alive in the same way that most of the things in the woods were alive. . . . He now had that same re-laxed, enjoying look of belonging anywhere he happened to be, and particularly in the woods."[80] Here Dickey makes a fine ironic twist: Ed, delirious with injury, fatigue, and atrocity, starts singing a victory-song, "a current popular favorite, a folk-rock tune."[81] This is a tiny but sharp reflection of how Ed lives in a culture which has appropriated the mountaineer's "folk" world, turned "nature" into something in-nocuous and domestic—a formal design where life and death are the same—which is here returned grotesquely to its own.

But simultaneously the mountaineer is identified with Ed him-self, as if he were a middle term between Ed and the forest. Ed is able to pick the spot to wait for the mountaineer, and later finds his body, because he puts himself into the latter's mind. As he lies in wait, Ed notes "the feeling of a peculiar kind of intimacy";[82] in the act of shoot-ing, he wounds himself badly falling onto one of his own arrows, and as he tracks the shot man, once "I could not tell which was my blood and which was his."[83] One image unites both identifications, connect-ing the shot man with "nature" and also evoking the story of Cain and Abel: "He got carefully down to his knees; blood poured when his mouth opened and seemed to splash up out of the ground, to have the force of something coming out of the earth, a spring revealed when the right stone was moved."[84] In the film, these identities are conveyed when Ed and the shot man fall from the cliff. The moun-taineer's body does not hit the rocks but falls in the water with Ed; there is a moment in the underwater, uterine dimness when they seem to embrace, and it is hard to tell which is which. The body of the natu-ral man causes Ed to fall—but only because he has killed it first. As Norman O. Brown said, "Murder is suicide with mistaken identity."[85]

Indeed, not only the slain mountaineer but all the other pro-tagonists are Ed's body. He leaves the violating body and the innocent murdered body behind him dead, and is left with the violated and the murdering wounded. Over the next few days he and the other survi-vors escape with their lives and manage, barely, to conceal the true course of events from the authorities. The ending of the film contrasts with that of the book. In the latter, the experience leads to a deepening of Ed's life, and "every night as the water rose [behind the dam] I slept better . . . until finally I slept as deeply as Drew was sleeping."[86] In

Boorman's version, there is no such sentiment and no such denial. We see the surface of the lake, shot from an inch or so above it, as if we were in the water. The theme of "Dueling Banjos" suddenly turns into a menacing sustained buzz, as a shape appears below the surface and becomes a waxen dead hand, rising stiffly, its palm turned upward and its fingers clutching at life and air. With a cry Ed jerks awake. His wife comforts him, but he lies staring for a minute, as the "Dueling Banjos" theme begins again, softly and very cheerfully—the way Drew and the boy played it—and the credits run. As Ed closes his eyes, "Dueling Banjos" stops with a discordant twang, and we are in the lake again, a low ghostly hum filling our ears, as we are left staring out over the dark waters, piled over "nature" by "civilization," watching in terror for what does not appear again, but might at any moment break the surface, revealing what lies next to us.

This hand is the most powerful and memorable image in the work. Boorman seems to be fascinated with this motif, for it appears in a very different context and manner in *Excalibur*, as the hand rising from the lake with the sword of that name (but of this connection, more later). As for the use of this image in *Deliverance*, however, its treatment in advertisements is a measure of popular avoidance of the work's real meaning. On the cover of one paperback edition, the hand in the water is turned away from the viewer and toward the unsuspecting boaters in the middle distance. In old advertisements for the film, hands actually emerge from the water leveling a shotgun at the boaters. In this way the implied psychic and moral threat to the reader/viewer is vulgarized into a simple physical threat to the protagonists, the "heroes"; the reader/viewer is invited to ignore those aspects of this complex work which lie beneath, and may even subvert, the hero-and-villain (*wiros*-and-*villanus*) adventure surface.

Thus the deeper themes of *Deliverance* constitute, among other things, a sharply satirical critique of the basic presuppositions of the culture in which it was written—presuppositions which affect the work's choice of motifs and situations, which motifs and situations in turn pull against and across the work's underlying currents in a complex manner. This culture is the one which invented "civilization" and "nature," and the work reflects the dynamic of that culture's repressiveness. Basic needs of the human organism are repressed in such a way that they can only reappear in demonized form, distorted by forgetting and "ignore-ance" and tainted with overt violence which is a reply to the covert violence of the one-dimensionalization process.

The deformed and violent character of the "nature" which appears is then used as a justification for more repression.

"All men were once boys," says Ed, "and . . . boys are always looking for ways to become men. Some of the ways are easy, too; all you have to do is be satisfied that it has happened."[87] But, as Sartre said, "the European has only been able to become a man through creating slaves and monsters."[88] *Deliverance* has the structure of a rite of passage to adulthood, but since it is also a story of our civilization, that rite is maimed and abortive. The work's very plot structure is that of a boyhood adventure, or misadventure: four friends go off on an escapade which promises to be a Great Adventure; they botch it terribly and spend most of their time getting out of their fix and hiding the facts from the Big People. What is learned, if anything, is not maturity but fear and avoidance. A successful rite of passage, as practiced by traditional cultures, requires a secure (though immature and dependent) ego-structure to be first disassembled, then reconstituted in the adult mode by communion with the ancestral spirits, the *daimones*.[89] But in our civilization, a patriarchy of those whom Fiedler calls "more motherless child than free man,"[90] the ego-boundary is an insecure frontier which perpetuates the ego through violence[91]—and, since the ego is itself a boundary in a higher dimension, this instability and violence permeate the entire personality vis-à-vis its universe. Our rites of passage, then, have violence at their hearts because the disassembly of the ego threatens self-destructive collapse, which must be warded off by an equal and opposite movement of aggression. The communion with the ancestral *daimones* becomes an invasion by the demonic, for demons are the forms which *daimones* take in an environment in which every motion of the soul is expressed in terms of violence; and these ancestral demons must be subdued by being projected onto the external world as "contemporary ancestors" and then killed, in what Rogin calls "the history of . . . psychic regression, . . . regeneration through violence and flawed maturity."[92]

Thus *Deliverance* epitomizes the rite of a civilization which has lost its thread through the labyrinth of time, and perpetuates itself by pseudo-resolutions, incomplete rites repeated endlessly, the repetition-compulsion of New Worlds to Conquer.[93] For at least eight hundred years, mountaineers' forebears have been involved in this process, as victims and (not contradictorily) at the same time as perpetrators: as the visible incarnation, the cutting edge, of Western violence, simultaneously despised for that violence whose realization the "civilized" Westerner has blanked out in his or her own heart. The degradation, in the context of a rite of passage, attaches its victim all the more strongly to the oppressor. But, being the distorted, never-consummated rite of a culture which cannot achieve its own passage, the degradation ends only when the victim opts out of the rite. And then the dominant culture, shaken to its core by the rejection of its means of self-validation, has no recourse but to cast the "rebel" out beyond the pale of validation, to label that outcast as a "savage," an uninitiated child, and not (as in reality) one who is struggling for a mature identity which shall have achieved its own, different and valid passage.

6 A Heritage and a Hermitage

Now we must choose, said Mercier.
Between what? said Camier.
Ruin and collapse, said Mercier.
Could we not somehow combine them? said Camier.
—Samuel Beckett

The struggle for such a valid identity, a struggle never crushed but never genuinely accepted by the dominant culture, helps to illuminate certain aspects of mountain culture, particularly in its relation to "general" (hegemonic) "American" culture—aspects which have been thought of as paradoxical, or even as going against the idea that Appalachia "exists." Most of what I have to say here will be general and abstract, but I am assured that it is confirmed by the experience of those who are actually engaged in efforts to help mountain dwellers and emigrants deal with assaults on their identity and self-worth. I hope, indeed, that what I have to say may be suggestive, first, toward future investigations of such concrete problems, both in Appalachia and in our society as a whole; and, second, toward the efforts of Appalachian scholars to sort out the questions of positive versus negative aspects of mountain culture and society, and the related questions of native versus outside efforts to redress matters.

One of the most significant works of modern Appalachian scholarship is an essay by Helen Lewis, Sue Kobak, and Linda Johnson which refutes the general notion that mountaineers' "regressive" religion and "outmoded" family structure existed from the beginning and are simple causes of Appalachian "backwardness" today. In "Family, Religion, and Colonialism in Central Appalachia: or, Bury my Rifle at Big Stone Gap," these scholars analyze the process by which outside agents—industrial and missionary—gained control of Appalachia and subjected its people to economic exploitation and cultural denigration. They then show that the rigidity and privatism of mountain family and religious life are results of this process—attempts at self-defense. Here they draw part of their framework from Albert Memmi, the Tunisian author of *The Colonizer and the Colonized*. The most specially relevant passage from Memmi runs:

> It is not an original psychology which explains the importance of the family, nor is it the intensity of family life which explains the state of social structures. It is rather the impossibility of enjoying a complete social life which maintains vigor in the family and pulls the individual back to that more restricted cell, which saves and smothers him. . . . Religion constitutes another refuge value, both for the individual and for the group. For the individual, it is one of the rare paths of retreat; for the group, it is one of the rare manifestations which can protect its original existence. . . . Formalism . . . is the cyst into which colonial society shuts itself and hardens, degrading its own life in order to save it. It is a spontaneous action of self-defense, a means of safeguarding the collective consciousness without which a people quickly cease to exist. . . .
>
> The calcified colonized society is therefore the consequence of two processes having opposite symptoms: encystment originating externally and a corset imposed from outside.[1]

The first time I read this passage, I was startled by its close analogy, in the collective sphere, to a passage of R. D. Laing dealing with the results of oppression in the individual sphere:

> If the whole of the individual's being cannot be defended, the individual retracts his lines of defence until he withdraws to a central citadel. He is prepared to write off everything he is, except his "self". But the tragic paradox is that the more the self is defended in this way, the more it is destroyed. The apparent eventual destruction and dissolution of the self . . . is accomplished by the inner defensive manoeuvres themselves.[2]

The parallel between these processes—their self-defensive origin, and their self-defeating and self-suffocating result—is exact. Elsewhere Laing refers to the resulting individual state as "existential gangrene,"[3] recalling Memmi's "encystment." What I wish to do here, then, is to explore this parallel in some detail, in order to place the phenomena discussed by Lewis, Kobak, and Johnson within a still wider and, I hope, still more illuminating context. And as for direct engagement with the contemporary experience of mountain people, I have found some of Allen Batteau's analyses of his observations in Eastern Kentucky to be especially adaptable to this context.

In what follows, I will cite other sources—in particular, the observations of other modern students and natives of Appalachia and of the migrant ghettoes. I have also seen fit to appeal to some of my own experiences—though indeed this whole book is informed by my experience. But I have been most struck by the parallelisms among the three I have mentioned, and here I wish to draw attention to my technique of interweaving quotations from them. In this way I have tried to outline the fabric of individual and collective experience as they affect mountaineers, in the hope of transcending the dichotomy between "individual" and "collective" experience altogether.

Those familiar with Laing may object that he does not deal in particular with poor or "colonized" people. But I find this fact significant in itself. Instead of the question "How can the experience of middle-class British psychiatric patients be relevant to Appalachians?" I would encourage the reader to ask, "What does it mean that these experiences transcend class, ethnic, and even national boundaries in the modern West, and yet have such sharp relevance to Appalachia?" I shall try to address this question, among others, in order to illuminate the relations between Appalachia and "America" in the wider context of both.

I have described a process of infantilization as central to others' relations to mountain people and to their ancestors. This infantilization process has other aspects, though, besides the strengthening of dependent patterns by what Batteau calls "the manipulation of regressive and self-defeating impulses within the dependent class."[4] The word "self-defeating" suggests another aspect of this process: the double-bind. This is described by Laing as a situation in which one injunction or expectation conflicts with a simultaneous one on a different level of abstraction, and is combined with forces which prevent the conflict from being consciously realized.[5] The result is an untenable position, what Batteau calls "a series of no-win situations"[6] in which the dominated is reduced, in Memmi's terms, to "only changing dilemmas."[7]

In the case at hand, the double-bind consists in a call to adults to "grow up," thereby both enjoining adulthood and denying that the object of the injunction already possesses it ("Let us begin to guide the mountain man toward wholeness"). Rogin notes that a century and a half ago "the paternal authority repressed out of liberal politics reappeared in Indian paternalism";[8] the same situation exists today with regard to Appalachians, among others. Thus the dominated is told to be a whole person in a way which denies the reality of that wholeness which he or she actually possesses. At the same time, this injunction imputes "wholeness" to a dominant other who, as we shall see, is not actually whole. This other's own partialness is in fact isomorphic with that of the dominated, and is only more perfectly repressed or rationalized. And besides being based on all these false premises, the domination is imposed in a context of pretended democratic equality, of what Laing calls "pseudo-mutuality"[9]—it is labeled as not being domination at all in a society which Batteau accurately calls "nominally egalitarian."[10] Finally, the injunction not to notice all these contradictions is provided by the sign-appropriation imposed on the dominated culture, the categorization and trivialization of the dominated's experience by the dominant sign-system with its "near bewitching self-verification."[11]

Thus there arises a disjunction between Laing's being-for-oneself and being-for-the-other—or, on the collective level, between "identification group" and "valuation group," as Appalachian scholars have called them.[12] What are the possible responses to this disjunction? In the Appalachian case, Batteau lists the three ways of dealing with this situation as *avoidance, denial,* and *regression.* Of the last he writes: "Regression to dependence, and identification through emulation . . . are socially integrative, obviating the isolation of feelings of shame."[13] For, as Laing says, "shame, rather than guilt, appears to arise when a person finds himself condemned to an identity as the complement of another he wishes to repudiate, but cannot."[14] Yet acceptance of this regression also conflicts with the larger situation of pseudomutuality imposed by the "nominally egalitarian" dominant culture. In this way Laing's "conjunction of identity-for-others and identity-for-self"[15] becomes impossible; the dominated, as Memmi says, "almost never succeeds in corresponding with himself."[16]

The dominated is therefore left with *avoidance* or *denial,* in which there is a turning in upon the self, an attempt to live by identity-for-self alone. But this is not satisfactory either. "The subordinates," as Batteau notes, "are bonded to the very system that they . . . find oppressive";[17] for the result is still "an investment of emotional energy upward, toward the superior, rather than horizontally toward one's peers."[18] As such, *denial* only strengthens the imposed identity-for-others—it does not abolish it but only inverts it. Batteau further observes that "a mulish or hostile rejection is a subjective denial of another's superiority; [but] the other individual will see such behavior as proof of childish stubbornness."[19] As Laing puts it, "the more un-

tenable a situation is, the more difficult it is to get out of it."[20] The subject, then, is left with *avoidance;* and since for most people nowadays
this is physically impossible, it takes the form of an internal, mental
avoidance which coexists with the outward rejection/dependency
system.

Similarly, one of Laing's patients "felt that in every way that
mattered others were more 'large scale' than he was," while "in practice he was not easily overawed. He used two chief manoeuvres to
preserve security. One was an outward compliance with the other. . . .
The second was an inner intellectual Medusa's head he turned on the
other. . . . Both techniques together were designed to avoid the dan-
gers of being engulfed or depersonalized."[21] This man described himself as "only a cork floating on the ocean";[22] thus "he forestalled the
danger to which he was perpetually subject, that of becoming someone else's *thing,* by pretending to be no more than a cork. (After all,
what safer thing to be in an ocean?)."[23] What safer thing to be than a
cork in the ocean? Or an apple on the flood? At least an apple on the
flood is in little danger of being eaten. But it is still an inanimate *thing,*
unable to do anything active on its own behalf. This person's means of
self-defense had left him in a state where "he felt he had no weight,
no substance."[24]

Thus, without confirmation of their being from the other, and
without any consistent way of obtaining such confirmation, the dominated turn in upon themselves. But this process is self-defeating. The
individual, or the culture, self-reduced to an apple on the flood, has
reduced the *feeling* of dependency while in fact becoming totally subject to the other's will.

Furthermore, one's own sense of self, deprived of outside confirmation, begins to wither. Giving up hope of confirmation of one's
being from others involves giving up an important part of one's own
sense of self. Rogin observes, concerning the Indian removals, that
when "individuals lose social support for their own personal experience of reality"[25]—when identity-for-others does not support identity-
for-self—infantilization is the result. And how does this infantilization take place? We come full circle as Laing elucidates the matter in
the passage I invoked at the beginning of this chapter: "If the whole of
the individual's being cannot be defended"—including, here, that part
of one's being which is located in others—"the individual contracts his
lines of defence until he withdraws to a central citadel. . . . But the
tragic paradox is that the more the self is defended in this way, the
more it is destroyed."[26]

Other close correspondences among these conditions of oppression abound, ramifying into the works of other students of modern domination in its various spheres and dimensions. For the person with impaired selfhood, says Laing, "the polarity is between complete isolation or complete merging of identity rather than between separateness and relatedness." [27] Just so, for Memmi's colonized, "the only possible alternatives . . . are assimilation or petrifaction." [28] To ward off these feelings of engulfment, the dominated individual tries to depersonalize the dominator, to see the latter as a mechanical producer of behavior. But in the process, the dominated inescapably does the same to himself. Laing, again, describes the ironic result: "To forgo one's autonomy becomes the means of secretly safeguarding it; to play possum, to feign death, becomes a means of preserving one's aliveness. . . . To turn oneself into a stone becomes a way of not being turned into a stone by someone else. . . . To be stony hard and thus far dead forestalls the danger of being turned into a dead thing by another person." [29] The dominated petrifies the other with an "intellectual Medusa's head," but succeeds only in becoming "a cork floating in the ocean," an apple on the flood.

For, as one retreats into a supposed "inner self" defined by its freedom from the other's presence, one's real self splits into an outer false-self system—accurately characterized by Batteau as "artificial and detached from one's true self" [30]—and a sharply set-off and bounded "inner self" which is quite different from a truly *centered* selfhood. Centrality is or should be a way of expressing totality, or a position from which the whole may be seen and grasped; the retreat into the "inner self" is dangerous (though sometimes necessary) precisely because, taken as an end in itself, it refuses to grasp and, eventually, to see that totality. By objectifying the "external" qualities, the *essences*, and drawing a sharp line between these and "inner" *existence*, the subject succeeds only in treating them as two things on the same level, distinguished merely by the boundary—succeeds only in dragging existence down to the level of essences, of qualities, and hence making it all the more vulnerable.

Thus, in Laing's words, "the self's isolation is . . . its effort to preserve itself in the absence of an assured sense of autonomy and integrity," [31] but this defense "tends to perpetuate and potentiate the original threatening quality of reality." [32] The inner self splits off from the false-self system; autonomy becomes autotomy, a heritage becomes a hermitage, and "existential gangrene" and "encystment" develop. "For without the inner the outer loses its meaning," says Laing, "and without the outer the inner loses its substance." [33] The sense of being-in-the-world is attenuated; as Memmi says, "even the present is cut off and abstract." [34] The boundary must be defended more and more desperately as what is inside it suffocates; hence what Memmi calls the "hollow rigidity" [35] of the colonized's institutions. Or to change situations and metaphors a bit, one Appalachian migrant put it this way: "The feller who loses his roots has got to grow claws to hang on." [36] The rigidity of the mountaineer or migrant is the rigidity of someone who is holding on for dear life, and what he is holding onto is his own dear life. [37]

Nor is it only the poor or the "colonized" who today find themselves hanging on for dear life. Batteau, following Robert Merton's description of the "bureaucratic personality," describes three defenses against shame and inadequacy: "By maintaining certain boundaries of privacy one can always retreat if the competition becomes too intense. . . . By depersonalizing relationships, one maintains a similar sphere of privacy, guarding against the overexposure of emotions and weaknesses. By role-playing and overconformity one arrives at an identity closure that, however artificial and detached from one's true self, can ward off shame." [38] These mechanisms, which Batteau calls "normative in modern societies," [39] correspond precisely to defenses against the three fears which Laing describes as characterizing the person insecure in his own being: engulfment, petrification/depersonalization, and implosion. [40]

These defenses are "normative in modern societies" because the dominator, too, is a victim of the system which produces the domination. As Laing, following Fanon, notes: "The colonists not only mystify the natives, . . . they have to mystify themselves." [41] For Appalachia itself, native scholars have noted that "members of the ruling class are no less impotent as a result of their own prowess at reification." [42] And for either class, these mechanisms are self-defeating.

What I have just said needs to be expanded upon. As it stands, some might take it as an apology for ruling-class behavior—"Ah, well, aren't we all human?" But it is just the opposite. My point is to refute the "culture-of-poverty" model by which patronizing elitists have blamed so many victims. The key, again, is Batteau's statement that these processes are "normative in modern societies." That fact is demonstrated by the extensive parallels I have drawn with Laing, who writes of the experience of the sort of people who consult private psychotherapists, not of the poor in the hollows or the ghettoes.

Yes, many poor mountain people behave in ways that are self-defeating and self-perpetuating. A "culture-of-poverty" explanation is inevitable—*if* we start with a "trait"-hunting model of culture and a "development" model of economics. Instead, it is all-important to realize that these "neuroses" of the poor are *essentially the same as those of the ruling class*—that they are the same distorted structures of meaning expressed in different surface "traits" according to the person's situation—and that, like poverty itself, *they are the result of "modernization" and "assimilation," not of "backwardness" and "isolation."* They are not some "subcultural" aberration but an integral part of a whole society whose behavior on *every* social level is frequently self-defeating and self-perpetuating. In short, they are not the result (much less the cause) of "poverty" but *the result of modernity in the conditions of poverty.* They are products—or rather, integral parts—of modernity in general, just as the army of the poor is an integral part of industrialism, and just as the "underdeveloped" periphery is an integral part of a "developed" economy. A single underlying reality manifests itself in different self-defeating "traits" among the powerful and the powerless—and that reality is the economics of industrialism and its cause/effect, the mentality of modernity. The "problem" of Appalachia is not what one professional modernizer has called "alienation produced by dysfunctions in the socioeconomic structure,"[43] but *that alienation which is produced by the socioeconomic structure in its "normal" and "necessary" functioning.*

Hence trying to eliminate these "traits" by acculturation or "adjustment" is self-defeating. The basic mental patterns underlying these "traits" are self-perpetuating *because* they are shared and reinforced by the whole society. That society, as Batteau says, "has . . . produced poverty at its periphery and alienation at its center,"[44] while, in individuals, it has produced affective poverty at the boundary with others and spiritual alienation in the inner heart. Here, in the center of modern society, lie the real "roots of futility"[45] in dealing with the "disadvantaged." The real futility lies in attempts "to guide the mountain man toward" a "wholeness" *which is not there in the larger society.* Attempts to "solve" the psychological "problems" of the poor are futile if they are made in isolation, on the one hand, from the other "problems"—the whole situation—of the poor; and, on the other hand, in isolation from the psychological "problems" of the non-poor. And the common basis of both sets of "problems" is the "problem" of modernity in general. These "problems" will never be eliminated un-

til and unless fundamental changes are made in our world as a whole.
Until then, dominator and dominated alike will simply "rearrange the
terms" [46] of their common dilemmas.

Of the self-defeating mechanisms we have explored, Batteau
mainly discusses dependency, and then primarily as a means of dealing with shame. But, as we have seen, Laing and Memmi deal more
directly with the other mechanisms—denial and avoidance. I have
found this approach most fruitful in applying this nexus of ideas to
Appalachia. Furthermore, I have tried to deal with these mechanisms,
not on the social level where shame arises, but on the level of personal
identity, and of the kinds of assaults on it that cause shame among
other things. Let me, then, proceed to specifics in applying these concepts to modern Appalachian reality.

In the Appalachian case, denial and avoidance show themselves
in the mountaineer's notorious "paranoia" and "refusal to adapt."
These "traits" are familiar to anyone who has worked with Appalachians, known Appalachians—or, like the author, is one. They have
been discussed *ad nauseam* as "culture-of-poverty" traits; but it is important to realize that, like other such "traits," (1) they are partly in
the eye of the beholder; (2) insofar as they exist, they are adaptations
to a real situation; and (3) that situation is not "poverty" as some
aberrant phenomenon, but the modern world in general in one of its
integral aspects.

Are mountain people really "paranoid," then, or do they simply
show justifiable offense at unconscious insult, and ingrained suspicion at smooth talk which has so often led to exploitation and abandonment, whether by agents of the captains of industry or by "agents
of social change"? Lewis, Kobak, and Johnson note that "early visitors
[to the mountains]—including industrialists, missionaries, and tour-
ists—found great hospitality, open goodwill, as well as the begin-
nings of cautious suspicion. The mountain people learned to dis-
trust." [47] As for more modern instances, we can do no better than
quote one of Robert Coles' mountaineer interlocutors:

> As I see it, up there in the hollow it's real bad. . . . But there's plenty
> they just don't want to lose, an awful lot of plenty, I'll tell you. People
> come in here and they don't know that. I heard on the TV a man saying
> we're supposed to be suspicious up in the mountains, and we don't
> trust no one, except ourselves. What a lot of hooey he had in his mouth,
> saying that. Sure we're not going to like someone if he comes in here

and tells us we're a bunch of damn fools, and we should do this and that and everything they want us, and then we'll be all right. . . .

We need to change the whole thing around, so that there's work here for the people, and they bring home a good wage. And when that happens, if that day ever comes, then I'll tell you no one's going to find us being "suspicious" like they said, and hard to talk with, and all that. A hunter, he develops a good nose, just like the dogs here. If a man has a good nose he can smell trouble a long way off, but he can smell something good, too. It's as simple as that, if you ask me. Sure we're afraid of them all coming here; we can smell the trouble before it gets to the first hill in Kentucky—or over in West Virginia. But if they came to us and wanted to bring in some work here, and it didn't mean tearing up the whole county, and it didn't mean eating up our lungs, then we'd be just like any American—glad to have a job, you bet your life. We'd want to sit here and be ourselves, of course. We wouldn't want to act like some of the people you see on television. We wouldn't want to dress as they do, and talk as they do, no matter how much money we made. We'd want to live as we do. But we'd be working, and that would sure be a welcome change hereabouts.[48]

Well, maybe it's not *quite* as simple as that; but this man from my mother's torn-up home county puts his finger unerringly on the problem. We note especially that for him, under decent conditions of life and of human respect, the alternative to isolation is not assimilation but relatedness. Being "just like any American" has a particular, restricted sense for him. "We'd want to live as we do." The all-or-nothing dilemma does not exist for him because he is not innerly divided—his selfhood is intact. He is not paranoid, but he understands "suspicion" as a rational response to conditions. Another such response is noted by a native scholar-activist:

What on the surface may strike Jack Weller . . . as ignorance, that keeps people from taking polio shots even when they are offered free transportation,[49] may, in fact, be better explained by Frantz Fanon, a physician himself, who argues (in *The Wretched of the Earth*) that the Algerians resisted "modern medical techniques" as long as the French were in control of them but adopted the new techniques immediately when they felt themselves to be in control. I have seen parents who had refused to have their children vaccinated at the public health clinic willingly have them vaccinated when it was "our" medical students who were giving the shots.[50]

When native mountaineers give the shots—and call the shots—a great many problems disappear.

So then, as for my first point, mountaineers' "paranoia" is at least partly in the eye of the beholder. And what about "lack of adaptability"? Do mountaineers really refuse to adapt? Do they really wall themselves inside a shell of "provincialism" or "isolation"? On the contrary, mountain people are a nation of adapters—as well they might be; as they have needed to be. Why, then, is the opposite impression so widespread?

In the first place, mountaineers have not always adapted in the *ways* expected by their would-be benefactors. But this is because, once more, a culture is not a bagful of "traits" but a matter of Laing's *"fundamental structures of experience."* Faced with the same events, different people *experience* them in different ways—they fit them into different structures with different interrelations of parts. Hence they respond to these different experiences with different "adaptations."[51] As Bob Snyder says, "Appalachia is not isolated nor parochial; what distinguishes its people is the conclusions they reach after they have travelled around."[52] He and I can both vouch personally for the truth of this statement.

But of course, there is a limit to anyone's "adaptability." Given what I have just said, a would-be benefactor who expects "adaptability" to result inevitably in the disappearance of "deviant traits" will inevitably be disappointed. And when these alleged benefactors therefore consistently refuse to recognize one's constant and painful efforts at adaptation for what they are—when they persist, indeed, in labeling these as the opposite—then of course one may give up in disgust and decide to save one's energy by retreating into real isolation and provincialism, with all the self-defeating results I have already described.

My first point thus merges with my second and third, since outsiders' illusory perceptions of mountaineers' "lack of adaptability" and the like can become a self-fulfilling prophecy by creating (or refusing to recognize) actual conditions that foster such "traits." Thus a native organizer told Coles:

> You shift the burden from the society as a whole and from you as an activist over to the people you're concerned with. . . . It's their backwardness and suspiciousness and parochialism and resistance to change and rigid adherence to an outmoded kinship structure, and it's their isolation and their refusal to accommodate themselves to a technological society. . . .
> The truth is that the people in this region have tried *everything*. They fought their way out here and adjusted themselves to that. When

businessmen came in here and tried to develop the region, use its timber and coal, they adjusted to that. In fact, they adjusted to the most advanced kinds of technology. . . . The people up the hollows even adjusted to the "war on poverty." . . . And of course the whole thing turned out to be one more bitter disappointment.[53]

Coles comments: "Who, then, is to say that such people are 'suspicious' or 'doubtful' or 'egocentric' or 'depressed' or 'now-oriented,' and all the other things they are called? Why don't we simply summarize the problem and call them 'realistic,' which means smart about the world, plain and simple smart about *their* world?"[54]

But of course such attitudes do tend to become fixed habits of perception. When one gives up on "adaptability," the only "realistic" alternative *is* isolation and provincialism, with all their self-defeating results. Thus "paranoia" and "lack of adaptability" *do* exist in Appalachia, but not as unexplainable aberrations. As for paranoia, consider for example what happened in September 1967, when a film crew observing "poverty" in Letcher County, Kentucky, was confronted by an irate landowner, Hobart Ison. Ison advanced, brandishing and firing his pistol and repeatedly shouting, "Get off my property!" But since he was not behaving "rationally," he was not taken seriously; the crew assumed he was firing blanks. They started to leave, but they were not moving fast enough for Ison. He drew a bead on the crew's leader, Hugh O'Connor, and shot him in the chest, killing him.[55]

At Ison's trial, the prosecution argued for their client's sanity on the ground that "paranoid coloring" was normal for his culture.[56] "Well, you know, us hillbillies is a queer breed," remarked the Harlan County court clerk, ". . . and I'm just as proud as punch to be one."[57] Ison does seem to have been an unusually "eccentric, mean-spirited"[58] person; but "for present purposes," as Laing says, "it is much more important to recognize the sense in which such 'delusions' are true than to see them as absurd."[59] Laing elsewhere calls paranoid delusions "partially achieved derealization-realizations,"[60] that is, incompletely integrated recognitions that one is being treated as an object. Thus it can hardly be ignored that Ison had shot the leader of a film crew which had come on his land without permission, attracted by "the appalling poverty of his tenants":[61]

Theodore Holcomb, the associate producer of the film, was particularly struck by the looks of a miner, still in work clothes and still covered with coal dust, sitting in a rocking chair on one of the porches. "He was just sitting there scratching his arm in a listless way," Holcomb said later. "He had an expression of total despair. [What about total fatigue?] It was an extraordinary shot—so evocative of the despair of the region."[62] [Once more, what about fatigue?]

The pattern of invasion, objectification, and false categorization is clear; and we see the truth of what Laing says, after Lemert—that "much more often than is generally supposed there is some sort of conspiracy around people who feel conspired against."[63] It is notable that the courts found it impossible to try Ison in his own county, due to "the overwhelming sentiment . . . that the defendant did right."[64]

Of course Ison did not do right, but his actions are understandable in a sense which does not explain them away. Personal circumstances had made his life into an exaggerated expression of a theme, but in his environment the theme was, and is, universal. Ison was the antennae of his society. His boundaries had been invaded, the boundaries of his land as an extension of his self, and the permission of "his" renters was irrelevant to him, as their relation to the land did not entitle them to give it.[65] He saw his land being used as an object, and not only that, but appropriated for use as a negative image. His reaction of anger was indeed normal, and he simply took it further than an entirely "normal" person would.

Nevertheless, some psychology in its function as a tool of control would deny the validity of the anger itself. A survivor of the Buffalo Creek disaster of 1972 remarked of the coal company whose negligence had precipitated it: "I have a deep-seated resentment against Pittston which probably isn't normal, but I just cannot help it. . . . This is probably the wrong way to feel, but I just cannot help it."[66] The speaker of these words had clearly absorbed some "enlightened" popular psychology; Laing describes the same phenomenon again and again as the "gamesmanship"[67] which much standard psychology imposes in order to invalidate people's own feelings and perceptions.

And as for "lack of adaptability," I was the victim of such "gamesmanship" myself on that score from a graduate-school housemate of mine, a counseling major from the Northeast, who berated me constantly for that "trait." His alarm extended not only to my musical tastes and my occasional pre-Johnsonian syntax, but even to the size of my breakfast. I would look up from my heaping bowl of cereal, over his own half-full one, and meet his pitying gaze: "But Rodger, look at *mine!*" he would counsel. The extent of his own adaptability was measured by his refusal to allow me to mention in his presence the name of an acquaintance who drove about those southern Indiana hills in a pickup truck. This, I was assured, was "a typical anti-Semitic trait." Life was increasingly unpleasant for both of us during those six months. But the reader will already see what neither of us very young men did at the time: that my housemate was suffering an intense identity crisis of his own, that he was dealing with it by projection, and that I was doing neither of us any good by indignantly expecting this northeastern liberal "helping professional" to be perfectly secure in his own being in the face of what I now see as the underlying structures of modernity.

But the best exploration of this theme that I know of is found in fiction. In Harriette Arnow's *The Dollmaker*, East Kentuckian Gertie Nevels, living in wartime Detroit, has a conference with her son's teacher over a poor grade in conduct. Gertie defends Reuben, but:

> "I see no point in carrying this discussion further. He will have to adjust."
>
> "Adjust?" Gertie strode ahead, turned and looked at the woman.
>
> "Yes," Mrs. Whittle said, walking past her. "That is the most important thing, to learn to live with others, to get along, to adapt one's self to one's surroundings."
>
> "You teach them that here?" Gertie asked in a low voice, looking about the dark, ugly hall.
>
> "Of course. It is for children—especially children like yours—the most important thing—to learn to adjust."
>
> "You mean," Gertie asked—she was pulling her knuckle joints now—that you're a teachen my youngens so's that, no matter what comes, they—they can live with it."
>
> Mrs. Whittle nodded. "Of course."
>
> Gertie cracked a knuckle joint. "You mean that when they're through here, they could—if they went to Germany—start gitten along with Hitler, er if they went to—Russia, they'd git along there, they'd act like th Russians an be"—Mr. Daly's word was slow in coming—"communists—an if they went to Rome they'd start worshipen th pope?"
>
> "How dare you?" Mrs. Whittle was shrill. "How dare you twist my words so, and refer to a religion on the same plane as communism? How dare you?"
>
> "I was just asken about adjustments," Gertie said, the words coming more easily, "an what it means."
>
> "You know perfectly well I mean no such thing." Mrs. Whittle bit her freshly lipsticked lips. "The trouble is," she went on, "you don't want to adjust—and Reuben doesn't either."
>
> "That's part way right," Gertie said, moving past her to the stairs. "But he cain't hep the way he's made. It's a lot more trouble to roll out steel—an make it like you want it—than it is biscuit dough."[68]

Fine words; I wish I had known them to show my housemate. But human flesh is neither steel nor dough. Withdrawing to Laing's inner citadel, becoming Memmi's stony-hard cyst, turning oneself into steel, is certainly a description of a common type of "adjustment" to mountain and migrant life. The Appalachian people was formed in the beginning of a process of penetration into the literal stony-hard citadels of the mountains—a process of dropping out of "civilization's" sight altogether, of becoming a nothing in the latter's sight in order to remain, and become, something in its own sight. And faced with all-or-nothing choice between total isolation and total engulfing absorption, mountain culture has often chosen isolation, and hence perhaps chosen a slow death by suffocation over a quick one by drowning. For the ironic fact is that this process is simply another version of the one by which the outside observer forms a fixed sentimental image of the dominated culture, whether the former laments its passing or desires to see it preserved in every "colorful" detail. By this self-objectification, embattled mountaineers simply set their own "traits" against their own selfhood, become their own contemporary ancestors. In resisting evil rather than striving to overcome it with good, the dominated simply fall into treating themselves in a disguised form of the evil's own terms. The result, in Fanon's words, is "a hard core of culture which is becoming more and more shrivelled up, inert and empty . . . rigid in the extreme, or rather . . . the dregs of culture, its mineral strata."[69]

Thus it is that, in defending this stony-hard citadel, mountaineers and their forebears have defended many a cause not only lost but, looked at solely on its merits, well-lost, from the Scottish Covenant to the Kanawha County, West Virginia, textbook protest. The latter, however, offers a particularly clear example of the dialectic which keeps this self-defeating process in motion. The clash of meanings in that situation has been well explored in several aspects.[70] We may note, for example, that a pivotal incident in it occurred when the county hired, to represent it against the protesters, a legal firm which was accustomed to defending coal operators against the UMW. It was because of this sort of thing that class and cultural boundaries were sharply and irrevocably drawn and the protest entered its disruptive stage. But the "national" media generally ignored such key facts, preferring for example to give free publicity to the handful of Klansmen who showed up at some of the demonstrations in full regalia, doubtless in the sure knowledge that all cameras would turn in their direction. (This process of seizing on fringe aspects of a situation and labeling them as central in an imposed system is familiar to any intelligent viewer of the evening news. It corresponds in individual life to what Laing, following Ruesch, calls "tangential response."[71]) This was the only way in which "mainstream" America and its media could grasp the behavior of their "contemporary ancestors," whose system of meanings they had engulfed in their own and whose actions must therefore be recoded to fit that system—who, in this case, must be assigned motives expressing the shadowy, rejected side of "America's" own psyche. And as these motives and this identity were continually forced on the protesters, some of them seem to have taken it up, so that their most visible actions tended to become dominated by outsiders with racist connections. (Groups like the Klan thus benefit from the assumptions of media liberalism in much the same way that Leninist groups in the Third World benefit from the assumptions of the U.S. government.) Hence an attempt at isolation turned, in a backhanded way, into a particularly ugly form of engulfment by the dominant society's values—its avowedly rejected values, but still *its* values.

It will thus be seen, once again, that I do not attribute pathology to Appalachians in general, much less characterize Appalachian culture in general (whatever that is) as a "pathological" one in the sense of some "syndrome" forming part of a "culture of poverty." Rather, the phenomena I have discussed are the forms that the natural strivings of being-in-the-world, to maintain and enlarge that being, take in conditions hostile to authentic existence. Further, if there is any "pathology," then it is also—and indeed primarily—that of the wider modernized culture, a culture notoriously hostile to authentic existence and increasingly hostile to existence in general. That culture's dominant class shares all the disease's essential features, with different manifestations which are appropriate to its own situation. And finally, this "pathology" is not universal to all persons, nor—especially, and most importantly—is it totally prevalent over those of the dominated culture who are caught in it. Authentic being still exists for those who "know [their] own story," who "remember who [they] are."[72]

These phrases might be taken in a variety of senses, both individual and collective, and all of them true. In the context from which I have cited them, a study of Appalachian migrants, they refer to a sense of group and regional identity. And I believe that such a sense can be an important part of the process of self-recovery. Nevertheless, a sense of separate "ethnic" identity can also express itself in self-defeating terms, becoming trapped in the terms of the problem. Consciousness of identity, which is one step on the road "from self-consciousness to self-possession,"[73] can be rested in for its own sake, and become a fixed image of itself, reified, its own Blakean Spectre. Laing notes: "An 'identity' sometimes becomes an 'object' that a person feels he has lost, and starts to search for. Many primitive phantasies are attached to identity and 'its' objectification and reification. The frequently described modern search for 'identity' becomes another phantasy scenario."[74] This process on the individual plane is analogous to (and accompanies) commoditization on the economic plane.[75] It is an example of that process by which, in Kierkegaard's terms, though "revelation may have already conquered, shut-upness ventures to employ its last expedient and is cunning enough to transform revelation itself into a mystification, and shut-upness has won."[76]

Thus Appalachian scholars, and others interested in regional consciousness, must deal with the paradoxes generated by self-defense mechanisms in situations of domination and impaired identity. Chapman notes about another case: "The nervousness about self-identity which characterizes so much Scottish art, at least in the twentieth century, is evidence of the lack of a confident and robust identity as much as it is a means of producing it."[77] If identity were fully secure it would not need to be thus objectivized. Donald Macaulay, too, writes with respect to his own culture:

> Members of a cultural minority have many things to guard against. These things, it would appear, are not always obvious. They may, on the one hand, give up and resign themselves to be taken over. On the other hand they may institutionalise and become assertive in their parochialism, seeing this as their only defence against the continual pressure exerted by the majority, and failing to recognise that this alternative is itself culturally destructive and constitutes one of the pressures they must resist.[78]

Here we see all the features of the process which Laing and Memmi explore in other spheres. What Batteau calls the "artificial closure of identity"[79] once more creates a boundary which, beginning as a defense, becomes a suffocation.

Hence we find those, in Appalachian and other contexts, who combine an uncritical acceptance of the "positive" aspects of such a fixed image with a paranoid boundary-rigidity against all "outsiders" and their attempts to help. Lewis, Kobak, and Johnson call this "a form of defensive racism" in which "the burden of understanding is placed not upon the Appalachian but upon the good shepherd in wolf's clothing who desires to 'help' mountain people."[80] This is of course where the burden belongs; and yet, as the authors note, "this can lead to . . . becoming oversensitive to criticism, more negative, more unchanging and traditional in approach to problems."[81] Such persons—whether rural family members, as in this case, or academics—do not realize that accepting the positive stereotype is tantamount to acquiescing in the objectivized condition, just as is accepting the negative one. Thus the undermining of selfhood persists, and the subject defends against it by projecting onto the outsider the negative aspect of that subject's own self-image. This projection, though, robs the "outsider" of a center as well, denying the latter's selfhood. For in this state, as Laing observes, "the very act of experiencing the other as a person is felt as virtually suicidal."[82] Such a process denies many real possibilities of creative response to change. For as Fanon said, "the consciousness of self is not the closing of a door to communication. Philosophical thought teaches us, on the contrary, that it is its guarantee. National consciousness, which is not nationalism, is the only thing that will give us an international dimension"[83]—just as individual consciousness, which is not individualism, is the only thing that gives us relatedness with other individuals.

Malcolm Chapman, discussing the process by which mainstream British culture sets up itself and Gaelic culture in a set of oppositions and thus implicitly compartmentalizes the latter, notes:

> We are faced with an intellectual structure whose capacities for gathering and ordering reality, and for generating internal coherence, are convincingly real. . . . It is an artefact of the "near bewitching self-verification" . . . of this system that any critique of it appears inevitably like the espousal of one or other of its permissible polarisations. If, therefore, we seem to be questioning the communal beauty of Gaelic life our vision immediately becomes the harsh gaze of rationalist utility. If, on the other hand, we deny to science the capacity to encapsulate, englobe, or invade Gaelic folk-life, then we appear to be advocating a retreat into the meaningful womb of the alternative society.[84]

It is indeed difficult to write about the Scottish Highlands, the Southern Highlands, or any analogous area without not only seeming to endorse one or the other pole of the dichotomy, but talking oneself into endorsing or concealing it. Inverting an oppressive system is not the same as overturning it. In Fanon's words, "it is always easier to proclaim rejection than actually to reject."[85] Have I fallen into this trap? Specifically, have I committed the error I have just been attacking? Have I slid toward the "romantic" side of the opposition; have I criticized negative stereotypes only in the name of the positive ones, and have I, consequently, tended to advocate or approve a "small-is-beautiful" romanticism which hinders effective action against concrete oppression? Further, have I tended toward that nationalism which Batteau criticizes justly and accurately (if not grammatically) as "an artificial closure of identity, a rigid and reflexive distinction between 'we' and 'they'"?[86] And finally, as a corollary to all these, have I indulged in an outdated rhetoric of anti-American and anti-Western simplicities?

Such questions have occurred to me, and they may have occurred to some readers. But in the first place, I do not believe that a desire for human scale in society is inherently "romantic" or "primitivist." Chapman goes on from the above statement to say that his "examination of the imagery by which the virtues of Gaelic society are expressed is not in any simple sense a denial of those virtues. At the same time, I think that there is a great deal more to be said."[87] In this book I have tried to say a bit of that about our own highland society. With regard to Appalachia it is important to realize that what is invalid in the sign-system which Chapman and Batteau criticize is not the individual oppositions taken each by each, but their lining up in a package-deal single opposition which, explicitly or implicitly, leaves the dominant culture in possession of the attributes of power. I indeed believe that technical-instrumental "rationality," especially in its tendency to exclude other modes of being, is a feature of modern societies, and that it represents in that measure a decline in human potentialities; but this is not to exalt a "pre-logical" or "pre-rational" mind. Our ancestors were as rational as people can be, and so are our "contemporary ancestors"; it is the identification of instrumental rationality with reason which is the falsehood embodied in modern domination. Romantic primitivism simply takes that falsehood for granted as true and reverses its value judgments. As Fanon said, "there is no question of a return to Nature. It is simply a very concrete question of not dragging men toward mutilation, of not imposing upon the brain rhythms which very quickly obliterate it and wreck it."[88]

What is necessary, I think, is a transvaluation of the positive features of Appalachian and "folk" life, among others, in the name of a different general conception of humanity—one in which such qualities will not be seen as opposed to and incompatible with their polar alternatives, let alone inferior or doomed. It would be a conception in which, for example, imagination which is not uselessly dreamy would unite with rationality which is not ruthlessly instrumental in that synthesis which is Reason—not a compromise or mixture of the two, but the reality underlying the terms of the dichotomy, of the "cloven fictions." As for "primitivism," my model is Blake, who said, "Where man is not, nature is barren";[89] and who invoked England's green and pleasant land in order to call for a City in it—that is, a world fashioned by conscious human activity—but a City very different from our dark Satanic mills.

Hence, furthermore, I am not idealizing the past, whether Appalachian, "Celtic," Regular Baptist, pagan, or whatnot. On this level, "past" versus "present" is merely one more oppositional term in the discourse which, whether the idealizers of the past realize it or not, assigns non-dominant cultures to oblivion. The "human scale" of past and present nonindustrial societies did not and does not preclude many human inhumanities—social and sexual oppression and all the distortions which mechanical "folk"-solidarity can impose on the human spirit. It is true that many such evils in Appalachian society and its predecessors originate or are strengthened as defensive responses to intrusion and outwardly imposed degradation of various sorts; this study has illustrated that point time and time again. Nevertheless it is still dishonest to conclude that the features we dislike about those cultures are somehow "unreal" or less integral to the cultures than the ones we do like. Such ontological discriminations have meaning, if at all, only on quite different levels.

And yet there is a complex, dialectical connection here. Wholeness is not contained in the past, but the process of losing what we have lost is a part of the process by which modern humanity in general has lost, has abandoned some of its vital potentialities. It is not any idealized original *content* of "Celtic" culture which is the point of decrying the losses that have overtaken "Celtic" nations; similarly it is not any unique "distinctiveness" of Appalachian "folk" culture which is the point of our human problem, but rather the universal human values which have been violated as part of our particular *process* of change. Our goal must be to liberate the potentialities of humanity in general by meeting the universal needs of the human spirit. But one of the universal qualities of the human spirit is particularity; and a group's or an individual's history is part of their whole being in the present.

The strivings which sometimes express themselves in pastoral idealization are not vacuous. They concern potentialities which, if they contrast with the present, pertain not simply to the past but to the timeless, and thus equally to the future. What is needed is not the reconstitution of some "folk culture" but the recovery of human values in the context of the present. But the present is the result of the past, and wholeness in the present involves a proper relation to the past. Of Appalachia it has been said: "Only if remembrance of the past is not appropriated by the dominant culture can it remain a vision in opposition, a weapon in the struggle for a better social order."[90]

Since the past is part of the present, it follows that the liberation we hope and strive for is not a "liberation" from the past into a rootless present. The past is necessary as a springboard for the future; the isolated present is a knife edge too narrow to stand on. (The mountaineer's notorious "present-orientation" is the result, not only of an uncertain future, but of being cut off from the past.)[91] And similarly, since particularity is a part of wholeness, this liberation is not one from "particularism" into simple "universalism"; the mirage of a single ideal "universal" culture is not the triumph of reason but the airiest of all mystifications.

Thus this particularism does not add up to an exclusivist nationalism. And yet there is, to be sure, a real problem here which must not be minimized. Helen Lewis, comparing Wales and Appalachia, provides a synopsis of the pertinent questions:

> Is class consciousness more progressive than regional consciousness? Can regional or ethnic consciousness, which grows out of experiences of exploitation, lead to an analysis of the reasons for the exploitation and inequality and reach the same point as that reached in class analysis? Can class consciousness emerge but fail to take the analysis to the root cause of the inequities? Can class consciousness and regional consciousness together develop an analysis and conceptualization which locates the source of power in society and provide a means of joining together workers and community? Can both be co-opted so that people only see equal distribution of the same pie?
> . . . It is hard for the poor of South America to believe there are poor in the U.S. or unemployed from the factories which have migrated to their country. Does regional pride lead necessarily to a sense of regional uniqueness which prevents the development of a sense of community with other exploited in other regions?[92]

Of the questions in the first paragraph, the expressions of fear are, ruefully, as true as those of hope. And Lewis' remark about the poor of South America is sharply confirmed in my experience by a conversation I had with a young co-worker in San Diego, a citizen and resident of Mexico ten miles away. During breaks from my showing him how to operate the baling machine, we engaged in the California pastime of comparing notes on our native regions. When I told him that I came from a poor area, he asked with surprise: "*¿Hay americanos pobres?*" And when I described for him some of the conditions I had grown up seeing—the trailer-filled hillsides, the tar-paper shacks, a grade-school classmate who had vomited an enormous roundworm ("*La llamamos la solitaria*")—he shook his head and said quietly: "*Es muy difícil creer.*" Then, as often, I was tempted to echo Mother Jones: "When I get to the other side, I shall tell God Almighty about West Virginia."[93]

Appalachia has suffered from this kind of naïveté not only in its own spokesmen but in those of other groups, without the excuses of youth or unfamiliarity with this country, who somehow cannot see the problems of "Anglo-Saxon Protestants" as real. And as for failure to develop community with other exploited, an especially lamentable and instructive example of this was played out during the confusion and decadence of the early and mid-seventies, when Appalachian white Protestants who thought in regional terms and northeastern white Catholics who thought in "ethnic" terms sometimes tangled with each other amid mutual accusations of belonging to the "Establishment."

If the negative potentialities are there, however, so are the positive. One may be permitted skepticism at the assumption (if I read Lewis correctly) that regional and other analyses are to be judged by how closely they "reach the same point as that reached in" an already formed class (political-economy) analysis. To me, at any rate, regional analysis and class analysis are not mutually exclusive but mutually supporting in intersecting dimensions, and it is possible for regional and class consciousness to join in mutual support, just as the forms of oppression are mutually supporting, are metaphors of one another. The key to success is to refuse either to ignore any of the forms of oppression or to try to reduce all of them to simple transformations of one.[94]

Of these oversimplified approaches, though, exclusive nationalism is certainly one of the most incoherent and self-defeating. As it is false to see the positive features of a culture as "real" and the negative ones as unreal, just so it is false to see the positive features as the "native" ones and the negative ones as "impositions." It has often been pointed out, and this book has explored the fact again, that

many of the negative features of Appalachian culture and its predecessors are in fact responses to intrusion and oppression; but response to oppression is itself a positive phenomenon. At any rate, to
take the fact that negative "traits" may be self-defeating responses to
intrusion—or simply the best that may be made of a bad situation—
and jump from there to identifying these "traits" as "imported" from
a corrupt outside world into a pre-existing ideal society, is to commit a
category error of the first magnitude. This sort of nationalism assumes
the dichotomy which it ought to criticize at that dichotomy's root.

And at any rate, there is no uniform "America" to set alongside
"Appalachia." Not only is "mainstream" America itself only a fraction
of America as a whole, but as commonly spoken of by its critics (including myself), it is not wholly identifiable with the *actuality* of any
region, class, ethnic group, or intersection of these. (It is certainly not
identifiable with the Northeast, or New York/New Jersey, as some Appalachians seem to think. People from those areas, indeed, tend to
locate "America" somewhere "out here," and often try to approximate
it in their own way—sometimes, as in the case of some "neoconser-
vatives," with grotesque results.) Here we may avail ourselves once
more of the Scottish analogy. Malcolm Chapman writes:

> It might seem obvious . . . that if the populace of Edinburgh can find
> it in their sophisticated and urbane hearts to despise the Highlander for
> his rusticity and barbarity, then the population of London, that much
> bigger, more sophisticated, more urbane and more southerly, must de-
> spise him that much more. This extension is not, however, entirely
> justified. . . .
>
> If the aspirant to social status in the Highlands chooses to ape
> Lowland ways and despise his own, then a contemporary understand-
> ing of such activity is to be found in the Highlands, and not in the
> Home Counties. If the Scottish Lowlanders, particularly the articulate
> middle class, choose to use "English" manners and modes of expres-
> sion in order to establish a social primacy, or to distance themselves
> from the Highlander or the rustic Scot, this is not in any simple sense
> the fault of the English. The "Englishman" of Scottish resentment is in
> many respects the product of a purely internal dialogue—a product
> that it is a convenient falsity to locate elsewhere. It is a common Scottish
> Nationalist jibe [sic] that the English view Scotland as a mere "Scot-
> shire", an unimportant northern county. We can, I think, with both
> justice and gravity, turn the resentment around, and point out that Eng-
> land is not merely a southerly extension of the Lowlands of Scotland,
> however much it might seem to be so from Inverness.[95]

As we have seen, this was as true eight hundred years ago as it is today. And as for analogies across space as well as time, I can do no better than to repeat Chapman's statement with the names changed:

> It might seem obvious that if the populace of Cincinnati can find it in their sophisticated and urbane hearts to despise the Appalachian for his rusticity and barbarity, then the population of New York, that much bigger, more sophisticated, more urbane and more northerly, must despise him that much more. This extension is not, however, entirely justified.
>
> If the aspirant to social status in Appalachia chooses to ape Midwestern ways and despise his own, then a contemporary understanding of such activity is to be found in the mountains, and not in Manhattan. If the Midwesterners, particularly the articulate middle class, choose to use "Northeastern" or Californian manners and modes of expression in order to establish a social primacy, or to distance themselves from the mountaineer or the rustic Midwesterner, this is not in any simple sense the fault of the coasts. The "Yankee" of Southern resentment is in many respects the product of a purely internal dialogue—a product that it is a convenient falsity to locate elsewhere. It is a common Appalachian nationalist gibe that the Yankees view the South as a mere "Sunbelt," an unimportant Southern Rim. We can, I think, with both justice and gravity, turn the resentment around, and point out that New York is not merely a northeasterly outlier of the Cincinnati-Dayton area, however much it might seem to be so from Berea.

If there are a few kinks and overlaps in this translation, the fact only strengthens my point. Like "Appalachia"—indeed, even more so— "America" is a state of mind, an imaginary garden hopping with real toads and grinding with real machines. It is an enslaving illusion for others as much as for Appalachians to take it for "the" reality, whether to emulate or to oppose.

And too, there are other states of mind in, and of, "America" and "the West." Evil is separation; Blake's England became dark and Satanic only when sundered from her consort Albion. The Romans, too, may have thought that *Roma* meant force; but among her inner circle of priests, Rome bore the secret name *Flora*. And America, too, bears a secret name, known not by her priests but to some part of her people, and to some part of each of them; one not spoken but acted.

A defense of Appalachia's particularity is not, then, a nationalistic call for Appalachians to rise up against "America," or to seal themselves off from it. It is rather a call for the liberation of America and the world from the common factors, the mind-forged manacles that hold all in bondage, manifested everywhere in different ways. We must emulate Lewis' Welsh miners, who "easily understand regional discrimination and have a strong regional consciousness, but do not see solutions regionally."[96] The point is that *even regional oppression is not simply a regional problem*. Appalachia's "liberation" will not come without a basic change in America, in the West, and in the world—a change which will liberate the potentialities not only of the oppressed but also of the oppressor, who clings to his form of power as all there is to attain in his version of the world; a change still more needed as both the oppressed and the oppressor are found inside each and all.

7 INCONCLUSION:
The Region of Merlin

Fear & Hope are—Vision.
—Blake, *The Gates of Paradise*

Human beings cannot create what they cannot imagine.
—Steve Fisher

Each Man is in his Spectre's power
Untill the arrival of that hour,
When his Humanity awake
And cast his Spectre into the Lake.
—Blake, *Jerusalem*

In the preceding chapters I have emphasized the negative experiences of the Scotch-Irish and Appalachian peoples to such an extent that I may well be asked, not only what hope there is for Appalachian culture and identity—or for simple humanity—but what there ever could have been that was worth preserving. In spite of my disclaimers, some may think the tale contradicts the teller: what could be the result of the forces I have described except a victimized, demoralized, infantilized "culture of poverty," devoid of all sense of identity and worth? And if these forces are not simply endemic to the poor and oppressed, but rather are pervasive in different forms all through modern society, then what hope is there for any of us?

Such have been the questions of many, but they are not only inadequate but, taken by themselves, radically false. The system of meanings which shapes the experience of this "enduring people" includes life-enhancing values, existence-confirming values, wholeness-creating values, which have prevailed among individuals, families, and groups among mountaineers and their forebears as often as wholeness, existence, and life have been defeated in the larger battles. And often enough have these meanings motivated men and women to strike blows in those greater battles—from the rebels of Galloway eight hundred years ago, to the rent protesters of Ulster, to the myriad struggles of mountain people in our own era. And as the problems of the oppressed are basically those of their larger society, just so endurance, resistance, and life itself have survived among the oppressed in the same way in which they have survived among the "advantaged."

And what way is that? How *has* humanity managed to endure in spite of the forces we have examined? The key to the paradox lies in the word "forces." This essay has concentrated on discussing certain forces because it attempts to treat them from a new perspective. But if one concentrates exclusively on the "external" forces that act on an individual or a culture, then the prospect will inevitably seem hopeless, for the realm of hope lies outside the realm of "forces." Such forces are properly studied by the analytic method, for analysis is the appropriate tool for cutting through the mystifications which bind persons. But analysis belongs inherently to the realm of the bound and not the free, of necessity and not possibility, of discourse and not dialogue, of process and not praxis; and hence, with regard to the self, of the forces working against it and not the fact of its integrity. Analysis can expose the foundations of these forces, but it cannot encompass that which overcomes them. Creativity, like violence, cannot be seen through the sights of positivism. The essences of freedom, integrity, and creativity must be explored by other means, as by art and myth.

Myth is a four-letter word to most social critics, and I myself have shown how myth-patterns can be forced into the mold of power-structures, to which these myth-patterns give strength. The structural patterns of myth, however, must not be confused with the underlying capacity for symbolization, which is the specifically human characteristic. The structural patterns of signs are only the symbols' *exposition*, and this is why they are subject to *imposition*. But the structures most susceptible to imposition by distorting forces of power are precisely those whose symbolic core has been forgotten (as when the mythologems of human wholeness and its ultimate recovery become "scientific socialism"). The mark of a true myth is that it, like a whole human selfhood, contains a core which is subversive of its own distortions. And this fact is nowhere more true than in those myths which deal directly with human wholeness.

Myth and symbol have often been seen as instruments of oppression, and indeed much has been said here about what Chapman calls "symbolic appropriation" and its destructive effects. But when an anthropologist like Chapman uses the word "symbol," he means something different from, and less than, what the word means for the student of myth and symbol as valid human creations. By "symbol" the structural anthropologist really means "sign," something algebraic and definite in meaning, and for this very reason reducible to an element in that set of formal oppositions which constitutes a structural system; while the true mythical symbol, like the natural object it is, is not fully reducible to stataeble meanings and is itself a source of meaning. The sign stands for a thought, while the symbol, in Paul Ricoeur's words, gives rise to thought.[1] Ricoeur explains this difference further:

> One might be astonished that the symbol has two such rigorously inverse uses. Perhaps the reason should be sought in the structure of signification, which is at once a function of absence and a function of presence: a function of absence because to signify is to signify "vacuously," it is to say things without the things, in substituted signs; a function of presence because to signify is to signify "something" and finally the world. Signification, by its very structure, makes possible at the same time both total formalization—that is to say, the reduction of signs to "characters" and finally to elements in a calculus—*and* the restoration of a full language, heavy with implicit intentionalities and analogical references to something else, which it presents enigmatically.[2]

Although here Ricoeur draws no sociopolitical conclusions from this distinction, we may attempt to explore some of these implications. The sign as algebraic "character" is adaptable as an instrument of power and domination precisely because it is a function of absence, of division, reduction, necessity, and *I-it* relationship. But the true symbol is not totally co-optable because it is a function of presence, of unity, wholeness, possibility, and *I-thou* relationship—of that integral meaningfulness which, like the human personality of which it is one of the major functions, is not reducible to its component parts. The mention of algebraic "symbols" brings to mind the structural diagrams of Lévi-Strauss, the grim interlaces of Laing's *Knots*, and especially the equations, so much like "symbolic" logic, appearing in Laing, Phillipson, and Lee's *Interpersonal Perception*. These are disgrams of necessity and fate because they belong to the realm of the symbol degraded to sign, the icon treated as idol, the relation flat-tened to experience. It is precisely because these signs are "neutral," "public," and "transparent" that they can become the total property of the perceiver; the full symbol resists such appropriation by its very opaqueness and irreducibility, which are functions of its origins in the depth of selfhood. The sign is dichotomous, a "cloven fiction," and in Paulo Freire's words, such a dichotomy, "by creating unauthen-tic forms of existence, creates also unauthentic forms of thought, which reinforce the original dichotomy."[3] The symbol is not dichoto-mous but double in meaning, and thus heals dichotomies; it deals in contraries, not negations:

> Negations are not Contraries: Contraries mutually Exist:
> But Negations Exist Not: Exceptions & Objections & Unbeliefs
> Exist not: nor shall they ever be Organised for ever & ever.[4]

The sign sets up opposite meanings as mutually exclusive; the symbol contains mutually existing opposites simultaneously, in creative ten-sion. Or, to use Coleridge's distinction, the sign belongs to the realm of fancy, that "luxuriant fancy" which in Chapman's words "a people or a sex are only allowed . . . if they renounce political effectivity, and vice versa";[5] the symbol belongs to the realm of imagination, the power which unites and creates, and which is necessary for effectivity in the political and many another sphere. The dichotomous sign per-tains to objects, and to people as objects; the symbol is the property of the subject in freedom. Sign-mediated relationships are transac-tional; myth is potentially transexperiential, intersubjective.[6] The ma-nipulation of sign-as-algebraic-character is the precondition of what Freire called "mythicization"; this opprobrious adaptation of the word "myth" stands to the sign as true myth stands to the symbol. It is pre-cisely when this oppressive mythicization is cut away that we can see the liberating power of true myth, which is not a mode of imaginary "explanation" but a tool of real exploration. It is when we have seen through myth as pseudo-history that we can look through myth as symbol. One becomes a "master of the word," in Freire's terms, a namer of reality, precisely within this framework of what the word really is.

Perhaps indeed—the suspicion never quite disappears from any modern "educated" mind—perhaps indeed mythology is a disease of language, and language itself a disease of mind. And perhaps the an-cient Gaels saw this if in fact they worshiped Ogma, the god of words, as the conductor of souls to the underworld,[7] and the cheerful divine smith and builder Goibniu as the bringer of life.[8] But Ogma was a complex god, whose Gaulish equivalent Ogmios appeared to his people under two guises: as an old man leading other men by golden chains running from his tongue to their ears, and as a burly young man with a club, whom the Romans identified with Hercules, and in whose form the Irish Ogma occurs in later literature.[9] The word by which the elders instruct the young—the cultural process, and the cultural network of "collective representations"—is the strength of the people. The myths and representations which give meaning to existence are what have motivated our forebears to demand "that their existence be recognized."[10] As binder of the dead, Ogma is *discourse*, structure as a bond of necessity; as champion of the gods he is *dialogue*, structure as a framework of possibility. He could lead souls successfully through the perils of the state after death because that passage symbolizes the passage of individuals and nations through the state after birth. The poetic tongue by which Ogma teaches and inspires, and the club by which he defends the soul from demons and the people from its enemies, are one and the same instrument.

In particular, myth must be defended against the charge that it is an individualistic distraction from collective struggles in the concrete world. Interest in myth has often enough taken such a form in modern society, but the criticism takes for granted the bourgeois dichotomy between "inner" and "outer" and the implicit lining-up of this dichotomy with the one between "individual" and "society."[11] These dichotomies are neither equivalent nor, in the first place, objectively "given." Personhood itself is not individual, or at any rate is not the same thing as individuality. Indeed, we have seen how, in the dominated situation, the equation of personhood with the isolated "inner" self leads to the destruction of that self. Myth in general, and especially mythologems of personhood, are collective and social, and give life to the search for social solutions—indeed, express the essential content of what those solutions aim at. Myth is not the enemy of reason, only of instrumental rationality. To ask what myth has to do in a positive sense with political action (the word is of course often enough used loosely in a negative sense) is like asking what political analysis has to do with the "simple wisdom of the folk." These are equal and opposite sides of the same false dichotomy, and equally disabling to whole thought and action. Art, rational analysis, myth, political struggle, and so on, are all real activities engaged in by real people, and only in people who are divided and compartmentalized—and to that degree unreal—are they mutually exclusive.

Thus now, as my subject changes from the past to the future, which are characterized by necessity and possibility respectively, I find a shift in tone necessary; for to treat the future with the analytic tools of the past has been the downfall or corruption of all the great historicist ideologies.

The picture I painted of Appalachia in the last chapter was a very gloomy one because I was dealing with the present mainly as a product of the past forces I had explored. I have used the iron tools of analysis to delineate the iron laws of necessity. But in so doing I have told only half the story—even about that past, which was once a living present. Appalachians and their ancestors, like others, have always acted from their wholeness as well as from their partialness, from their freedom as well as from their necessity, from their choices as well as from their chances. As Tom Plaut says, "Appalachian history is full of rebellions and rebels: of men and women who demand, in Camus' terms, that their existence be recognized."[12] Appalachia survives, not only in the sense of cultural "survivals," but in that survival of the spirit which has produced the continuing struggle for justice, respect, and control by people over their own lives. Thus they transcend their limiting circumstances both individually and collectively. As personhood is a dialectic of necessity and possibility, so also is the present, which is the only time-dimension in which personhood can exist. Hence a full discussion of the present—and of hope for the future, which will one day be a present—must incorporate a dialectic between analytic tools of explanation and synthetic tools of exploration. Thus, in order to complete my description of the present—to throw light on our situation not only as a result of a certain past but as a springboard for possible futures—I here offer some applications of myth as it has touched our people in the distant past, and done so in ways which I think still have relevance.

If "myths are . . . to be studied as . . . maturative or pathogenic,"[13] what maturative myths are available to us? Let us return to the roots of the Scotch-Irish experience in Britain, where the geography and conditions of the Atlantic Zone presented its inhabitants with patterns—a spirit of place, if we may say it—which antedate not only the English but also the Celts. In particular, the pattern of repeated invasions and cultural overlayerings has fostered myths which express the relations of conqueror and conquered in a variety of ways—both from the standpoint of each of the two, and from complex synthetic standpoints.

Among the few precious bits of British historical tradition dating from before the depredations of Geoffrey of Monmouth is a compilation called *Enweu Ynys Prydein* (*Names of the Island of Britain*). Its first triad states that before the coming of the Britons, Britain was called *Y Vel Ynys*, "The Honey-Isle"; while before it was settled at all it was *Clas Merdin*, "The Region of Merlin."[14] Merlin seems originally to have been a figure connected with the lost origin-myths of Britain. Later his name appears attached to historical legends of "wild men of the woods" with shamanistic powers; much later, Geoffrey was the first to connect him with Arthur.[15] We seem to have here one of the few surviving fragments of authentic pre-Christian myths of Britain's origin. The point in our present context is this: Just as the English invested the Atlantic Celts with the qualities of the wild, the dreaming, the right hemisphere, so the Celts had done the same to the Atlantic world that had preceded them. On the level of stereotype, this is the "positive" side of the same oppressive process which created the negative stereotype of Goemagog and his giant brethren. The preternatural powers of original personhood are relegated to the wild woods, outside the pale of settlement, and made the possession of powerless solitaries. This is the "romanticism" of dominant cultures; preternatural efficacy is made a substitute for concrete power. This process has been applied to many dominated groups, including women. In this way the sign becomes a tool of domination. "The raw begs for cooking and serving up";[16] and the Isle of Honey is rapidly becoming the Isle of Ashes.

So much for the level of stereotype. But on the level of archetype we have something different. The stereotype, the idol, competes with concrete "reality" on the latter's own level. But the archetype, the icon, is higher and deeper than the concrete, and informs it with archetypal possibilities. What we glimpse here in the original figure of Merlin is the *Urmensch*, original personhood with the full enjoyment of human potentialities. On this level his solitariness is merely a token of his singleness, his wholeness. He is not something outside the pale of humanity, but rather is the essence of humanity itself, placed outside the pale of consciousness by a process of self-blinding. As Norman O. Brown said, "To see with our own eyes is second sight."[17] Thus Merlin's prophetic power can be seen as a shadowing-forth, a primitive analogue or *Urform*, of that prophetic dimension which rescues revelation from the shells of mystification, objectification, and shut-upness that grow up around it, and which opens it up and restores it to its function in eternity and the present—that prophetic dimension which originates in the existential depths of autonomy and personal integrity. (It is intriguing to recall that the historical legends incorporating the Merlin-figure refer precisely to those parts of North Britain where the Scotch-Irish mainly originated, and to that forest much of which was not settled until men with bronze tools and weapons came to the Honey-Isle.[18]) The myth of Merlin is a myth of survival; and though mere survival is a poor substitute for resistance, it is the necessary condition of potential resistance.

Other apparent fragments of early Atlantic myth expand upon this theme and lead it in vitally suggestive directions. We have remarked how the imperial Roman mind, at once brutalized and hypersophisticated, saw the primitive peoples of the North in terms of the age of Saturn, the Greek Kronos, the Titan who, before being deposed by the later gods, had ruled over the Golden Age. But this sophisticated primitivism was not *simply* a projection of the dominant culture's meanings onto the "barbarian." An element of something quite different is found in two extraordinary passages from the first-century author Plutarch. His dialogue "On the Decay of Oracles" contains the following passage:

> Demetrios said that among the islands lying near Britain there were many lonely scattered ones, of which some were named after spirits [*daimonon*] and heroes. He himself had sailed, to investigate and observe by Imperial command, to the nearest-lying of these lonely isles, which had a few inhabitants, holy men who were all held inviolate by the Britons. . . . They said that there is one island there in which Kronos is imprisoned, and is guarded by Briareus as he lies there; for sleep has been devised as a chain for him. But around him there are many spirits, his companions and attendants.[19]

The passage is striking because it seems to embody, in a form only superficially classicized in names and the like, a very early form of the legend of Arthur—how after his last battle he did not die but was carried instead to the isle of Avalon, where he sleeps in a cave. In classical mythology, Kronos or Saturn is exiled, but in general he does not sleep; that motif is found only in a few fragments preserved from the Orphic mysteries,[20] which themselves are believed to have originally been based on Northern shamanism.[21] This detail, reappearing a thousand years later in the Arthurian cycle, vouches for the authenticity of the story as a version of a real British/Atlantic myth. The expedition mentioned could well be that of Agricola's navy around Scotland in A.D. 82. Thus this would be only one of the many features of pre-Christian belief which survived by being grouped around the historic figure of Artorius, the last great hope of Britain. And its nature and location suggest that it is not only pre-Christian but pre-Celtic, perhaps even pre-Indo-European.

In a later dialogue, "Concerning the Face on the Moon," Plutarch seems to have embroidered the story with more Greco-Roman motifs; nevertheless, the thematic structure is undamaged and indeed clarified. The island of Kronos is now placed far beyond the ocean, and the details of his imprisonment are elaborated. Three islands are mentioned,

> in one of which the barbarians tell the tale that Kronos is imprisoned by Zeus, and the Ancient One, Briareus, has been stationed near him, to keep guard over both these islands and the sea, which they call the Kronian Main. . . . For Kronos himself lies in a deep cave, surrounded by rock that shines like gold, for sleep is the chain devised for him by Zeus; but birds, flying over the summit of the rock, bring him ambrosia, and the whole island is pervaded by the fragrance which scatters like a fountain from the rock. And those spirits wait on Kronos and attend him, for they were his companions when he was king over gods and men. These foretell many things on their own, for they are second-sighted. But as for the greatest prophecies, and those concerning the greatest things, they come down and report them as dreams of Kronos; for whatever Zeus plans out, these things Kronos dreams, and the titanic experiences and movements of his soul cause him to stiffen, until Sleep restores him to rest.[22]

If this myth is what it appears to be—both a survival from the Atlantic world, ancient even in Plutarch's day, and the origin of the story of Arthur's exile—then the part of the world from which most Appalachians' ancestors came has given us what may be the oldest surviving story in Western Europe, one which outlived the Celtic settlement of Britain, the Roman occupation, the coming of Christianity, and even the overwhelming of Celtic Britain by another foreign invasion and change of language, to become part of the heritage of the "Anglo-Saxon" world culture. The remarkable survival power of this myth is a function of its theme: it is *about* survival, the survival of wholeness in a world of limitation and domination. And its motifs concern the necessary means of that survival: they have not only survival power but survival value. Kronos is asleep, but not dead; he lies in the west, the direction of the setting sun of death, but he is asleep in a cave—not only an entrance of the underworld but also a womb of birth; and the sea which is named after him has the same double value. (Albion in Christianized pseudohistory is the descendant of Ham, the embodiment of that inner impulse which, in the form in which it surfaces in consciousness, is deranged and perverted. But he is also the son of Neptune, a god not only of the sea but of fresh wellsprings.)

Above all, Kronos' sleep is not inert and deathlike but active and creative. "For whatever Zeus plans out, these things Kronos dreams." Thus the myth, like all true myths, contains a core which transcends and subverts its distortions. Zeus, the god of the present world of iron, has devised (*memechanesthai*, "mechanized") sleep as a chain for Kronos. But wholeness subverts the bond forged for it by mechanistic power: for it has access to a power which Zeus does not understand and anticipate, the power of dreaming. Thus Kronos' sleep is not the sleep of death which Zeus had intended, and the tomb which Zeus had devised becomes a womb of potential rebirth. And Kronos' dreams are not the fantasies of one cut off from the world but are in touch with the conscious decisions by which the world as we experience it is ordered. It is Zeus who has cut himself off from realizing the bases of his own "reality." The myth of the sleeping Kronos/Arthur conveys that authenticity and wholeness are never lost, that there remains what Freire calls "untested feasibility."[23] The motif of dreaming conveys that a living relation exists between this surviving personhood and the world of action. An essential feature of Kronos' dreaming and prophetic sleep is that its nature contradicts Zeus' view of Kronos, and manifests a living and active self beyond the terms of that view; for "to see with our own eyes is second sight."

With *our* own eyes: for Kronos' sleep is not the "inner" fantasy of an isolated individual consciousness. Its content is the world of planning and action, and that content is communicated to the world. Kronos himself is not the symbol of an individual but of something which is common to all persons. Susanne Langer has proposed that dreams were an important origin of human thought in general.[24] Or rather, the relationship between dreams and waking life: for as David Bleich points out, all the higher mammals dream, but the human dream is significant because it is remembered in waking life and interpreted in terms of that life.[25] Thus the myth of the British Kronos touches on themes that lie close to the very origin of our humanity, and therefore it deals with the preservation of that humanity under conditions in which we are forced to fall back on our most fundamental sources of life.

Nevertheless, Kronos remains on his island. Just so, Blake's Albion sleeps on the sea-washed rock to which his world has shrunk, the starry heavens fled from his mighty limbs. Here again is the problem of trading archetypal efficacy for effectiveness in the world of concrete power-relations. The image of the dreamer has been used to keep oppressed groups—Appalachians, "Celts," women—in subjection by granting them a realm of their own without actual power. In individual terms this is what Laing calls "a transcendence in a void,"[26] produced by "a technique of concealing and preserving one's own true possibilities, which, however, risk never becoming translated into actualities if they are entirely concentrated in an inner self for whom all things are possible in imagination but nothing is possible in fact."[27] In this negative aspect, the island of Kronos is the realm of Laing's stony-hard citadel, of Memmi's encystment.

But this is to see only the aspect of Kronos' imprisonment which Zeus has consciously devised. From Kronos' viewpoint, matters are quite different. "For whatever Zeus plans out, these things Kronos dreams." The dream is the mode of *survival* in the world of potentiality. Memmi and Laing have described, in the social and individual cases respectively, how destructive this situation can be if this potentiality is left only to itself; nevertheless, it is still the essential mode of survival, necessary though not sufficient. The dream must be gone on from, not denied. And what is the nature of Kronos' dreams? Plutarch is ambiguous as to whether they telepathically perceive what Zeus is planning, or the other way around; but in the Orphic fragments, it is explicitly Kronos whose dreams perceive or create the future events of the world *before* Zeus consciously plans (*prodianoeitai*, "thinks-through-forward") them.[28] The debate between the two interpretations is still going on today in different terms; but the second is the one which penetrates more deeply into the myth's overall meaning—its nature as a myth not only of survival, but of transcendence and subversion. For if we see beyond Zeus' view of Kronos' buried impotence to the actual inner life of Kronos' dreams, and if furthermore we look beyond the simple view of those dreams to the possibility of their deeper importance even for Zeus himself—an importance to which he has blinded himself—then there is no reason not to go another step and deny Zeus' fundamental assumption: that Kronos must needs remain on his island.

For of course, if Plutarch's story is what it seems to be, namely an earlier form of the myth of Arthur in Avalon, then we must remember that Arthur does not remain there but will one day return to restore Britain. (It is surely even possible that, though Plutarch does not mention it, this feature was present in the Atlantic myth as conveyed to him; such a feature would strengthen the connection of the Atlantic deity with Kronos/Saturn.) The sleep, then, that is Zeus' machination to bind Kronos, is not only subverted by dreams but will one day be supplanted by waking, by concrete action to unite the dreams of potentiality with the works of actuality. And the "one day" is not a future occurrence, but is in potentiality now, and capable of being made actual in every ongoing situation: not only in some final, projected (in two senses) hour of need, but in every moment of need. The participation of the usurped in the world is no longer only in dream; they go forth in power to confront the usurper—both the usurper without, and the one within their own minds:

> The Breath Divine went forth upon the morning hills. Albion mov'd
> Upon the Rock, he opened his eyelids in pain; in pain he mov'd
> His stony members, he saw England. Ah! shall the Dead live again?
>
> The Breath Divine went forth over the morning hills. Albion rose
> In anger: the wrath of God breaking bright flaming on all sides around
> His awful limbs; into the Heavens he walked clothed in flames
> Loud thundring, with broad flashes of flaming lightning & pillars
> Of fire, speaking the Words of Eternity in Human Forms, in direful
> Revolutions of Action & Passion, thro the Four Elements on all sides
> Surrounding his awful Members. Thou seest the Sun in heavy clouds
> Struggling to rise above the Mountains. in his burning hand
> He takes his Bow, then chooses out his arrows of flaming gold.
> Murmuring the Bowstring breathes with ardor! clouds roll round the
>   Horns
> of the wide Bow, loud sounding winds sport on the mountain
>   brows. . . .
> And the Bow is a Male & Female & the Quiver of the Arrows of Love
> Are the Children of his Bow: a Bow of Mercy & Loving-kindness:
>   laying
> Open the hidden Heart in Wars of mutual Benevolence Wars of Love.[29]

And what is the source of this power? Arthur's sword Excalibur was forged in the isle of Avalon, in that world of potentiality beyond the waters of death/birth where Arthur would one day go in exile/refuge. And it was given him by (and given back to) the Lady of the Lake, his own creativity. (One thinks again of Boorman's striking image of its giving, and that image's ironic twin in *Deliverance;* and one begins to see the subtle and profound linkage of the two images.)

Have I grown too bold? Have I slipped into mystification? It has been said that failed prophecy becomes apocalyptic and failed apocalyptic becomes gnostic withdrawal from the world. And this was indeed the story of many people's journeys in the sixties and seventies. As for mystification, I have mentioned the "battle" of Wounded Knee, where U.S. troops massacred scores of Sioux men, women, and children; these victims had drawn a delusion of invulnerability from the Ghost Dance religion, whose illusory promises of the white man's disappearance are paralleled in early versions of the myth of Arthur's return.

But I am not trying to interpret prophecy as a literal foretelling of the future. "The dissolution of the myth as explanation is the necessary way to the restoration of the myth as symbol." [30] By prophecy we must mean not an attempt to *foretell* what will happen, but rather an attempt to *tell forth* that which transcends the present. And this transcendence takes place on the plane, not of a future as fixed and determined as the present is, but of a potentiality which is the realm of freedom—a potentiality which is not simply to be passively waited for but instead to be brought into being through action. In this sense the prophetic meaning of the Ghost Dance was not unfolded in its miraculous promises which brought on the massacre at Wounded Knee in 1890; rather, it was revealed in that promise of human dignity which motivated those who put Wounded Knee into history again in 1973. And this prophetic gift is no property of an elite few; for it was in this sense that Moses said, and Blake repeated: "Would to God that all the Lord's people were prophets." [31]

Freire writes that in "the silence of profound meditation, . . . men only apparently leave the world, withdrawing from it in order to consider it in its totality, and thus remaining with it. But this type of retreat is only authentic when the meditator is 'bathed' in reality; not when the retreat signifies contempt for the world and flight from it, in a type of 'historical schizophrenia.'" [32] The last clause is almost a technical definition of gnosticism, while the authentic retreat is that of Plutarch's British Kronos, withdrawn from the world only apparently and bathed in the plans of Zeus, if not indeed giving form to those plans. The dreams of Kronos are no fantasy of magical prophecy, but are the clear vision of himself and his world as they are, freed from the categories imposed by the usurper: "To see with our own eyes is second sight." The Plutarchan Kronos-myth recognizes that "dreaminess" is a result of oppression, and dialectically the instrument of that oppression; but it images forth the fact that it is the *sleep* (the loss of

consciousness) which is the tool of domination, while the *dream* subverts that domination in the terms which are left to it. Plutarch's version goes no further; being cast in Roman terms, it does not escape a
"civilized" viewpoint concerning the "noble, dreamy savage." Nevertheless, it contains within itself the ironic contradiction of that view; it
embodies that "image which keeps control over false images." [33] And
what seems to be the people's version of the tale embodies not only the
sleep but also the awakening and the return.

Kronos/Arthur sleeps in a far-off misty isle, but this simply
images forth the fact that he embodies a transpersonal archetype.
"Dreaminess" is an unintegrated lump of that transpersonality lodged
within the personal; its cause in the dominated situation is the projective identification of other real persons with fixed images springing
from the projected archetypes (negative or positive) of the dominator.
Since the archetypes are transpersonal and even transhuman, this
identification is depersonalizing and dehumanizing. Thus the myth
of Kronos/Arthur has power precisely because it is a myth about
(Freirean) "mythicization" and shows forth mythically its demytholo-
gizing corrective. In this way it illustrates the potential of the true
symbol to escape the limitations imposed upon it by particular sign-
systems.

Specifically, in the return-motif, this mythologem directly contradicts the dichotomy imposed by the modern Celtic-romantic view
of Matthew Arnold, Ernest Renan, and others, which says, in Renan's
words: "Alas! . . . Arthur shall never return from his enchanted
isle, and rightly did Saint Patrick say to Ossian: 'The heroes that you
mourn are dead; can they be reborn?'" [34] That view is a fantasticized
shell of the truth, schizoidly split-off from its real purport. This magical dreaminess is a mirage, seen through the sights of domination, of
the repressed wholeness which seems magical to those whose horizon is limited by the lines of instrumental rationality. What is necessary to overcome "dreaminess" is not rationalistic denial (which
merely takes for granted the terms of the dichotomy), but reintegra-
tion. Then our heroes are reborn the only way they can be, namely in
us: "To see with our own eyes is second sight." The myth is not about
the value of dreaming in itself but about the hidden wellsprings of
critical consciousness and creative action—about the necessity of
knowing who, and what, and *that* one is, so that one may come to consciousness of one's own interest and develop (*prodianoeisthai*) plans of
action to achieve it.

The healing of the divided self comes in making present one's thought and action;[35] the myth of the return of Arthur springs from people's perception of what is required *of themselves* in the present. True, a myth can become a split-off fixed image, a substitute for action rather than an energizer of it. What is needed, however, is that as the oppressed become self-conscious and overcome the false categories imposed on them by the oppressor, they must become not only dreamers but doers, not only seers with their own eyes but actors on their own behalf. "To see with our own eyes is second sight," and to act on our own behalf is the rebirth of the heroes whom we have mourned.

All action in the world comes forth from the wellspring of the creative. The embodiment of the creative has been banished to his sea-cave, in the realm of possibility; but there his selfhood is still in contact with the patterns of the universal order, still bathed in reality, and in the moment of need he returns to drive out the usurper. Process becomes praxis; fate becomes freedom. The myth, to be sure, does no more than point at this, for the means of realization lie beyond the vision-quest in the world which is returned to but which appears transfigured by the vision. Not in some imagined future, for that would be to defeat the purport of the myth and swallow up the return inside the dream; but rather in the present life of everyone who is in touch with those currents, the creative possibility leaves its cave of birth beyond the sea of death, emerges into actuality, and takes up arms in the waking world against the usurper of personhood; so that, we may yet hope, there may rise, not from the waters of death the dead and empty hand of murdered selfhood, but from the waters of birth the living hand of strength, bearing the sword of victory.

NOTES

INTRODUCTION

1. Whisnant, *Modernizing the Mountaineer*, 268.
2. Mannoni, *Prospero and Caliban*, 125.
3. Ardener, "Belief and the Problem of Women"; "The 'Problem' Revisited."
4. Cf. Rogin, *Fathers and Children*, 121–22.
5. A lack of understanding on this fact tends to becloud Hechter's work, though his own data point in this direction for those alerted to the fact.
6. Cf. Cunningham, "Heritage or Hermitage?," 253–54.
7. Kushner, "Reflections on Mountain Adaptations," 171, discussing Edward H. Spicer.
8. Laing, *Politics of Experience*, 65; emphasis original.
9. O'Toole, "Culture and Development," 268, summarizing Foster, Robinson, and Fisher, "Class, Political Consciousness, and Destructive Power."
10. Chapman, *Gaelic Vision*, 218.
11. A remarkably prescient treatment of these same themes was written at the turn of the century with regard to Ireland by Chesterton ("Celts and Celtophiles").
12. Memmi, *Colonizer and the Colonized*, 11.
13. Couto, "Political Silence and Appalachia," 117.
14. Cf. Reid, "Appalachian Studies," 142.
15. Batteau, "Appalachia and the Concept of Culture," 24.
16. Lawrence Thompson, cited in Miller, "Appalachian Studies Hard and Soft," 105.
17. Ashe, *Camelot*, 220.

CHAPTER 1

1. Cf. Evans, "Atlantic Ends of Europe."
2. Atkinson, "Fishermen and Farmers," 7.
3. Piggott, "Traders and Metal-Workers."
4. Renfrew, "Social Archaeology of Megalithic Monuments," 162.
5. For whatever it might be worth, Geoffrey of Monmouth, whom we shall meet later, connects Basques with both the Orkneys and the original settlers of Ireland (*History of the Kings of Britain*, 100–101). The Norse word for "menhir" was *bautasteinn*, whose first element is of unknown origin (Kluge, *Ety-*

mologisches Wörterbuch, s.v.
"dolmen").

6. Cf. Gimbutas, "Old Europe."
7. Holinshed, *Chronicles*, 428–43.
8. Ibid., 434.
9. Ibid., 432.
10. Geoffrey, *Historia Regum Britan-niae*, 250–51; cf. *History*, 72–73.
11. E.g. Holinshed, 443.
12. Cf. Kovel, *White Racism*, 63.
13. Burl, *Stone Circles*, 203–204.
14. Powell, "Coming of the Celts," 116–18.
15. Radford, "From Prehistory to History," 152.
16. Powell, 119.
17. Radford, 146.
18. Powell, 119–21.
19. Lévi-Strauss, *Tristes Tropiques*, 244.
20. Sheehan, *Savagism and Civility*, 4.
21. Ibid., 96.
22. Ibid., 5.
23. Cf. Rogin, *Fathers and Children*, 10.
24. Virgil, *Aeneid VI*, 851.
25. Tacitus, *De Vita Agricolae*, 23.
26. Cf. Tacitus, *On Britian and Germany*, 128.
27. Cf. Morris, *Age of Arthur*.
28. K. Jackson, ed., *Gododdin: The Oldest Scottish Poem*.
29. Morris, 149, 151.
30. Ibid., 400–405.
31. L. Jones, "Old-Time Baptists," 120.

CHAPTER 2

1. Mac Cana, *Celtic Mythology*, 35.
2. F. Henry, *Irish Art*, 63, 78–79, 81, 83, 91, 98–99, 150–51, 164–66, 176, 179, 184, 198–99.

3. K. Jackson, *Language and History*, 124–25, 147.
4. Turner, "Sigificance of the Frontier," 199.
5. Ibid., 227.
6. Ibid., 201.
7. Fanon, *Wretched of the Earth*, 313.
8. Cf. Rogin, 330n8.
9. Sartre, preface to Fanon, 26.
10. J. Henry, *On Sham*, 150.
11. Bede, *History of the English Church and People*, 92; cf. *Opera Historica*, 71.
12. K. Jackson, ed., *Gododdin*, 63.
13. Bromwich, ed., *Trioedd Ynys Prydein*, 241.
14. Ibid., cxxxii.
15. *Gododdin*, 64; cf. K. Jackson, *Language and History*, 116–17.
16. Cf. *Gododdin*, 65–66.
17. Radford, 146.
18. Murison, "Linguistic Relationships in Medieval Scotland," 71–72.
19. Donaldson, *Scotland: Church and Nation*, 12–13.
20. Ibid., 19.
21. Barrow, *Anglo-Norman Era*, 7.
22. Ibid., 74–83.
23. McEvedy, *Penguin Atlas of Medieval History*, 60.
24. Almgren, *Viking*, 128.
25. Donaldson, 20–23.
26. Bur, "Social Influence of the Motte-and-Bailey Castle," 140.
27. McNeill and Nicholson, eds., *Historical Atlas of Scotland*, 128.
28. Bur, 140.
29. Ibid.
30. Dickinson and Duncan, *Scotland from the Earliest Times to 1603*, 111.
31. Murison, 73; Dickinson and Duncan, 113; cf. Geoffrey Stell,

"Mottes," in McNeill and Nicholson, eds., 29.

32. Barrow, *Anglo-Norman Era*, 153.
33. Frost, "God's Plan for the Southern Mountains," 416.
34. Murison, 74.
35. Dickinson and Duncan, 113.
36. Ibid., 111. This coinage was increasingly dependent on that of England (Barrow, *Kingship and Unity*, 58).
37. Dickinson and Duncan, 114
38. Ibid., 113.
39. Murison, 72–73, 74; cf. Barrow, *Anglo-Norman Era*, 48–49.
40. Ranald Nicholson, "The Highlands in the Fourteenth and Fifteenth Centuries," in McNeill and Nicholson, eds., 68.
41. Ibid.
42. Murison, 73, 74.
43. White, *Medieval Technology*, 41–69.
44. Falls, *Birth of Ulster*, 11.
45. Eliade, *Sacred and the Profane*, 47.
46. Cf. Hanning, *Vision of History*, 149, 234–35 n 113.
47. Lovejoy, *Great Chain of Being*, 100–103.
48. Alanus, *De Planctu Naturae*, prosa 3; cited in C. S. Lewis, *Discarded Image*, 58.
49. Laing, *Politics of Experience*, 51.
50. Hanning, 104.
51. Ibid., 105.
52. Geoffrey, *History*, 62–64; cf. Joseph Campbell, *Hero with a Thousand Faces*, 342–45.
53. Hanning, 157.
54. Geoffrey, *History*, 56–57.
55. Hanning, 157–58.
56. Geoffrey, *History*, 65.
57. Fanon, 313.

58. Cf. Joseph Campbell, *Hero with a Thousand Faces*, 345–54.
59. Joseph Campbell, *Flight of the Wild Gander*, 6.
60. Murison, 82.
61. Cf. Rogin, 121–22.
62. Cf. ibid., 208.
63. Ritchie, *Normans in Scotland*, 151.
64. Cf. Rogin, 6–7; Sheehan, 2; Newcomb, "Appalachia on Television," 160.
65. Batteau, "Rituals of Dependence," 158–59.
66. Fanon, 211.
67. Rogin, 14.
68. Coles, *Migrants, Sharecroppers, Mountaineers*, 241.
69. Cf. Rogin, 79–80; Plaut, "Conflict, Confrontation, and Social Change," 275–76.
70. Moncreiffe and Pottinger, "Scotland of Old."
71. Hicks, *Appalachian Valley*, 52.
72. Plaut, 276.
73. Cf. Rogin, 101–103.
74. Cf. ibid., 44.
75. Ibid., 116.
76. Cf. ibid., 208.
77. Cf. ibid., 210; Laing, *Self and Others*, 144–46.
78. Weil, *Need for Roots*, 48.
79. Fr. Tomás Ó Ceallaigh, 1911; cited in Murphy, "Irish Question," 30.
80. Murison, 78–79.
81. Cf. Chapman, 223–24.
82. H. Lewis, "Colony of Appalachia," 5.
83. McNeill and Nicholson, 178; Withers, *Gaelic in Scotland*, 25.
84. Cf. Murison, 80.
85. Dunbar, "The Flyting of Dunbar and Kennedy," *Poems*, 80.

86. Kennedy in ibid.
87. Murison, 80.
88. Kinsley in Dunbar, 284.
89. Withers, 24.
90. Montgomerie, *Poems*, 280; *u, v,* and *yogh* normalized.
91. Cf. Kovel, 87–91.
92. Montgomerie, 281.
93. Cf. Duncan, *Scotland*, 90.
94. Memmi, 11.
95. Murison, 81.
96. Ibid.
97. Hechter, in *Internal Colonialism*, has explored the concept of peripheralization in precisely this zone, but his efforts, though useful, are marred by a vagueness and shallowness of historical perspective and a naïve use of the word "Celt," both of which he seems to have absorbed largely from Celtic nationalist literature. For a discussion of Scotland in the sixteenth to eighteenth centuries in terms of a core-periphery model, see Whyte, "Early-Modern Scotland."
98. Donaldson, 65–66.
99. Stewart, "History of the Church of Ireland," 316–17.
100. Cf. Chapman, 15–17. Cf. also Kundera, "Tragedy of Central Europe," 33: "True, the Russian language is suffocating the languages of the other nations in the Soviet empire, but it's not because the Russians themselves want to 'russianize' the others; it's because the Soviet bureaucracy . . . needs a tool to unify its state." Just so, the Scottish monarchy simply found English a better tool of state power than Gaelic.
101. Memmi, xiii.
102. Leyburn, *Scotch-Irish*, 7.
103. Ibid., 7n.
104. Ibid., xv.

CHAPTER 3

1. McHugh, lecture.
2. Cf. Mathew, *Celtic Peoples and Renaissance Europe.*
3. Canny, *Elizabethan Conquest of Ireland,* 121–22.
4. Murray et al. (eds.), *Oxford English Dictionary,* s.v.
5. Canny, 123–25.
6. Ibid., 15, 126–27.
7. Ibid., 126.
8. Ibid., 133–34.
9. Dudley, letter to Ashton, May 1575; in ibid., 134–35.
10. Smith, letter to Sir William Fitzwilliam, 8 Nov. 1572; in ibid., 129.
11. McDougall, *Racial Myth in English History,* 31–50.
12. Cited in French, *John Dee,* 180; cf. 188–99, esp. 190–93.
13. Canny, 131–32, 161–62.
14. Sartre, 26; translation modified.
15. Weil, 48.
16. E.g. Canny, 160–63.
17. Rees and Rees, *Celtic Heritage,* 122–23.
18. Morris, 149, 152.
19. Perceval-Maxwell, *Scottish Migration to Ulster,* 14.
20. Macleod, *American Indian Frontier,* 161.
21. Leyburn, 91–98.
22. For a less impressionistic docu-

mentation of this fact, see
Perceval-Maxwell, 289.
23. Opie, "Sense of Place," 116.
24. Stewart, 313.
25. Coles, *South Goes North*, 333.
26. Leyburn, 139.
27. Ibid., 135–36.
28. *The Hireling Ministry None of Christ's* (London, 1652), cited in Miller, *Roger Williams*, 200.
29. Hill, "Puritans and 'The Dark Corners of the Land,'" 78.
30. J. A. Manning, *Memoirs of Sir Benjamin Rudyerd* (London, 1841), 135–38; cited in Hill, 96. For examples of what horrified Sir Benjamin, see Carmichael, ed., *Celtic Invocations*; K. Jackson, *Celtic Miscellany*, 85–86.
31. Cited in Miller, 201.
32. Cf. Rogin, 29–30.
33. Frost, "God's Plan for the Southern Mountains," 416.
34. Leyburn, 125–26.
35. Cited in Ford, *Scotch-Irish*, 148.
36. Leyburn, 127.
37. Ibid., 160–63.
38. Ibid., 164–68.
39. Ibid., 168.

CHAPTER 4

1. Leyburn, 255.
2. See Caudill, "Anglo-Saxon vs. Scotch-Irish." Caudill has since modified his views (conversation with the author, 31 October 1984).
3. Leyburn, 135–36, 182.
4. Cf. L. Jones, "Preliminary Look at the Welsh Element."
5. John C. Campbell, *Southern Highlander*, 65.

6. McDonald and McDonald, "Ethnic Origins." Cf. Newton, "Cultural Preadaptation," 150.
7. *National Atlas*, 63; cf. Otto, "Oral Tradition in the Southern Highlands," 21 map.
8. Walls, "Naming of Appalachia," 56–59.
9. Johnson, *America Explored*, 34–35, 44, 46, 140, 164, 170, 171, 174, 190.
10. Silverberg, *Mound Builders*, 233–93; Purrington, "Status and Future of Archeology," 46, 47.
11. Silverberg, 285–88.
12. Ibid., 166–221.
13. Conley and Stutler, *West Virginia*, 35–40; Scalf, *Kentucky's Last Frontier*, 19–20.
14. Silverberg, 65–67.
15. E.g. Fell, *America B.C.*
16. Silverberg, 294–337; Purrington, 47–48.
17. Leyburn, 327–34.
18. Cf. ibid., 171, 172, 199.
19. Toynbee, *Study of History*, II, 310.
20. Piggott, *Druids*, 118.
21. Canny, 159.
22. Ibid., 160.
23. Cf. ibid., ch. 8; Sheehan.
24. Tolles, "Culture of Early Pennsylvania," 615.
25. Rogin, 39.
26. Ibid., 133.
27. Ibid., 231–32.
28. Ibid., 44.
29. Ibid., 12.
30. Asbury, "Journal," 295.
31. William Strickland, *Observations on the Agriculture of the United States of America* (London: W. Bulmer, 1801), 71; facsimile appendix to Strickland, *Journal*.
32. Cuming, *Sketches of a Tour*, 118.

33. Ibid., 119–20.
34. Mooney, *Ghost Dance Religion*, 676. The author of this celebrated work was an Irish-American whose interest in Irish national liberation movements led him to the study of other movements of resistance to "Anglo-Saxon" encroachment.
35. Scalf, 34.
36. Rogin, 4, 32, 41, 252, 307.
37. Leyburn, 325.
38. Ibid., 331.
39. McDonald and McDonald, 119.
40. Coles, *Migrants*, 205.
41. Ibid., 523.
42. Nicolson, *Mountain Gloom and Mountain Glory*, 72–112.
43. Lyndsay, *Ane Dialog betuixt Experience and ane Courteour*; cited in Nicolson, 94.
44. Nicolson, 96–100.
45. Humphrey, "Religion and Place," 123–31.
46. Cf. Eller, *Miners, Millhands, and Mountaineers*, 15; Otto, 27.
47. Shapiro, "Place of Culture," 134.
48. Cf. Evans, "Scotch-Irish," 85–86; Newton, 150–52.
49. Edward H. Spicer, *The Yaquis: A Cultural History* (Tucson: Univ. of Arizona Press, 1980), 347; cited in Kushner, "Reflections on Mountain Adaptations," 173. Cf. Cunningham, 253–54. Cf. also Batteau, "Appalachia and the Concept of Culture," 11–12: "We need a better way of conceiving of the integrity of Appalachian culture than simply listing cultural traits" (12).
50. Coles, *Migrants*, 203–204.
51. Ibid., 204. Cf. Fisher, "Appalachians as 'Redskins.'"
52. Williams, 15.
53. Ibid.
54. Scholes, address at St. Olaf's College, Fall 1973; cited in England, "Great Books or True Religion?," 40.
55. Matthews, *Experience-Worlds of Mountain People*, 14.
56. Lucretius, *The Way Things Are*.
57. C. S. Lewis, *Discarded Image*, 35–39.
58. *Oxford English Dictionary*, s.v.
59. E.g. Weller, *Yesterday's People*, 6.
60. Coles, *Migrants*, 239–41, 252, 262.
61. Ibid., 241.
62. Cf. K. Jackson, *Studies in Early Celtic Nature Poetry*; K. Jackson, *Celtic Miscellany*, 63–75.
63. Coles, *Migrants*, 241.
64. Ibid.
65. Vincent, "Retarded Frontier."
66. Cf. Wilhelm, "Appalachian Isolation," 88–89.
67. Evans, "Scotch-Irish," 80–81, 84–85.
68. Eller, *Miners*, 7; emphasis mine.
69. Kovel, 190.
70. E.g. West, *Freedom on the Mountains*, 10–12.
71. Cited in Williams, 237; cf. Wilhelm, 78, 87–88.
72. Wilhelm, ibid.
73. Humphrey, 134–35.
74. Ibid., 132.
75. Cf. Shapiro, *Appalachia on Our Mind*, 3–31; Williams, esp. chs. 2, 4, 5, 6.

CHAPTER 5

1. Shapiro, *Appalachia on Our Mind*, 62.

2. Ibid., 63.
3. Ibid.
4. Frost, "The Last Log School-House," address before the Cincinnati Teachers' Club, 15 Dec. 1895; cited in ibid., 119–20.
5. Frost in ibid., 120.
6. Fox, *Trail of the Lonesome Pine*, 40.
7. Shapiro, *Appalachia on Our Mind*, 3–31; Williams, chs. 2, 4, 5, 6.
8. Sheehan, 2.
9. Ibid., 4.
10. Ibid., 181.
11. Shapiro, *Appalachia on Our Mind*, 131.
12. Cf. Rogin, 245; Chapman, 92–95; Eller, "Industrialization and Social Change," 35–36; Newcomb, "Appalachia on Television," 160.
13. Cf. Rogin, 113.
14. Toynbee, II, 309.
15. Ibid.
16. Ibid., 310–12. My apologies for the choppiness of this quotation: the late professor's publishers have not been forthcoming with permissions.
17. Ibid., I, 467.
18. Cf. Rogin, 12.
19. D. C. Somervell, in his abridgment of Toynbee's work, summarizes the latter's attitude toward Appalachians in the notorious sentence: "The Appalachians present the melancholy spectacle of a people who have acquired civilization and then lost it" (149). This is Somervell's more colorful version of Toynbee's remark that Appalachian "barbarism" represents "not a survival but a reversion." The one recorded protest to Toynbee him-self against these strictures bounced off the eminent scholar's carapace (James S. Brown, "Appalachian Footnote").
20. Cited in Rogin, 210.
21. Cited in Davids, *Man Who Moved a Mountain*, 34–35.
22. Weller, *Yesterday's People*, 28.
23. Sheehan, 2.
24. Coles, *Migrants*, 497.
25. Snyder, "Image and Identity," 130.
26. Moore, intro. to Guerrant, xi.
27. Guerrant, 3.
28. Weller, conversation reported by Norman Simpkins, May 1983.
29. Gerrard, "Churches of the Stationary Poor," 108.
30. Ibid., 106.
31. Ibid., 113n14.
32. Cf. H. Lewis et al., "Family, Religion and Colonialism," 133, 136.
33. C. S. Lewis, *Preface to Paradise Lost*, 132.
34. Semple, "Anglo-Saxons"; cf. Shapiro, 80–81, 91, 108.
35. E.g. Heron, "Making of the Ulster Scot"; Toynbee, I, 467.
36. Frost, "God's Plan for the Southern Mountains," 412.
37. Cf. Whisnant, *All That is Native and Fine*, 181–252, esp. 206–207, 237–46.
38. Grant, *Passing of the Great Race*, 35–36.
39. E.g. Kahn, "New Strategies for Appalachia," 57–59.
40. Laing, *Divided Self*, 52.
41. Cf. Weller, *Yesterday's People*, 2.
42. Seltzer, "Media vs. Appalachia," 11.
43. Cf. Branscome, "Annihilating the Hillbilly," 211–12, 221; Seltzer.

44. A. Jackson, "To See the 'Me' in 'Thee,'" 23.
45. Cf. also Branscome, 221.
46. Laing, *Divided Self*, 95.
47. Ibid., 139; emphasis in original.
48. Memmi, 81.
49. Walls, "Internal Colony or Internal Periphery?," 330.
50. Laing, *Self and Others*, 101.
51. Weller, *Yesterday's People*, 150. Weller has since come to recognize the essentials of the situation I am describing (cf. Weller, "Appalachia: America's Mineral Colony"). But his earlier call to an unspecified "us," presumably in possession of "wholeness," to "guide" Appalachians in that direction, is still in print and still required reading for many students in the mountains and elsewhere. Thus it can stand conveniently for a whole school of still current opinion.
52. Vance, intro. to Weller, *Yesterday's People*, v.
53. Laing, *Politics of Experience*, 51.
54. Cf. Rogin, 210.
55. Harrington, 96.
56. Memmi, 105. Cf. H. Lewis et al., 133.
57. Cf. Fanon, 223–24.
58. Newcomb, 160.
59. Eliade, *Myths, Dreams, and Mysteries*, 43.
60. Kirby, "Our Own Music," 242, 250 n 17.
61. Cf. Kushner, 175–77.
62. Macaulay, "Penny for the Guy, Mister . . ." in *Seobhrach as a' Chlaich* (Glasgow: Gairm, 1967), 16, tr. 88; cited in Chapman, 164.
63. Blake, *Jerusalem*, 17, in Erdman, *Illuminated Blake*, 296.
64. Cf. Chapman, 128–29.
65. An exception, and one which has influenced my interpretation, is Farber, "'Deliverance'—How It Delivers." Farber, however, concentrates on a critique of "machismo" and presses some points further than I would.
66. Cf. Eliot, "Burbank with a Baedeker: Bleistein with a Cigar," *Collected Poems*, 33.
67. Fiedler, *Love and Death in the American Novel*, 148.
68. Ibid., 149.
69. Dickey, *Deliverance*, 7.
70. Ibid., 82.
71. I am indebted to Loyal Jones for pointing out the latter fact to me (letter, 7 Sept. 1983).
72. Dickey, 92.
73. Cf. Farber, 9.
74. Dickey, 38.
75. Cf. Rogin, 114–25.
76. Dickey, 13.
77. Cf. Farber, 9.
78. Geoffrey, *Historia Regum Britanniae*, 250–51; my translation.
79. Dickey, 195.
80. Ibid., 205.
81. Ibid., 206.
82. Ibid., 197.
83. Ibid., 202.
84. Ibid., 199.
85. Norman O. Brown, *Love's Body*, 162.
86. Dickey, 280.
87. Ibid., 78.
88. Sartre, 26.
89. Cf. Joseph Campbell, *Flight of the Wild Gander*, 108–10.
90. Fiedler, 6.
91. Cf. Rogin, 121–22.
92. Ibid., 13.
93. Cf. Norman O. Brown, *Life*

Against Death, 91–93; Becker, *Denial of Death,* 180–81.

CHAPTER 6

1. Memmi, 101–102.
2. Laing, *Divided Self,* 77.
3. Ibid., 33.
4. Batteau, "Rituals of Dependence," 144.
5. Cf. Laing, *Self and Others,* 144–45.
6. Batteau, "Rituals," 146.
7. Memmi, 109.
8. Rogin, 10.
9. L. C. Wynne et al., "Pseudo-Mutuality in the Family Relations of Schizophrenics," *Psychiatry* 21 (1958), 205; cited in Laing, *Self and Others,* 185. Cf. Rogin, 100.
10. Batteau, "Rituals," 157.
11. M. McDonald, "Language 'At Home' to Educated Radicalism," *Journal of the Anthropological Society of Oxford* 9, 1 (1978), 27; cited in Chapman, 206.
12. Reck and Reck, "Living is More Important than Schooling," 21.
13. Batteau, "Rituals," 157.
14. Laing, *Self and Others,* 87.
15. Laing, *Divided Self,* 95.
16. Memmi, 140.
17. Batteau, "Rituals," 144.
18. Ibid., 158–59.
19. Ibid., 158.
20. Laing, *Divided Self,* 41.
21. Ibid., 48.
22. Ibid.
23. Ibid.
24. Ibid.
25. Rogin, 208.
26. Laing, *Divided Self,* 77.

27. Ibid., 53.
28. Memmi, 102.
29. Laing, *Divided Self,* 51.
30. Batteau, "Rituals," 147.
31. Laing, *Divided Self,* 90.
32. Ibid.
33. Laing, *Politics of Experience,* 46.
34. Memmi, 102.
35. Ibid., 100.
36. Cited in Obermiller, "Appalachians as an Urban Ethnic Group," 148.
37. As a sort of anti-type to Laing, Goshen, in "Characterological Deterrents to Economic Progress in People of Appalachia," compares Appalachian culture with schizophrenia in a way which, besides its free attributions of pathology, employs negative and external definition in both cases in a fashion which Laing criticizes repeatedly and trenchantly in discussing schizoid phenomena—a way whose rejection may even be said to form one of the chief bases of Laing's approach (cf. *Divided Self,* 33–34, 162–65; *Politics of Experience,* 85–95).
38. Batteau, "Rituals," 147.
39. Ibid.
40. Laing, *Divided Self,* 43–53.
41. Laing, *Politics of Experience,* 49; cf. Plaut, "Extending the Internal Periphery Model," 353–54, 357.
42. Foster, Robinson, and Fisher, "Class, Political Consciousness, and Destructive Power," 300.
43. Photiadis, "New Aims," 259.
44. Batteau, "Appalachia and the Concept of Culture," 27.
45. Cf. Polansky et al., *Roots of Futility,* an Appalachian "culture-of-poverty" study which

has strongly affected this discussion by way of critique.

46. Batteau, "Rituals," 145.
47. H. Lewis et al., 133.
48. Cited in Coles, *Migrants*, 267–69.
49. See Weller, *Yesterday's People*, 119.
50. Branscome, 222–23.
51. Cf. Cunningham, 254.
52. Snyder, "EdubyGodcation," 43.
53. Cited in Coles, *Migrants*, 292–93.
54. Ibid., 295.
55. Trillin, "U.S. Journal," 178.
56. Ibid., 182.
57. Ibid., 183.
58. Ibid., 180.
59. Laing, *Divided Self*, 100.
60. Laing, *Self and Others*, 39.
61. Trillin, 181.
62. Ibid., 178.
63. Laing, *Self and Others*, 134.
64. Trillin, 180.
65. Cf. Batteau, "Rituals," 147–49.
66. Cited in Erikson, *Everything in its Path*, 182.
67. Laing, *Self and Others*, 151.
68. Arnow, *Dollmaker*, 334–35.
69. Fanon, 238.
70. E.g. Billings and Goldman, "Religion and Class Consciousness"; Seltzer, *passim*.
71. Laing, *Self and Others*, 102–103.
72. Obermiller, 148.
73. Snyder, "Image and Identity," 132.
74. Laing, *Self and Others*, 86–87.
75. Cf. Reid, 142.
76. Kierkegaard, *Concept of Dread*, 114.
77. Chapman, 31.
78. Macaulay, "On Some Aspects of the Appreciation of Modern Gaelic Poetry," 136.
79. Batteau, "Rituals," 163.

80. H. Lewis et al., 133.
81. Ibid.
82. Laing, *Divided Self*, 47.
83. Fanon, 247; cf. Whisnant, "Developments in the Appalachian Identity Movement," 44–45.
84. Chapman, 206; cf. Shapiro, *Appalachia on Our Mind*, 113.
85. Fanon, 219.
86. Batteau, "Rituals," 163.
87. Chapman, 206.
88. Fanon, 314.
89. Blake, *Marriage of Heaven and Hell*, 10, in Erdman, *Illuminated Blake*, 107.
90. Einstein, "Politics of Nostalgia," 39.
91. H. Lewis et al., 133.
92. H. Lewis, "Wales and Appalachia," 356.
93. M. Jones, *Autobiography*, 235.
94. Cf. Kushner, 173.
95. Chapman, 16.
96. H. Lewis, "Wales and Appalachia," 355.

CHAPTER 7

1. Ricoeur, *Symbolism of Evil*, 19.
2. Ibid., 17–18.
3. Freire, *Pedagogy of the Oppressed*, 76.
4. Blake, *Jerusalem*, 17, in Erdman, 296.
5. Chapman, 147.
6. Cf. Laing, *Politics of Experience*, 44.
7. Mac Cana, 41.
8. Ibid., 36.
9. Ibid., 37.
10. Plaut, "Extending the Internal Periphery Model," 358.
11. Cf. Reid, 142.

12. Plaut, "Extending," 358.
13. Joseph Campbell, *Flight of the Wild Gander*, 6.
14. Bromwich, 224–29.
15. Clarke in Geoffrey, *Life of Merlin*, 200–201.
16. Speer, "Culture as Barter," 366.
17. Norman O. Brown, "Apocalypse," 49.
18. Clarke, 170–71, 201; cf. Burl, 203–204.
19. Plutarch, *Moralia*, V, 402, 404; my translation. Cf. Ashe, 48.
20. Kern, *Orphicorum Fragmenta*, 190, 194.
21. Dodds, *Greeks and the Irrational*, 147.
22. Plutarch, XII, 180, 182, 186, 188; my translation. Cf. Ashe, 48.
23. Freire, 105–106.
24. Langer, *Mind*, II, 288–91.
25. Bleich, lecture, 20 Sept. 1972.
26. Laing, *Divided Self*, 80.
27. Ibid., 98.
28. Cherniss in Plutarch, XII, 188–89; Kern, 190, 194.
29. Blake, *Jerusalem*, 95, 97, in Erdman, 374, 376.
30. Ricoeur, 350.
31. Numbers 11:29; Blake, *Milton*, iA, in Erdman, 216.
32. Freire, 76n3.
33. Derick Thomson, "Cotriona Mhór," in Macaulay, ed., *Nua Bhàrdachd Ghàidhlig*, 166.
34. Renan, "Poésie des races celtiques," 253; my translation.
35. Cf. Laing, *Self and Others*, 126–27.

BIBLIOGRAPHY

Almgren, Bertil, et al. *The Viking.* 1975; rpt. New York: Crescent, 1984.

Ardener, Edwin. "Belief and the Problem of Women." In Shirley Ardener, ed., *Perceiving Women.* London: Malaby, 1975.

———. "The 'Problem' Revisited." In Shirley Ardener, ed., *Perceiving Women.* London: Malaby, 1975.

Arnow, Harriette Simpson. *The Dollmaker.* 1954; rpt. New York: Avon, 1972.

Asbury, Francis. "Journal." In Samuel Cole Williams, ed., *Early Travels in the Tennessee Country.* Johnson City, Tenn.: Watauga, 1928.

Ashe, Geoffrey. *Camelot and the Vision of Albion.* New York: St. Martin's, 1971.

Atkinson, R. J. C. "Fishermen and Farmers." In Stuart Piggott, ed., *The Prehistoric Peoples of Scotland.* London: Routledge, 1962.

Barrow, G. W. S. *The Anglo-Norman Era in Scottish History.* Oxford: Clarendon, 1980.

———. *Kingship and Unity: Scotland 1000–1306.* Toronto: Univ. of Toronto Press, 1981.

Batteau, Allen. "Appalachia and the Concept of Culture: A Theory of Shared Misunderstandings." *Appalachian Journal* 7 (Autumn-Winter 1979–80), 9–31.

———. "Rituals of Dependence in Appalachian Kentucky." In Allen Batteau, ed., *Appalachia and America: Autonomy and Regional Dependence.* Lexington: Univ. Press of Kentucky, 1983.

Becker, Ernest. *The Denial of Death.* 1973; rpt. New York: Free Press, 1975.

Bede. *A History of the English Church and People,* tr. Leo Sherley-Price. Harmondsworth, U.K.: Penguin, 1968.

———. *Opera Historica,* ed. Charles Plummer. Oxford: Clarendon, 1896.

Bickmore, D., and M. A. Shaw, eds. *Atlas of Britain and Northern Ireland.* Oxford: Clarendon, 1963.

Billings, Dwight B., and Robert Goldman. "Religion and Class Consciousness in the Kanawha County School Textbook Controversy." In Allen Batteau, ed., *Appalachia and America: Autonomy and Regional Dependence.* Lexington: Univ. Press of Kentucky, 1983.

Bleich, David. Lectures in the Dept. of English, Indiana Univ., Fall 1972.

Branscome, James G. "Annihilating the Hillbilly: The Appalachians' Struggle with America's Institutions." 1971. In Helen Lewis et al., eds., *Colonial-*

ism in Modern America: The Appalachian Case. Boone, N.C.: Appalachian Consortium Press, 1978.

Bromwich, Rachel, ed. & tr. *Trioedd Ynys Prydein: The Welsh Triads*. Cardiff: Univ. of Wales Press, 1978.

Brown, James S. "An Appalachian Footnote to Toynbee's *A Study of History*." *Appalachian Journal* 6 (Autumn 1978), 29–32.

Brown, Norman O. "Apocalypse: The Place of Mystery in the Life of the Mind." *Harper's* 222 (May 1961), 46–49.

———. *Life Against Death: The Psychoanalytic Meaning of History*. New York: Random, 1959.

———. *Love's Body*. New York: Random, 1966.

Bur, Michel. "The Social Influence of the Motte-and-Bailey Castle." *Scientific American* 248 (May 1983), 132–40.

Burl, Aubrey. *The Stone Circles of the British Isles*. New Haven: Yale Univ. Press, 1976.

Campbell, John C. *The Southern Highlander and his Homeland*. 1921; rpt. Lexington: Univ. Press of Kentucky, 1969.

Campbell, Joseph. *The Flight of the Wild Gander: Explorations in the Mythological Dimension*. South Bend, Ind.: Gateway [1977].

———. *The Hero with a Thousand Faces*. 2d ed. Princeton: Princeton Univ. Press, 1968.

Canny, Nicholas P. *The Elizabethan Conquest of Ireland: A Pattern Established, 1565–76*. New York: Harper, 1976.

Carmichael, Alexander, ed. *Celtic Invocations: Selections from Volume I of Carmina Gadelica*. 1972; rpt. Noroton, Conn.: Vineyard, 1977.

Caudill, Harry. "Anglo-Saxon vs. Scotch-Irish: Round 2." *Mountain Life and Work* 45 (March 1969), 18–19.

Chapman, Malcolm. *The Gaelic Vision in Scottish Culture*. London: Croom Helm; Montreal: McGill-Queen's Univ. Press, 1978.

Chesterton, Gilbert Keith. "Celts and Celtophiles." in *Heretics*. 1905; 3d ed. New York: Devin-Adair, 1950.

Coles, Robert. *Migrants, Sharecroppers, Mountaineers*. Vol. 2 of *Children of Crisis*. Boston: Little, Brown, 1972.

———. *The South Goes North*. Vol. 3 of *Children of Crisis*. Boston: Little, Brown [1972].

Conley, Phil, and Boyd D. Stutler. *West Virginia Yesterday and Today*. Charleston, W.Va.: Education Foundation, 1966.

Couto, Richard A. "Political Silence and Appalachia." *Appalachian Journal* 5 (Autumn 1977), 116–24.

Cuming, Fortescue. *Sketches of a Tour to the Western Country. . . .* Pittsburgh: Cramer, Spear and Eichbaum, 1810.

Cunningham, Rodger. "Heritage or Hermitage? John Shelton Reed's *Southerners*." *Appalachian Journal* 12 (Spring 1985), 252–56.

Davids, Richard C. *The Man Who Moved a Mountain*. Pittsburgh: Fortress, 1970.

Dickey, James. *Deliverance*. Boston: Houghton, 1970.

Dickinson, W. Croft, and A. A. M. Duncan. *Scotland from the Earliest Times to 1603*. Oxford: Clarendon, 1977.

Dodds, E. R. *The Greeks and the Irrational*. Berkeley: Univ. of California Press, 1951.

Donaldson, Gordon. *Scotland: Church and Nation through Sixteen Centuries*. Naperville, Ill.: SCM Book Club, 1960.

Dunbar, William. *The Poems of William Dunbar*, ed. James Kinsley. Oxford: Clarendon, 1979.

Duncan, Archibald A. M. *Scotland: The Making of the Kingdom*. New York: Harper, 1975.

Edwards, Ruth Dudley. *An Atlas of Irish History*. London: Methuen, 1973.

Einstein, Frank. "The Politics of Nostalgia: Uses of the Past in Recent Appalachian Poetry." *Appalachian Journal* 8 (Autumn 1980), 32–40.

Eliade, Mircea. *Myths, Dreams, and Mysteries: The Encounter between Contemporary Faiths and Archaic Realities*, tr. Philip Mairet. New York: Harper, 1960.

———. *The Sacred and the Profane: The Nature of Religion*, tr. Willard R. Trask. New York: Harcourt, 1959.

Eliot, T. S. *Collected Poems, 1909–1962*. New York: Harcourt, 1963.

Eller, Ronald D. "Industrialization and Social Change in Appalachia, 1880–1930: A Look at the Static Image." In Helen Lewis et al., eds., *Colonialism in Modern America: The Appalachian Case*. Boone, N.C.: Appalachian Consortium Press, 1978.

———. *Miners, Millhands, and Mountaineers: Industrialization of the Appalachian South, 1880–1930*. Knoxville: Univ. of Tennessee Press, 1982.

England, Eugene. "Great Books or True Religion?" *Dialogue: A Journal of Mormon Thought* 9:4 (1974), 36–49.

Erdman, David V. *The Illuminated Blake: All of William Blake's Illuminated Works with a Plate-by-Plate Commentary*. Garden City, N.Y.: Anchor/Doubleday, 1974.

Erikson, Kai T. *Everything in its Path: Destruction of Community in the Buffalo Creek Flood*. New York: Simon and Schuster, 1976.

Evans, E. Estyn. "The Atlantic Ends of Europe." *Advancement of Science* 25 (1958), 54–64.

———. "The Scotch-Irish: Their Cultural Adaptation and Heritage in the American Old West." In E. R. R. Green, ed., *Essays in Scotch-Irish History*. London: Routledge, 1969.

Falls, Cyril. *The Birth of Ulster*. 1936; rpt. London: Methuen, 1973.

Fanon, Frantz. *The Wretched of the Earth*, tr. Constance Farrington. New York: Grove, 1968.

Farber, Stephen. "'Deliverance'—How It Delivers." *New York Times* 20 Aug. 1972, sec. 2:9, p. 16.

Fell, Barry. *America B.C.: Ancient Settlers in the New World*. New York: Quadrangle/New York Times Book Co., 1976.

Fiedler, Leslie A. *Love and Death in the American Novel.* 2d ed. New York: Dell, 1969.

Fisher, Steve. "Appalachians as 'Redskins': The Assault on the Land Continues." *Mountain Review* 4 (April 1979), 4–6.

Ford, Henry Jones. *The Scotch-Irish in America.* Princeton: Princeton Univ. Press, 1915.

Foster, Jim, with Steve Robinson and Steve Fisher. "Class, Political Consciousness, and Destructive Power: A Strategy for Change in Appalachia." *Appalachian Journal* 5 (Spring 1978), 290–311.

Fox, John, Jr. *The Trail of the Lonesome Pine.* New York: Scribner, 1908.

Freeman-Grenville, G. S. P. *Atlas of British History.* London: Rex Collings, 1979.

Freire, Paulo. *Pedagogy of the Oppressed,* tr. Myra Bergman Ramos. 1970; rpt. New York: Herder and Herder, 1972.

French, Peter J. *John Dee: The World of an Elizabethan Magus.* London: Routledge, 1972.

Frost, William Goodell. "God's Plan for the Southern Mountains." *Biblical Review* 6 (July 1921), 405–25.

———. "Our Contemporary Ancestors in the Southern Mountains." *Atlantic Monthly* 83 (Mar. 1899), 311–19.

Geoffrey of Monmouth. *Historia Regum Britanniae.* 1136. Ed. Acton Griscom and Robert Ellis Jones. London: Longmans, 1929.

———. *The History of the Kings of Britain,* tr. Lewis Thorpe. Baltimore: Penguin, 1966.

———. *Life of Merlin,* ed. Basil Clarke. Cardiff: Univ. of Wales Press, 1973.

Gerrard, Nathan L. "Churches of the Stationary Poor in Southern Appalachia." In John D. Photiadis and Harry K. Schwarzweller, eds., *Change in Rural Appalachia: Implications for Action Programs.* Philadelphia: Univ. of Pennsylvania Press, 1970.

Gimbutas, Marija. "Old Europe in the Fifth Millennium B.C.: The European Situation on the Arrival of the Indo-Europeans." In Edgar C. Polomé, ed., *The Indo-Europeans in the Fourth and Third Millennia.* Ann Arbor: Karoma, 1982.

Goshen, Charles E. "Characterological Deterrents to Economic Progress in People of Appalachia." *Southern Medical Journal* 63 (Dec. 1970), 1054–59.

Grand Atlas de la France. Paris: Sélection du Reader's Digest, 1969.

Grant, Madison. *The Passing of the Great Race.* New York: Scribner, 1916.

Guerrant, Edward O. *The Galax Gatherers: The Gospel among the Highlanders.* Richmond: Onward, 1910.

Hanning, Robert W. *The Vision of History in Early Britain: From Gildas to Geoffrey of Monmouth.* New York: Columbia Univ. Press, 1966.

Harrington, Michael. *The Other America: Poverty in the United States.* Baltimore: Penguin, 1963.

Hechter, Michael. *Internal Colonialism: The Celtic Fringe in British National Development, 1536–1966.* Berkeley: Univ. of California Press, 1975.

Henry, Françoise. *Irish Art during the Viking Invasions (800–1020 A.D.)*. Ithaca, N.Y.: Cornell Univ. Press, 1967.

Henry, Jules. *On Sham, Vulnerability and Other Forms of Self-Destruction*. New York: Random, 1973.

Heron, James. "The Making of the Ulster Scot." 1910; Appendix C of Henry Jones Ford, *The Scotch-Irish in America*. Princeton: Princeton Univ. Press, 1915.

Hicks, George L. *Appalachian Valley*. New York: Holt, 1976.

Hill, J. E. C. "Puritans and 'The Dark Corners of the Land.'" *Transactions of the Royal Historical Society*, 5th Ser., v. 13 (1962), 77–102.

Holinshed, Raphael. *Holinshed's Chronicles of England, Scotland, and Ireland*. 1577; 2d ed. 1587; rpt. London: Richard Taylor, 1807.

Humphrey, Richard A. "Religion and Place in Southern Appalachia." In Patricia D. Beaver and Burton L. Purrington, eds., *Cultural Adaptation to Mountain Environments*. Athens: Univ. of Georgia Press, 1984.

Jackson, Agnes Moreland. "To See the 'Me' in 'Thee.'" *Soundings* (Nashville) 56 (1973), 21–44.

Jackson, Kenneth H. *A Celtic Miscellany: Translations from the Celtic Literatures*. 1951; rev. ed. Harmondsworth, U.K.: Penguin, 1971.

———. *Language and History in Early Britain*. Edinburgh: Edinburgh Univ. Press, 1953.

———. *Studies in Early Celtic Nature Poetry*. Cambridge: Cambridge Univ. Press, 1935.

———, ed. *The Gododdin: The Oldest Scottish Poem*. Edinburgh: Edinburgh Univ. Press, 1969.

Johnson, Adrian. *America Explored: A Cartographical History of the Exploration of North America*. New York: Viking, 1974.

Jones, Loyal. Letter to the author, 7 Sept. 1983.

———. "Old-Time Baptists and Mainline Christianity." In J. W. Williamson, ed., *An Appalachian Symposium: Essays Written in Honor of Cratis D. Williams*. Boone, N.C.: Appalachian State Univ. Press, 1977.

———. "A Preliminary Look at the Welsh Component of Celtic Influence in Appalachia." In Barry M. Buxton et al., eds., *The Appalachian Experience: Proceedings of the Sixth Annual Appalachian Studies Conference*. Boone, N.C.: Appalachian Consortium Press, 1983.

Jones, Mary Harris. *The Autobiography of Mother Jones*. 1925; 3d ed. rev. Chicago: Charles H. Kerr, 1976.

Kahn, Si. "New Strategies for Appalachia." *New South* 25 (Fall 1970), 57–64.

Kern, Otto, ed. *Orphicorum Fragmenta*. Berlin: Weidmann, 1922.

Kierkegaard, Søren Aabye. *The Concept of Dread*, tr. Walter Lowrie. Princeton: Princeton Univ. Press, 1957.

Kirby, Rich. "Our Own Music." In Helen Lewis et al., eds., *Colonialism in Modern America: The Appalachian Case*. Boone, N.C.: Appalachian Consortium Press, 1978.

Kluge, Friedrich. *Etymologisches Wörterbuch der deutschen Sprache.* 17th ed. Berlin: De Gruyter, 1957.

Kovel, Joel. *White Racism: A Psychohistory.* 1970; 2d ed. New York: Columbia Univ. Press, 1984.

Kundera, Milan. "The Tragedy of Central Europe." *New York Review of Books* 31 (26 April 1984), 33–38.

Kushner, Gilbert. "Reflections on Mountain Adaptations." In Patricia D. Beaver and Burton L. Purrington, eds., *Cultural Adaptation to Mountain Environments.* Athens: Univ. of Georgia Press, 1984.

Laing, Ronald David. *The Divided Self: An Existential Study in Sanity and Madness.* Harmondsworth, U.K.: Penguin, 1965.

———. *Knots.* New York: Random, 1972.

———. *The Politics of Experience and The Bird of Paradise.* Harmondsworth, U.K.: Penguin, 1967.

———. *Self and Others.* 2d ed. 1969; rpt. Harmondsworth, U.K.: Penguin, 1971.

———, with H. Phillipson and A. R. Lee. *Interpersonal Perception: A Theory and a Method of Research.* Harmondsworth, U.K.: Penguin, 1970.

Langer, Susanne K. *Mind: An Essay in Human Feeling.* Vol. II. Baltimore: Johns Hopkins Univ. Press, 1972.

Lévi-Strauss, Claude. *Tristes Tropiques.* New York: Atheneum, 1969.

Lewis, Clive Staples. *The Discarded Image: An Introduction to Medieval and Renaissance Literature.* Cambridge: Cambridge Univ. Press, 1964.

———. *A Preface to Paradise Lost.* London: Oxford Univ. Press, 1942.

Lewis, Helen Matthews. "The Colony of Appalachia." Introduction to Helen Lewis et al., eds., *Colonialism in Modern America: The Appalachian Case.* Boone, N.C.: Appalachian Consortium Press, 1978.

———. "Wales and Appalachia—Coal Mining, Culture, and Conflict." *Appalachian Journal* 10 (Summer 1983), 350–57.

———, Sue Easterling Kobak, and Linda Johnson. "Family, Religion, and Colonialism in Central Appalachia: or, Bury my Rifle at Big Stone Gap." In Helen Lewis et al., eds., *Colonialism in Modern America: The Appalachian Case.* Boone, N.C.: Appalachian Consortium Press, 1978.

Leyburn, James G. *The Scotch-Irish: A Social History.* Chapel Hill: Univ. of North Carolina Press, 1962.

Lovejoy, Arthur O. *The Great Chain of Being: A Study of the History of an Idea.* 1936; rpt. New York: Harper, 1960.

Lucretius (Titus Lucretius Carus). *The Way Things Are,* tr. Rolfe Humphries. Bloomington: Indiana Univ. Press, 1968.

Macaulay, Donald. "On Some Aspects of the Appreciation of Modern Gaelic Poetry." *Scottish Gaelic Studies* 11 : 1 (1966), 136–45.

———, ed. *Nua Bhàrdachd Ghàidhlig / Modern Scottish Gaelic Poems.* Edinburgh: Southside, 1976.

Mac Cana, Proinsias. *Celtic Mythology.* London, 1970.

McDonald, Forrest, and Ellen Shapiro McDonald. "The Ethnic Origins of the American People, 1790." *William and Mary Quarterly* 37 (Apr. 1980), 179–99.

McDougall, Hugh A. *Racial Myth in English History: Trojans, Teutons, and Anglo-Saxons.* Hanover, N.H.: Univ. Press of New England, 1982.

McEvedy, Colin. *The Penguin Atlas of Medieval History.* Harmondsworth, U.K.: Penguin, 1961.

McHugh, Roger. Lectures in the School of Letters, Indiana Univ., Summer 1968.

Macleod, William Christie. *The American Indian Frontier.* New York: Knopf, 1928.

McNeill, Peter, and Ranald Nicholson, eds. *An Historical Atlas of Scotland, c. 400–c. 1600.* St. Andrews: Atlas Committee of the Conference of Scottish Medievalists, 1975.

Mannoni, Dominique O. *Prospero and Caliban: The Psychology of Colonization,* tr. Pamela Powesland. 1956; 2d ed. New York: Praeger, 1964.

Mathew, David. *The Celtic Peoples and Renaissance Europe: A History of the Celtic and Spanish Influences on Elizabethan History.* London: Sheed & Ward, 1933.

Matthews, M. Taylor. *Experience-Worlds of Mountain People: Institutional Efficiency in Appalachian Village and Hinterland Communities.* New York: Teachers College, Columbia Univ., 1937.

Memmi, Albert. *The Colonizer and the Colonized,* tr. Howard Greenfeld. 1965; rpt. Boston: Beacon, 1967.

Miller, Jim Wayne. "Appalachian Studies Hard and Soft: The Action Folk and the Creative People." *Appalachian Journal* 9 (Winter-Spring 1982), 105–14.

Miller, Perry. *Roger Williams: His Contribution to the American Tradition.* New York: Atheneum, 1962.

Moncreiffe, Iain, and Don Pottinger. "Scotland of Old" (map). Edinburgh: Bartholomew, n.d.

Montgomerie, Alexander. *The Poems of Alexander Montgomerie,* ed. James Cranstoun. Edinburgh and London: William Blackwood and Sons, 1887.

Moody, T. W., F. X. Martin, and F. J. Byrne, eds. *A New History of Ireland.* Vol. 9, *Maps, Genealogies, Lists.* Oxford: Clarendon, 1984.

Mooney, James R. *The Ghost Dance Religion and the Sioux Outbreak of 1890.* Washington, D.C.: Government Printing Office, 1896.

Moore, W. W. Introduction to Edward O. Guerrant, *The Galax Gatherers: The Gospel among the Highlanders.* Richmond: Onward, 1910.

Morris, John. *The Age of Arthur: A History of the British Isles from 350 to 650.* New York: Scribner, 1973.

Murison, David Donald. "Linguistic Relationships in Medieval Scotland." In G. W. S. Barrow, ed., *The Scottish Tradition.* Edinburgh: Scottish Academic Press, 1978.

Murphy, Cullen. "The Irish Question." *Atlantic* 256 (Sep. 1985), 28–37.

Murray, James A. H., et al., eds. *The Oxford English Dictionary: Being a Corrected Re-Issue with an Introduction, Supplement, and Bibliography of A New English Dictionary on Historical Principles.* . . . Oxford: Clarendon, 1970.

National Atlas of the United States of America. Washington, D.C.: Dept. of the Interior, Geological Survey, 1970.

Newcomb, Horace. "Appalachia on Television: Region as Symbol in American Popular Culture." *Appalachian Journal* 7 (Autumn-Winter 1979–80), 155–64.

Newton, Milton. "Cultural Preadaptation and the Upland South." *Geoscience and Man* 5 (1974), 143–54.

Nicolson, Marjorie Hope. *Mountain Gloom and Mountain Glory: The Development of the Aesthetics of the Infinite.* 1959; rpt. New York: Norton, 1963.

Obermiller, Phillip. "Appalachians as an Urban Ethnic Group: Romanticism, Renaissance, or Revolution?" *Appalachian Journal* 5 (Autumn 1977), 145–52.

Opie, John. "A Sense of Place: The World We Have Lost." In J. W. Williamson, ed., *An Appalachian Symposium: Essays Written in Honor of Cratis D. Williams.* Boone, N.C.: Appalachian State Univ. Press, 1977.

O'Toole, Thomas. "Culture and Development: Through Romantic Relativism into the Emerging Present." *Appalachian Journal* 6 (Summer 1979), 264–71.

Otto, John Solomon. "Oral Tradition in the Southern Highlands." *Appalachian Journal* 9 (Fall 1981), 20–31.

Perceval-Maxwell, M. *The Scottish Migration to Ulster in the Reign of James I.* New York: Humanities, 1973.

Photiadis, John D. "New Aims for Programs of Directed Change: The Case of Cooperative Extension in an Appalachian State." In John D. Photiadis and Harry K. Schwarzweller, eds., *Change in Rural Appalachia: Implications for Action Programs.* Philadelphia: Univ. of Pennsylvania Press, 1970.

Piggott, Stuart. *The Druids.* 1968. Harmondsworth, U.K.: Penguin, 1974.

———. "Traders and Metal-Workers." In Stuart Piggott, ed., *The Prehistoric Peoples of Scotland.* London: Routledge, 1962.

Plaut, Thomas. "Conflict, Confrontation, and Social Change in the Regional Setting." In Allen Batteau, ed., *Appalachia and America: Autonomy and Regional Dependence.* Lexington: Univ. Press of Kentucky, 1983.

———. "Extending the Internal Periphery Model: The Impact of Culture and Consequent Strategy." In Helen Lewis et al., eds., *Colonialism in Modern America: The Appalachian Case.* Boone, N.C.: Appalachian Consortium Press, 1978.

Plutarch. *Plutarch's Moralia.* Vol. 5, ed. Frank Cole Babbitt. Cambridge, Mass.: Harvard Univ. Press, 1936.

———. *Plutarch's Moralia.* Vol. 12, ed. Harold Cherniss and William Helmbold. Cambridge, Mass.: Harvard Univ. Press, 1957.

Polansky, Norman A., Robert O. Borgman, and Christine De Saix. *Roots of Futility.* San Francisco: Jossey-Bass, 1972.

Powell, T. G. E. "The Coming of the Celts." In Stuart Piggott, ed., *The Prehistoric Peoples of Scotland.* London: Routledge, 1962.

Purrington, Burton L. "The Status and Future of Archeology and Native American Studies in the Southern Appalachians." *Appalachian Journal* 5 (Autumn 1977), 40–54.

Radford, C. A. R. "From Prehistory to History." In Stuart Piggott, ed., *The Prehistoric Peoples of Scotland.* London: Routledge, 1962.

Reck, Una Mae Lange, and Gregory G. Reck. "Living is More Important than Schooling: Schools and Self-Concept in Appalachia." *Appalachian Journal* 8 (Autumn 1980), 19–25.

Rees, Alwyn, and Brinley Rees. *Celtic Heritage: Ancient Tradition in Ireland and Wales.* London: Thames & Hudson, 1961.

Rees, William. *An Historical Atlas of Wales.* 2d ed. London: Faber, 1959.

Reid, Herbert G. "Appalachian Studies: Class, Culture and Politics—II." *Appalachian Journal* 9 (Winter-Spring 1982), 141–48.

Renan, Ernest. "La Poésie des races celtiques." 1854. In *Oeuvres Complètes,* vol. 2. Paris: Calmann-Lévy, 1947–64.

Renfrew, Colin. "The Social Archaeology of Megalithic Monuments." *Scientific American* 249 (Nov. 1983), 152–63.

Ricoeur, Paul. *The Symbolism of Evil,* tr. Emerson Buchanan. Boston: Beacon, 1969.

Ritchie, R. L. Graeme. *The Normans in Scotland.* Edinburgh: Edinburgh Univ. Press, 1954.

Robinson, Philip S. *The Plantation of Ulster: British Settlement in an Irish Landscape, 1600–1670.* Dublin: Gill & Macmillan; New York: St. Martin's, 1984.

Rogin, Michael Paul. *Fathers and Children: Andrew Jackson and the Subjugation of the American Indian.* New York: Knopf, 1975.

Sartre, Jean-Paul. Preface to Frantz Fanon, *The Wretched of the Earth,* tr. Constance Farrington. New York: Grove, 1968.

Scalf, Henry P. *Kentucky's Last Frontier.* 2d ed. Pikeville, Ky.: Pikeville College Appalachian Studies Center, 1972.

Seltzer, Curtis. "The Media vs. Appalachia: A Case Study." *Mountain Review* 2 (May 1976), 10–11.

Semple, Ellen Churchill. "The Anglo-Saxons of the Kentucky Mountains: A Study in Anthropogeography." 1901. *Bulletin of the American Geographical Society* 42 (Aug. 1910), 561–94.

Shapiro, Henry D. *Appalachia on Our Mind: The Southern Mountains and Mountaineers in the American Consciousness, 1870–1920.* Chapel Hill: Univ. of North Carolina Press, 1978.

———. "The Place of Culture and the Problem of Identity." In Allen Batteau, ed., *Appalachia and America: Autonomy and Regional Dependence.* Lexington: Univ. Press of Kentucky, 1983.

————. "A Strange Land and Peculiar People: The Discovery of Appalachia, 1870–1920." Diss. Rutgers Univ., 1966.

Sheehan, Bernard. *Savagism and Civility: Indians and Englishmen in Colonial Virginia*. New York: Cambridge Univ. Press, 1980.

Silverberg, Robert. *Mound Builders of Ancient America: The Archaeology of a Myth*. Greenwich, Conn.: New York Graphic Society, 1968.

Snyder, Robert. "EdubyGodcation." In Mike Clark, Jim Branscome, and Bob Snyder, *Miseducation in Appalachia*. Huntington, W.Va.: Appalachian Press, 1974.

————. "Image and Identity in Appalachia." *Appalachian Journal* 9 (Winter-Spring 1982), 124–33.

Speer, Jean Haskell. "Culture as Barter." *Appalachian Journal* 10 (Summer 1983), 366–71.

Spicer, Edward H. "Persistent Cultural Systems." *Science* 174 (1971), 795–800.

Stewart, Andrew. "History of the Church of Ireland after the Scots were Naturalized." In Rev. Patrick Adair, *A True Narrative of the Rise and Progress of the Presbyterian Church in Ireland (1623–1670)*. Belfast: C. Aitchison, 1866.

Strickland, William. *Journal of a Tour to the United States of America*, ed. Rev. J. E. Strickland. New York: New-York Historical Society, 1971.

Tacitus, Quintus Cornelius. *De Vita Agricolae*, ed. H. Furneaux et al. 2d ed. Oxford: Clarendon, 1922.

————. *On Britain and Germany*, tr. H. Mattingly. Baltimore: Penguin, 1948.

Tolles, Frederick L. "The Culture of Early Pennsylvania." In Paul Goodman, ed., *Essays in American Colonial History*. New York: Holt, 1967.

Toynbee, Arnold J. *A Study of History*. London: Oxford Univ. Press, 1934.

————. *A Study of History*. Vols. I–VI, abridged by D. C. Somervell. New York: Oxford Univ. Press, 1947.

Trillin, Calvin. "U.S. Journal, Jeremiah, Ky.: A Stranger with a Camera." *The New Yorker* 45 (12 April 1969), 178–83.

Turner, Frederick Jackson. "The Significance of the Frontier in American History." *Annual Report of the American History Association for the Year 1893*. Washington, D.C.: Government Printing Office, 1894; rpt. Ann Arbor, Mich.: University Microfilms, 1966.

Vance, Rupert B. Introduction to Jack E. Weller, *Yesterday's People: Life in Contemporary Appalachia*. Lexington: Univ. of Kentucky Press, 1966.

Vincent, George E. "A Retarded Frontier." *American Journal of Sociology* 4 (July 1898), 1–20.

Virgil (Publius Virgilius Maro). *Aeneis (The Aeneid)*. Many editions.

Walls, David S. "Internal Colony or Internal Periphery? A Critique of Current Models and an Alternative Formulation." In Helen Lewis et al., eds., *Colonialism in Modern America: The Appalachian Case*. Boone, N.C.: Appalachian Consortium Press, 1978.

————. "On the Naming of Appalachia." In J. W. Williamson, ed., *An Appa-*

lachian Symposium: Essays Written in Honor of Cratis D. Williams. Boone, N.C.: Appalachian State Univ. Press, 1977.

Weil, Simone. *The Need for Roots*, tr. Arthur Wills. 1952; rpt. New York: Harper, 1971.

Weller, Jack E. "Appalachia: America's Mineral Colony." 1974. In Helen Lewis et al., eds., *Colonialism in Modern America: The Appalachian Case*. Boone, N.C.: Appalachian Consortium Press, 1978.

———. *Yesterday's People: Life in Contemporary Appalachia*. Lexington: Univ. of Kentucky Press, 1966.

West, Don. *Freedom on the Mountains*. Huntington, W.Va.: Appalachian Movement Press, 1973.

Whisnant, David E. *All That is Native and Fine: The Politics of Culture in an American Region*. Chapel Hill: Univ. of North Carolina Press, 1983.

———. "Developments in the Appalachian Identity Movement: All is Process." *Appalachian Journal* 8 (Autumn 1980), 41–47.

———. *Modernizing the Mountaineer: People, Power, and Planning in Appalachia*. New York: Burt Franklin, 1980.

White, Lynn, Jr. *Medieval Technology and Social Change*. 1962; rpt. London: Oxford Univ. Press, 1966.

Whyte, I. D. "Early-Modern Scotland: Continuity and Change." In G. Whittington and I. D. Whyte, eds., *An Historical Geography of Scotland*. London: Academic Press, 1983.

Wilhelm, Gene, Jr. "Appalachian Isolation: Fact or Fiction?" In J. W. Williamson, ed., *An Appalachian Symposium: Essays Written in Honor of Cratis D. Williams*. Boone, N.C.: Appalachian State Univ. Press, 1977.

Williams, Cratis D. "The Southern Mountaineer in Fact and Fiction." Diss. New York Univ., 1961.

Withers, Charles W. *Gaelic in Scotland 1698–1981: The Geographical History of a Language*. Edinburgh: John Donald, 1984.

INDEX